20

MOVIES
and
MEMORANDA

MOVIES

and

MEMORANDA

An Interpretative History of the National Film Board of Canada

by

D.B. JONES

Canadian Cataloguing in Publication Data

Jones, D.B. (David Barker), 1940-
  Movies and memoranda

(Canadian film series, ISSN 0705-548X ; 5)
Includes index.
Bibliography: p.
ISBN 0-919096-21-2

1. National Film Board of Canada — History.
2. Moving-pictures, Documentary — Canada — History.
I. Canadian Film Institute. II. Title. III. Series.

PN1993.N363J65   791.43'06'071   C81-090046-7

Series editor: Piers Handling
ISBN: 0-919096-21-2
ISSN: 0705-548 X
Printed in Canada by T.H. Best Printing Company Limited
Cover Design by Turquoise Graphics
The Canadian Film Series is published by The Canadian Film Institute
75 Albert Street, Suite 1105, Ottawa, Ontario K1P 5E7
Movies and Memoranda is co-published by Deneau Publishers
281 Lisgar Street, Ottawa, Ontario K2P 0E1
ISBN: 0-88879-073-2

©   1981 Canadian Film Institute/Institut canadien du film

CONTENTS

FOREWORD

I commend this book to all who are interested in the development of Canada as a nation, and in the significant role of the arts in that development. It is a scholarly and thoughtful analysis of the growth of one institution that is unique in the history of world cinema.

From what must have sometimes seemed to the author a complex and almost impossible task there has emerged an important contribution to better understanding the singularly Canadian and liberal-minded relationship that exists in this country between "culture" and the state.

On a personal level, I only regret that I am in the text for *Four New Apple Dishes* (its only claim to fame is that it was the first colour film released by the federal government, and it came out first only because *The Royal Visit of 1939* was longer and more difficult to edit). I would rather be remembered for my part in the production of *Alexis Tremblay, Habitant* or the *Canadian Landscape* films. Those films were at the heart of Grierson's "interpretation of Canada to Canadians," and we worked on them as independent filmmakers who were a part of what I believe to have been his vision of a national film community. There were not many of us in those days, but Grierson encouraged, badgered and inspired us in the same way as he did those on the inside. I believe that this influence affects the production style of the Canadian feature industry where most of the serious producers are cinematic descendants, albeit second or third generation, of the Grierson tradition. His departure was perhaps a greater loss to us in the "private sector" than it was to those who had joined the NFB staff because no commissioner who followed in the next 20 years had the same broad view.

This is not to say that they were not dedicated civil servants but I believe that they were primarily concerned with the NFB as an institution rather than with film as an instrument of national development. That was to come much later with the Canadian Film Development Corporation, the capital cost allowance and Pay-TV.

For many of us on the outside who, to quote from David Jones, could "make films much cheaper and who were more likely to execute the sponsor's aims without questioning them," it was a question of survival.

It's been a love-hate relationship. Throughout the years, in discussions with other filmmakers, frustrated by our inability to get funding for film projets that we felt to be nationally important, how many times have I said, "but you know, some of my best friends belong to the Film Board.'' Now David Jones has managed to give us an inside view of this extraordinary assembly of talent, social awareness and unavoidable bureaucracy — the National Film Board — generally taken for granted by the public and little understood except by a small group of cognoscentes in the fields of art and literature. And no one can deny that over the years this group of people have immeasurably enhanced the international reputation of Canada. The record is here and it's a record of which we can be proud.

Judith Crawley
President, Canadian Film Institute

ACKNOWLEDGEMENTS

This study was researched and written intermittently over a period of ten years. Between sojourns of various lengths in Montreal, I lived and worked in Australia, California, Kansas City, and Philadelphia. I taught, wrote scripts, consulted, produced films, worked on the night shift for an IRS regional office, and mowed lawns. Not foreseeing that this study might eventually reach print, I did not in those hectic years keep a detailed record of all the people who contributed to the project, and I am not capable of reconstructing an accurate and complete account now. Consequently, with the exception of the five people named below, I prefer not to attempt to cite individuals by name. However long the list would be, it would remain incomplete.

The assistance from the National Film Board itself was enormous. The Film Board allowed me to visit as long and as often as I liked, and left me alone when I was there. I talked with hundreds of people at the Film Board, saw hundreds of films, and read hundreds of documents. The Film Board's openness to me was startling.

At La Trobe University in Australia, I talked over this project with a number of colleagues who offered valuable insights and suggestions. The same occurred at Stanford University. The Communication Department at Stanford financed one of my briefer trips to Montreal. At Drexel University, where I teach as this book goes to press, I have met several people with whom I have discussed, profitably, the Film Board phenomenon.

The contributions from several people, however, were inordinately large. Tom Daly was always available to talk, and he meticulously read a draft of every chapter and called attention to errors. Guy Glover did the same. I'm particularly grateful to Guy, because he knew that his own enormous contribution to the Film Board was not within the central focus of my interests, yet he gave generously whenever asked — even after having officially retired. Martin Defalco is another NFB filmmaker who contributed enormously and without self-interest to the project. I owe him — and his family — a lot. Ron Alexander, an award-winning sound mixer at the Film Board before accepting a teaching post at Stanford, helped me in several ways during the latter stages of the project.

I want to cite one author whose work I found essential to the project, especially at the early stages: Forsyth Hardy and his collection of John Grierson's articles and talks (*Grierson on Documentary*, London: Faber and Faber, 1966). Although whenever possible I researched the original sources of the pieces collected in Hardy's book, and discovered new ones, without it I might not have realized, early enough, how rich Grierson's thinking really was. I believe Hardy's collection will endure as a resource for every person curious about the quality of thought that lay behind the development of documentary as we know it today.

I regret that the person who encouraged me the most, from my very first efforts at film study through to the completion of this book, is no longer with us to receive my gratitude. Janet Alexander died suddenly and unexpectedly in the spring of 1981. Her death saddened many people who had benefitted from her teaching and her friendship.

We would like to express our sincere gratitude to the National Film Board of Canada; the National Film, Sound and Television Archives, Public Archives Canada; the Canada Council; Kodak Canada Ltd.; and 3M Canada Inc., for their generous support in assisting the publication of this book.

We would also like to thank the University of California Press for their kind permission in allowing us to quote from Elizabeth Sussex's *The Rise and Fall of the British Documentary Film*; and the lines from "In Memory of W.B. Yeats" in "The Collected Shorter Poems" by W.H. Auden, were reprinted by permission of Faber and Faber Ltd.

INTRODUCTION

The redundancy in the subtitle of this book is intentional. All history is interpretative but, as Karl Popper lamented in *The Open Society and its Enemies*, the popular use of the word suggests that there is such a thing as "history as it actually did happen." If there is such a thing as "history as it actually did happen," it cannot be recorded or told. The writer of history necessarily selects comparatively few of the pieces of evidence available to him. These pieces of evidence themselves have been selected from what was available to the selector, whether the selector be an interviewee recalling events, an accountant, a memorandum writer, a photographer, an archivist, a file system, nature, or chance.

This is not *the* story of the National Film Board, but an interpretation of it, based on the pieces of evidence which were available to me and which seemed relevant to answering one question: how did the National Film Board of Canada, a government organization, achieve leadership in documentary film so early and maintain it through decades of production — a feat unmatched in the world.

This may seem like a simple question. It seemed simple to me when I first seriously raised it. I thought, and was so advised, that I could answer it by making a "structure-function" analysis of the Film Board. My plan was to spend six months or so at the Film Board, determine and describe how the Film Board is set up and how it works, and thereby explain the Film Board's unique accomplishments.

I was not long at the Film Board before I realized such an approach was futile. The "structure-function" method of analysis, when used alone and at a particular point in time, contains at least two fallacies. For one, a description of the organization in, say, 1975 can explain nothing of its prior performance — but the films of the past had raised the question, not the films of the future. Second, such a description, by itself, unfortunately explains everything, the bad films as well as the good (and the Film Board has produced its share of bad films), and thereby explains nothing.

I came to realize that to answer my question I had to pursue and combine two additional methods in which I had little training: history and criticism. I wasn't interested in explaining the Film Board's entire production, most of which is unspectacular. Relatively few documentaries of the Board's 10,000 or so films had spurred my interest. Although most of these films also spurred the world's interest, aesthetic judgment was still involved. This meant that I had to select the films which struck me as particularly important, justify my selection, and search the past for an understanding of how the Film Board came to produce such films. From what I found in this past, I had to decide what seemed relevant and what did not. To complicate matters, I discovered, early on, that the cause-and-effect relationship (if there was one) between organizational factors and the films was not simply a linear one. Certain organizational conditions might encourage or enable the production of certain kinds of innovative films, but these films could, in turn, affect the organization. My analysis had to account for this dynamic, interactive relationship between the films and the organization.

The reader will be the judge of how well or poorly I've managed this, but I could not have managed it at all were it not for a peculiar but immensely important factor in the Film Board's establishment and growth: John Grierson. More than forty years after Grierson set up the Film Board a filmmaker could remark justly that "it is Grierson's vision that still animates the place, even if it is a distant echo." Grierson's influence was enormous. His relationship to the Film Board was like God's to the world: he created it, but it got out of hand. More accurately, he created it such that it *would* get out of hand. He created something which was itself creative. (That was his genius.) But equally — and this is what was so helpful to me — Grierson's vision also provided an aesthetic standard, albeit a slippery one, against which to test films, and it suggested an organizational theory, however intuitive, on which to hang observations about the Film Board's structural development. Thus the phenomenon under study yielded a conceptual perspective from which to study it.

There were prices to pay for this. For example, I had to forego the security and detachment that comes from studying something from a received perspective, and I had to struggle with a certain vague circularity in my argument. But because the Film Board originated in a concern for documentary, this approach helped me resist the temptation to attempt a comprehensive study of the Board. I could in good conscience ignore the Film Board's excellent record in animated and experimental film, except as it seemed to contribute to the Film Board's documentary work. I could make but token reference to the Film Board's work in dramatic features, of great interest to Canadian film scholars and buffs, and to many NFB filmmakers, but of little consequence to the world. I could place the competent but unspectacular mainstream of the Film Board's documentary work in proper perspective, crediting it for providing space for those aesthetic adventures for which the Film Board is remembered. I could note the importance of the Film Board's technical facilities, experimentation, and development without attempting to detail it. And I was under no compulsion to dwell on the performance of the Film Board's various post-Grierson commissioners, none of whom seems to have played a crucial role in the emergence of the Film Board's best work.

But despite the necessity — and serendipitous advantages — of combining history and criticism, the original "structure-function" aspect of my approach was in some ways the most helpful of all. From extended visits to the Film Board, I came to know it more intimately than I ever could have from scrutinizing films and documents alone. I got to know a number of filmmakers, technicians, administrators, accountants, secretaries, and managers. Many of them were exceedingly generous to me with their thoughts, worries, and hopes. In several cases, I came to identify with their struggles, but was able to maintain perspective because often they were struggling against each other. I think this experience enriched my sense of what the Film Board is all about. I hope I've repaid their generosity by writing something they find interesting and perhaps even useful.

Although this book is blatantly interpretative, it is meant to be objective. Objectivity simply means, in science, criticism and scholarship; that the argument is present in such a way that others can examine the same evidence and follow the line of reasoning. The reader who notes that frequently I quote filmmakers without identifying them (in order to protect them) may question my objectivity, but any but the most casual, reclusive, or blind observer who would spend a little time at the Film Board could hear the same things. He just might interpret them differently.

And, finally, this book is *by no means* presented as "the last word" on the National Film Board. On the contrary, even if the Film Board should cease to exist tomorrow, there would remain much more to be said about its amazing history. I can imagine a book with almost the same structure as mine but picking different films and arriving at different conclusions. I can imagine extremely useful, detailed studies of aspects of the Film Board or its work which I have not emphasized. I can imagine revelatory studies of the Film Board from other points of view, such as national politics or the struggle for cultural identity. And I know that several people I met, and others I didn't meet, who either have been or were with the Film Board for a very long time, could write fascinating and insightful memoirs about their Film Board careers. I would be very pleased if this study were to help encourage the writing and publication of such books.

1
A WILL AND A WAY

When the National Film Board of Canada was established in 1939, no one had thought more about documentary's potential, and no one had worked harder to realize it, than John Grierson, the Film Board's inspirer, designer, and first Commissioner. As the leader of the British documentary movement of the nineteen-thirties, Grierson developed a purposeful aesthetic standard for documentary and a strategy for attaining it. Practice fell short of promise. The standard was high and the strategy delicate. And as Grierson struggled to realize his vision of documentary, his own thinking began to drift toward less challenging modifications of it. But it was Grierson's experience with the British documentary of the thirties, his efforts to tie an ambitious analysis of ends to a workable system of means, that would shape the strange character and unique development of the National Film Board of Canada.

The story of the British documentary film has been told often. We will not repeat those efforts here or try to improve upon them. Instead, we will scan the literature of, and about, the movement in order to distill the essential features of Grierson's documentary theory and practice. We will achieve only a partial clarification, because Grierson, in word and deed, exhibited a remarkable tolerance for ambiguity. He relished the apparently contradictory statement or action. As the Dutch filmmaker Joris Ivens recalled, Grierson would quote the Bible to a Communist and Lenin to a Catholic.[1] And his tactics as an administrator often baffled those nearest him. Yet Grierson's tolerance of ambiguity, his ease with contradiction, contributed to the fertility of his ideas and the effectiveness of his work, for it was tolerance in the metallurgical sense, based on inner strength and coherence. It was a resilience rooted in moral focus and intellectual breadth.

This same trait, which often manifested itself in Grierson's gift for the catchy, suggestive, or disconcerting phrase, may have something to do with the ignorance that documentary people today have of the depth and sophistication of Grierson's early concept of documentary. Grierson is remembered primarily for his interest in documentary as a social tool, for his avowed use of "cinema as a pulpit," his declaration that "art is not a mirror but a hammer," his claim to have "put the working man on the screen." But the most popular of Grierson's phrases — his definition of documentary as "the creative treatment of actuality" — is the least evidently utilitarian and yet the most deeply political.

The definition has a curious history. Grierson introduced it in the form of a throw-away line, without elaboration, in an article he wrote in 1933 about the job of the documentary producer.[2] The phrase caught the imagination of those working in, or following the progress of, the then-young field of documentary. It soon became the most widely quoted definition of documentary, a distinction which, half a century later, it retains. But on the rare occasions when the definition is not merely quoted but discussed, the purpose is to dismiss it. In a book published in 1935, Raymond Spottiswoode, himself a participant in the British documentary movement and later one of Grierson's Film Board lieutenants, complained of the definition's "misplaced catholicity." The definition was "as embracing as art itself." Spottiswoode proceeded to offer his own definition:

> The documentary film is in subject and approach a dramatized presentation
> of man's relation to his institutional life, whether industrial, social, or
> political; and in technique, a subordination of form to content.[3]

A. William Bluem, one of the infrequent writers on documentary to quote Spottiswoode's definition, prefers it to Grierson's, which he dismisses as an "easy phrase," and tautological.[4]

In evaluating Grierson's phrase as if it were meant for the dictionary, critics such as Bluem and Spottiswoode confuse Grierson's purpose with their own. This allows them to ignore completely the rich context of Grierson's phrase, avoid probing its ambiguity, and thus blind themselves to its meaning. In doing so, they blind themselves as well to the aesthetic possibilities of documentary, for Grierson was far less interested in specifying for academicians what documentary in 1933 was, than in suggesting to his working colleagues what documentary ought to be, what it might become.

Grierson liked to say that art arises not as a consciously sought goal but as "a by-product of a job of work done." His own rich conception of documentary art arose as a by-product of a more obviously practical concern: public education, or propaganda. After graduating from Glasgow University in 1923, with distinctions in English and Moral Philosophy, Grierson spent three years in the United States on a Rockefeller grant. He worked briefly with Walter Lippmann at the University of Chicago. Lippmann was deeply perplexed by a problem facing industrial democracies: how to create an adequately informed voting public when the issues of the day were becoming increasingly complex. Lippmann and the group around him accused the popular mass media of exacerbating the problem, but Grierson saw in them — particularly the Yellow Press and Hollywood films — the germ of a solution: their skill in dramatizing events so as to interest a broad public. These two cultural phenomena suggested to Grierson that a complex world could be popularly understood "if only we got away from the servile accumulation of fact and struck for the story which held the facts in living organic relationship together."[5]

Before returning to Great Britain, Grierson had two experiences which were to shape his thinking and his career. He helped prepare Eisenstein's *Battleship Potemkin* for American release, and he met Robert Flaherty, whose *Nanook of the North* he had seen several years earlier in Scotland. These two great directors represented opposite poles in their respective approaches to filmmaking.[6] Flaherty was an individualist. Grierson called him both a "poet" and an "explorer." Flaherty had spent years with the Eskimos before making *Nanook*. Flaherty observed his subject with a "strange innocence," seeing "things as they are." Flaherty "soaked himself in his material, lived with it to the point of intimacy . . . before he gave it form." Flaherty represented for Grierson the truth of Plato's remark that "no fire can leap up or light kindle till there is 'long intercourse with the thing itself, and it has been lived with.'"

Eisenstein and the Russians worked in groups. And unlike Flaherty, they drew their subjects from their own history. They made their own society's struggles "exciting and noble." Unlike Flaherty, Eisenstein was "detailed and cold in his shooting, and he warms his stuff to life only when he starts putting it together." It was Eisenstein's "power of juxtaposition" that impressed Grierson, "his amazing capacity for exploding two or three details into an idea."

From Flaherty Grierson derived his notion of what the plastic material for making documentaries should be: raw, unscripted film footage gathered in a relationship of intimacy with the subject. Flaherty's work inspired Grierson to conclude that the camera was "by instinct a wanderer." The camera's "capacity for getting around, for observing and selecting from life itself," implied that documentary would "photograph the living scene and the living story." Documentary would seek out the unforeseen, for "spontaneous gesture has a special value on the screen." Flaherty's method yielded an "intimacy of knowledge" unavailable to the studio approach. It was a method

> altogether alien in a cinema world which insists on forcing a pre-conceived shape . . . on all material together. Its chief claim to our regard, however, is that it is necessary, and particularly necessary in England.

But Grierson was a political man, and a moralist. His heroes were those of the Scottish Independent Labour Party. And, the early thirties were the years of the Great Depression and impending Fascism in Europe. As much as he admired Flaherty's method, he disapproved of Flaherty's choice of subjects and themes. Flaherty was a romantic. He was among those who loved "every time but his own," the kind of poet "who on every classic theory of society from Plato to Trotsky should be removed bodily from the Republic." However noble it is to struggle for existence against the forces of nature, Grierson argued, that struggle was not relevant to contemporary life, which involved a fight for "food in the midst of plenty," where the enemy might be "the crazy walrus of international finance." People must learn to "accept the environment in which they live, with its smoke and steel and its mechanical aids." For the subject matter appropriate to documentary, Grierson wrote:

> One may turn to the Russians for guidance rather than Flaherty. . . .They have made society on the move the subject matter of art. . . .Their sense of . . . social direction need not be identical with ours. The essential point . . . is that they have built up this rhythm and nobililty and purpose of theirs by facing up to the new material. They have done it out of the necessity of their social situation. No one will say that our own necessity is less than theirs.

Thus we see that "actuality" for Grierson had two dimensions, each of which he declared was *necessary* to the new documentary movement he was founding in England: raw, unscripted film footage taken in an intimate relationship with the subject; and the subject itself, which should be contemporary social reality. But it was necessary to do something more with this "actuality" than just string it together. "You photograph the natural life, but you also, by your juxtaposition of detail, create an interpretation of it." To be taken seriously, the interpretation had to be substantial. Grierson excluded newsreels, travelogues, and magazine films from "documentary" because they lacked significant structure. He admitted the impressionistic structure (such as in Ruttmann's *Berlin, The Symphony of a Great City* or Ivens's

Rain) to the realm of documentary, but only reluctantly. There was little point to such films. "And so," Grierson wrote of how they typically concluded, "nothing having happened and nothing positively said about anything, to bed." Grierson also admitted the story structure, but again grudgingly, for the individual's "particular belly-aches are [perhaps] of no consequence in a world which complex and impersonal forces command."

What then was Grierson's notion of the best kind of structure for documentary? We may never know for certain. The article in which he directly addressed the problem of structure was the third in a series of articles on documentary theory he was writing for *Cinema Quarterly*. After considering the combination of symphonic and dramatic forms, he concluded the article with this statement:

> The dramatic application of the symphonic form is not ... the deepest or most important. A future consideration of forms neither dramatic nor symphonic, but dialectic, will reveal this more plainly.

That "future consideration" never arrived, at least not in print. Grierson wrote two more articles for *Cinema Quarterly* before it ceased publication in 1935. Neither elaborated on "dialectic." Possibly Grierson feared that a favourable analysis of a concept like "dialectic" would offend too many of those government figures whose support for documentary he was seeking. It is at least equally possible, however, that Grierson lost interest in this attempt to categorize and explicate documentary forms. Perhaps he sensed that to try to define "dialectic" could lead him into a conceptual quagmire he'd do better to avoid. Grierson was not a denotative thinker. He was a connotative one. Formal system-making was alien to him. At any rate, by the middle of 1935, when the last issue of *Cinema Quarterly* appeared, Grierson apparently had retreated from his brief foray into systematization. Concluding an article called "Two Paths to Poetry," Grierson wrote:

> But this much is certain: in our realistic cinema, all roads lead by one hill or another to poetry. Poets [documentary filmmakers] must all be — or stay forever journalists.

"Poetry" (and "prophecy") for Grierson had its basis in the under-standing of social forces. The documentary filmmaker

> need not posit the ends ... but the ends must be there, informing his description and giving finality ... to the slice of life he has chosen. For that larger effect there must be the power of poetry or prophecy. Failing either or both in the highest degree, there must be at least the sociological sense implicit in poetry and prophecy.

And whatever else poetry or prophecy was, it was something positive forged out of full confrontation with the negative (a relationship which may contain the essence of what Grierson meant by "dialectic"):

> It is ... difficult to be sure of one's attitudes in a decade like this. Can we heroicize our men when we know them to be exploited? Can we romanticize our industrial scene when we know that our men work brutally and starve ignobly for it? Can we praise it — and in art there must be praise — when the most blatant fact of our time is the bankruptcy of our national management? Our confidence is sapped, our beliefs troubled, our eye for beauty is most plainly disturbed: and the more so in cinema than in any other art. For we have to build on the actual. Our capital comes from the actual. The medium itself insists on the actual. There we must build or be damned.

The sense of the second passage was echoed a few years later, in Europe's darkest hour, by a great poet, W.H. Auden (who coincidentally had worked on two British documentaries, *Night Mail* and *Coal Face*):

> Follow, poet, follow right
> To the bottom of the night,
> With your unconstraining voice
> Still persuade us to rejoice;
>
> With the farming of a verse
> Make a vineyard of the curse,
> Sing of human unsuccess
> In a rapture of distress;
>
> In the deserts of the heart
> Let the healing fountain start,
> In the prison of his days
> Teach the free man how to praise.[7]

It is this intent to forge praise out of the worst as well as the best aspects of reality that puts Grierson's idea of documentary on a level with the other arts. James Baldwin has written:

> Art and ideas come out of the passion and torment of experience: it is impossible to have a real relationship to the first if one's aim is to be protected from the second.[8]

Nietzsche put it even stronger:

> Health and disease — be careful! The standard must always be the efflorescence of the body, the resilience, courage, and cheerfulness of the spirit — but naturally also *how much morbidity it can absorb and conquer* — in other words, *make* healthy.[9]

And Grierson himself is remembered to have said that "All things are beautiful if you have got them in the right order."[10]

It thus seems fair to compare Grierson's "creative treatment of actuality" with Picasso's "You must begin with chaos if you would give birth to a dancing star," and perhaps to suppose that, if the Grierson of the early thirties had had his way, the "dancing stars" of the British documentary might have included at least one *Guernica*.

And yet Grierson often was — and still is — taken to have been anti-aesthetic. His apparently anti-aesthetic statements were largely a pose. Paul Rotha believes this was a tactic Grierson employed for allaying the fears of an unimaginative, suspicious Civil Service.[11] Edgar Anstey remembers Grierson as "sort of schizophrenic in the sense of the split between the social purpose and a passionate feeling about art, a word we were never allowed to breathe."[12] The real target of Grierson's prohibition was art-for-art's-sake. Too many of the young filmmakers who gathered around Grierson were attracted to film solely as an art, not to the social purposes to which it could be put. Grierson once described them as "too damned arty to get their noses into public issues." He wrote that the best of the young filmmakers

> believe that beauty will come in good time to inhabit the statement which is honest and lucid and deeply felt and which fulfills the best aims of citizenship. They are sensible enough to conceive of art as the by-product of a job of work done. The opposite effort to capture the by-product first (the self-conscious pursuit of beauty, the pursuit of art for art's sake to the exclusion of jobs of work and other pedestrian beginnings) was always a reflection of selfish wealth, selfish leisure and aesthetic decadence.

When Grierson insisted on the primacy of the social purpose, he did so, as Basil Wright, the director of *Song of Ceylon*, has pointed out, from a position

> founded on deep and accurate knowledge of Kant and Hegel and Marx and Lenin ... Plato and Aristotole ... and a highly informed appreciation of the visual arts from Michelangelo to Moore and from Massaccio to Magritte.

Wright also has recalled:

> Some of the words Grierson most often used were "purpose," "purposive," "creative." And these, godammit, represent an aesthetic formula which *he* never forgot even when he was beating daylights out of those of us whom he suspected of relapses into dilettantism.[13]

And Grierson's documentary aesthetic was rooted in a deep respect for truth. One of his favourite expressions, adapted from Mill, was that "it is in the hands of artists, and artists alone, that truth becomes a principle of action."[14] Art was thus an intermediary between the social condition, however disheartening, and the possibility of doing something

12

constructive about it. Documentary should be true, beautiful, and good. It should be "creative" in all three senses.

Karl Mannheim summarized well the dangers, but also the promise, of an aesthetic such as Grierson's. The attitude that art should carry a practical message

> threatens to abase art and turn it into propaganda; but we should not forget that the opposite extreme, art for art's sake, also drains the life-blood out of living art. The really great art of classical Greece, for example, had an organic function in the life of the *polis*.[15]

Grierson's concept of documentary was so Olympian in scope that perhaps it is more accurately called an ideal than a standard. Few, if any, documentaries have ever met it fully. And it is not an easy standard to apply in assessing a film. The true, the beautiful, the good — these are not measurable qualities. There is no consensus on them. Nations have taken arms over what they mean. Nevertheless, they do, in Grierson's formulation, take on certain meanings which are not entirely elusive. Grierson rarely, if ever, spoke of "objective" truth — or beauty or social good. These were largely relational qualities, having an important methodological component. When they were present in a film, they resided in a tension between the disorder of actuality, in both its senses, and the order achieved from structuring it, finding patterns in it, and drawing a message from it. Much as in a scientific explanation, the more disorder a film could give organic structure to, the larger its achievement.

However difficult "the creative treatment of actuality" may be to reach or apply, it sums up several years of profound thinking by a man who was struggling with documentary's problems on a daily basis. It was not an empty phrase. And it remains today the most interesting crystallization the documentary world has of what documentary does or should involve.

Grierson's first major attempt to apply his documentary idea occurred while he was just beginning to work it out. Fresh from America, he secured sponsorship from the Empire Marketing Board to make a film about the British herring fleet. In this film, *Drifters*, Grierson tried to synthesize what he valued in Flaherty and in the Russians. His subject belonged both to the natural world dear to Flaherty and the industrial world favoured by the Russians. Grierson directed the film somewhat in the manner of Flaherty, living with the fleet in an attempt to get to know it intimately. He did some of the shooting himself. In the editing, the film was modelled after the Russians, with rapid cross-cutting and contrasts. *Drifters* was a *succes d'estime* and drew several aspiring young filmmakers to Grierson. He was using an editing style not widely familiar in England, and which hadn't been applied to a British subject. *Drifters* was fresh. But it has not survived as a great film. The cutting looks artificial today. There is not the feeling of intimacy with its subject that one experiences from a Flaherty film, and there is little in way of a message. In trying to emulate both Flaherty and the Russians, Grierson fell short of both.

The most revealing insight *Drifters* yields into Grierson's values, however, lies not in this attempted synthesis but in a scene which he discarded. At one point the ship Grierson was on could not find any fish. Grierson borrowed some from another ship, had them lowered in the nets, and then filmed the men hauling in the "catch." Apparently, the entire scene, not just the fish, looked dead. From this Grierson concluded that in documentary "you cannot lie with impunity."[16]

Had Grierson kept making films, he no doubt would have enjoyed a notable career as a director. But he had a greater talent, and at that time a more needed one, as an organizer, entrepreneur, producer, arranger, teacher. He could lead, inspire, manoeuvre and accomplish. He soon would create and run the Empire Marketing Board Film Unit, and later the General Post Office Film Unit. He made possible just about every important English documentary of the thirties. In addition to the British government, Shell Oil, the Gas, Light, and Coke Company, and the BBC also sponsored films. In the course of those hectic years, Grierson developed principles of organization and leadership that he eventually would consolidate in Canada.

The first and overriding principle had begun with *Drifters*. Documentary was expensive. A film applying Flaherty's method might require a year or more of work and perhaps a hundred thousand feet of film. And the usual backers of expensive films were not likely to fund a documentary about "raw material which they in their own hearts despise." Consequently, the only conceivable source of on-going funding for documentary was government.

If attaching documentary to government sponsorship implied that documentary filmmakers were "propagandists first and filmmakers second," the arrangement had certain advantages. Government sponsorship "allows directors time to develop; it waits with a certain patience on their experiments; it permits them time to perfect their work." And when sponsorship was reasonably enlightened, it permitted a measure of freedom of content, for "half the virtue of propaganda is in the prestige it commands." Late in his life, Grierson remarked that "the greatest single discovery in the development of documentary came with the realization that its logical sponsorship lay with governments and with other bodies conscious of their public responsibilities."[17]

But sponsorship, for Grierson, was not simple patronage. He believed there should be a close link between the needs of government and the needs of the filmmakers. In the thirties Grierson himself maintained this link. Paul Rotha says that Grierson had "an expert sense of diplomatic strategy and manoeuvre which, clear enough to himself, could baffle some of those near him."[18] Grierson was a master at maintaining what another colleague, Stuart Legg, called "the delicate balance" between sponsor and filmmaker.[19]

The delicacy of this balance is perhaps best summed up in a pair of Grierson's favourite adages: "The King's shilling must not be abused," and "Public lies must not be told." On the one hand, filmmakers had to be sensitive to the needs of the public service and to give these needs the highest priority. On the other hand, by demonstrating this sensitivity, filmmakers secured "a measure of imaginative indulgence on the part of the powers that be."[20] When the measure of indulgence proved too small, Grierson, because of his close relationship to the sponsor, was able to shield his filmmakers from undue bureaucratic meddling. At the same time, Grierson protected the sponsor's interest, taking a detailed interest in every film for which he was responsible.

Grierson also saw a need to think of documentary production as part of a wider system. There was no use making the films if no one saw them. For films to have "an organic function in the life of the *polis*," they had to reach the public, not just other filmmakers. And the public for such films existed; Grierson said at the time that there was a larger audience outside the theatres than inside them. The EMB offered its films to schools and libraries on free loan. The movement founded film libraries. The GPO Film Unit sent out vans equipped with projectors and stocked with films.

But there was another systemic aspect to Grierson's strategy of sponsorship. He saw clearly that the documentary movement needed some sort of organizational base. The sponsorship of documentaries should be done "not on the basis of one director, one location and one film at a time, but on the basis of half-a-dozen directors with complementary talents and a hundred-and-one subjects all along the line." The next step after making *Drifters* was not simply to make another film for the Empire Marketing Board, but to form an Empire Marketing Board *Film Unit*. Later, in 1936, responding to the criticism that the GPO Film Unit films were "seldom electric," Grierson said that "it is not the individual directors, the separate films, that are significant, but the bulk of the output ... and the permanence of their future endowment.''[21]

The character of the organizations that Grierson built (first the EMB, and later the GPO Film Units) was not what might have been expected of a peace-time government organization. At the EMB, recalls Harry Watt,

> Everybody wandered in and out and there were no hours. We worked every God's hour there was, and wandered out to the pub and had a sandwich and a drink and came back and worked again and very often, if there was a rushed job, slept on the cutting room floor, all for a matter of two or three pounds a week.[22]

Alberto Cavalcanti, who worked with Grierson in the GPO Film Unit before Grierson left, remembered that Grierson ''had a very confused way of administration.'' Arthur Elton, another colleague, called Grierson ''an erratic administrator,'' but added that Grierson would probably say that ''the only possible sensible way of administering is to administer erratically.''[23]

If the Unit looked fluid and formless, it was at the same time extremely disciplined. The filmmakers would work very long hours, seven days a week, on low salaries which they rarely questioned. Harry Watt, who remembers the EMB Film Unit as a happy place of ''a million laughs,'' also remembers the Unit as monastic.[24] Filmmakers were forbidden to get married.

Filmmakers also were forbidden to talk about art, lest they drift into an attitude of art for its own sake, detached from public needs. Grierson hated the term and practice of ''self-expression,'' which he called ''the pursuit of disorder.'' Documentary was a group art, and some of the best films were group efforts. Several filmmakers worked on *Industrial Britain* and *Night Mail*. Personal credits on films were regarded as unimportant; they either were omitted or mischievously misallocated. Roles were interchangeable. All could edit well, write well, and even shoot.

The discipline and self-effacing commitment of the filmmakers of the thirties had an undeniably charismatic aspect, not in the popular sense of the word but in the sense that Max Weber originally used it.[25] For Weber, a leader invested with charismatic authority is ''set apart from ordinary men and treated as endowed with supernatural, superhuman, or at least specifically exceptional, powers and qualities.'' The basis for charismatic authority lies in ''the conception that it is the *duty* of those who have been called to a charismatic mission to recognize its quality and to act accordingly.'' A group subject to charismatic

authority is organized "on an emotional form of communal relationship." Charisma is "specifically foreign to economic considerations."
It is "specifically foreign to routine structure."

However, although Grierson was regarded by many with great awe,
he could not have been the sole source of the charismatic powers that
invoked such discipline, selflessness, and commitment. The metaphors
used to describe Grierson are invariably muddled, patronizing, or
uninspired: "an oxy-acetylene firebrand," "a small package of Scotch
dynamite," a "whirlwind," a "gin-drinking terror," a "fire-eating
Scot," and a "tornado-cum-thunderstorm." Grierson had faults. Some
people thought that Grierson was jealous of others' creativity, and that
he would often try to hurt creative people. Others felt exploited by him.
Rotha says that Grierson "fermented frictions and split loyalties."[26]
Harry Watt, after recalling an incident in which Grierson apparently lied
to him, concludes:

> Grierson was our guru, our "Chief," our little god, the man who had given
> us an aim and an ideal, who battled for us and protected us, and at whose
> feet we sat. We were adult enough to laugh at his foibles and play-acting,
> to joke about his verbosity and Calvinism, but basically, we adored
> him. . . .But it was never quite the same again.[27]

Grierson himself, when asked to explain the dedication of the
filmmakers of the thirties, identified the other source:

> Do you have to explain dedication? Film is exciting. Using film in a
> purposeful way was exciting. It was exciting new aesthetic territory.
> People were not only finding the art of the cinema, but they were finding
> themselves as artists. And not only that but the subject matter itself was
> exciting. . . .There were all kinds of intrinsic interests in the pursuit of
> documentary.[28]

The "creative treatment of actuality" had its own rewards.

The British documentary movement under Grierson's tutelage produced some important films, such as *Night Mail*, *Song of Ceylon*,
Industrial Britain, *Coal Face*, *Granton Trawler*, *Housing Problems*,
even *Drifters*. But it could not be maintained that the achievement lived
up to the very tough standard that had been set. The best of the films —
Night Mail and *Song of Ceylon* — are striking for their visual and aural
beauty, but they veer close to the forbidden territory of art-for-
art's-sake. They do not seriously address social problems or issues. The
films which did explore public issues did not do it so convincingly or
compellingly as the standard implied. Mannheim's warning proved
prophetic. The films were too propagandistic, and this was recognized
at the time:

> Mr. Grierson may like to talk about social education. . . .But even if it sounds like a sermon, a sales talk is still a sales talk.[29]

> But, all the ballyhoo to the contrary, they are basically government tracts, intended to applaud the progress of the Crown.[30]

> Mr. Grierson is not paid to tell the truth, but to make people use the parcel post.[31]

There appear to be several reasons for the failure of the British documentary to approach the standard that Grierson had set for it. One reason is that Grierson himself, as he assumed responsibility for production, acted more conservatively than his contemporary writings might have suggested. His effort in 1931 to bring Flaherty's talents to the service of the EMB Film Unit illustrates this practical conservatism. Grierson thought that an EMB film by Flaherty would enhance the Unit's prestige and inspire the young filmmakers. Here was a chance to turn an immense talent onto "socially relevant" material. But it was one thing to admire Flaherty's methods from a distance, and another to be accountable for them. When Flaherty started shooting, Grierson started worrying. Flaherty was profligate with time and money, and could spend as much of both on tests as another filmmaker might spend on a complete film. Exactly what happened between Flaherty and Grierson at the EMB is uncertain, but Arthur Calder-Marshall, in his biography of Flaherty, offers the most intriguing version. According to Calder-Marshall, Grierson — who had spoken against making films from preconceived notions — demanded a script from Flaherty. Flaherty reportedly grumbled, "I've never written a script before and I'm damned if I'm going to start now for some civil servant in Whitehall." Grierson said that the script didn't have to be too detailed. After a few days, Flaherty submitted four sheets of paper. The first was blank. The second carried the handwritten title, "Industrial Britain." The third said simply, "A SCENARIO: Scenes of Industrial Britain." And the fourth page was blank.[32]

With this experience as background, Flaherty reportedly offered his own critical analysis of the British documentary film movement, complaining that "what's wrong with the British documentary is that it hasn't any balls."[33]

But as Arthur Calder-Marshall notes, the end of Flaherty's association with *Industrial Britain* is "shrouded in legend." Eventually, several members of the Unit brought the film to completion.

Perhaps another reason why the movement produced no *Guernica* is that England, if not a perfect country, did not really need one. And as the decade progressed, and external threats to her security became more real, England's virtues became more apparent. Towards the end of the thirties, Grierson's writings assumed a softer, mildly chauvinistic tone when addressed to problems of England or the Empire, and a harder, militaristic one when addressed to problems of propaganda. In other words, Grierson himself drifted towards the more propagandistic aspect of his aesthetic, favouring the King's shilling to public truth. The outbreak of the war would push him even farther in that direction.

Furthermore, the social documentary was a new thing in England, and no sooner had it been launched than the new art had to cope with the introduction of sound. This technical innovation added a new dimension of actuality to any film using it, but at a great cost. Films became more expensive, the equipment more cumbersome, and the crews larger. Sound could, in an aesthetic sense, tyrannize a picture. The introduction of sound made Flaherty's method even harder to apply.

Although Grierson did manage to produce or inspire a large body of films, each film had to serve a particular commission. There was no general fund for production. This acute dependence on sponsorship left the movement vulnerable to ill-wishers. Despite the mildness of its films, the EMB Film Unit was accused of being a communist cell and of unfairly competing with the private film industry.[34]

The movement had to be cautious because it lacked the security of a permanent home. The EMB Film Unit lasted only about four years. The GPO Film Unit lasted six. (The Crown Film Unit, with which Grierson had little to do, was disbanded shortly after the war.) In between, sponsorship came from a variety of sources. Paul Rotha has noted that the collapse of Grierson's fragile institutions resulted from either Grierson's absence or his leaving.[35] Grierson had not devised a way to secure the documentary film movement on some basis not requiring his own ingenious involvement.

And finally, the standard was, after all, very high. Only one government organization has approached it with even a small degree of consistency, and that achievement came about in no small part because Grierson, by the time he became deeply involved with documentary in Canada, had a decade of intense experience behind him. He was prepared.

2
A MARRIAGE OF OPPOSITES: THE ESTABLISHMENT OF THE NATIONAL FILM BOARD

Although the National Film Board of Canada was established formally by an Act of Parliament on May 2, 1939, the process had begun in 1936 and was not fully concluded until 1941. The Film Board was born in a five-year struggle between inertia and purpose, or, in Max Weber's terms, between routine and charisma. Grierson brought an alien demand for excellence and an alien way of working into an organization that was slow to realize that it understood and desired neither. Grierson's participation in the latter part of the struggle was to some degree reluctant; history had placed him there. But history was also his ally — along with not a few Canadians.

An infrequently noted fact in the history of the documentary film movement is that Grierson's idea for a film *unit* at the Empire Marketing Board was inspired partly by Canada's own Government Motion Picture Bureau.[1] The MPB had been established in 1923 as an expansion of an Exhibits and Publicity Bureau, under the Department of Trade and Commerce.[2] In the twenties, the MPB made travel and other promotional films which were lively, visually pleasing, and unpretentious. As early as 1931, Grierson had got the EMB to send him to Canada to meet the MPB director, Captain Frank Badgley. By the mid-thirties, however, the MPB had stopped developing. The Depression had so depleted the MPB's budget that no sound-recording equipment was bought until 1934. And Captain Badgley, an Army veteran, had no serious interest in either the art or the social utility of film.

That kind of interest existed in Canada, not at the MPB but among groups of citizens in the major cities who wanted the opportunity to see a wider variety of films than that available through the American-dominated theatre chains. In 1935, Donald Buchanan and a young newspaper editor named Ross McLean helped form the National Film Society in Ottawa. The Society put on programmes which typically included European dramas and documentaries. In 1936, his newspaper having folded, McLean went to London as a private secretary to Vincent Massey, Canada's High Commissioner for England. There McLean sought out Grierson, who then was running the GPO Film Unit. Deeply impressed, McLean convinced Massey of the value and potential of the GPO work. Massey asked McLean to write, for his signature, a report concerning Canadian government film production and distribution. In his report, McLean noted:

> There is no sounder basis for the expansion of trade than a deeper, wider knowledge of differences in tasks and modes of life. These can be conveyed most effectively by interpreting in a wider sense the functions of the Motion Picture Bureau, by improving the quality and enlarging the quantity of Canadian films and by adapting them more consciously to the British public.[3]

McLean concluded with a recommendation that Canada invite Grierson to study the nation's film needs.

In 1938, Grierson received a cable inviting him to Canada to "study every phase of production and distribution" and offer "definite and detailed recommendations" for reorganization. Captain Badgley enthusiastically endorsed the invitation.

The situation that Grierson found in Canada appalled him. The MPB enjoyed an advantage that the British documentary film movement had lacked — security. Unfortunately (in Grierson's view), it was not documentary that was secure, but job tenure. The MPB was too much of a bureaucracy; it was just the opposite in character from the fluid, monastic, committed, goal-oriented EMB unit that it had helped inspire. Grierson wrote in his report that:

> The Bureau suffers ... from the permanence of its staff. Film-making, like all creative processes, requires a continual flow of fresh ideas....A permanent staff, particularly one comprised wholly of technical functionaries, is not likely to build up a body of criticism and be fully sensitive to new developments on the creative side of cinema.[4]

The MPB director, Captain Badgley, the one member of the Bureau who was not a technical functionary, nevertheless had to "seek prior authority for the minutiae of his departmental work."

Compounding the MPB's internal ossification, and perhaps related to it, was another problem. The Bureau had "neither central powers nor central purpose." There was no sense of "propaganda for Canada as a whole," no films that "dramatized [the idea of Canada] and brought [it] into the imagination of the home country." Various government departments had set up their own production units, and there was no central authority coordinating them. Some departments would jealously keep secret from other departments their production plans; in one case, two departments independently had developed very similar scripts on the same subject and had sent crews to the same location at almost the same time. Film distribution was similarly uncoordinated. Requests from overseas for films often would be met separately by two or more departments. There was very little effort to distribute films within Canada.

Grierson's principal recommendations were that the Canadian government establish a committee that would keep Canadian film policy in review and advise the Minister of Trade and Commerce (who had authority over the MPB) about problems and possibilities; develop a more sophisticated, more comprehensive sense of propaganda; centralize all production under the authority of a Government Film Officer, who would not be a member of the Civil Service; permit the hiring of temporary creative help, especially writers and directors; and centralize and develop film distribution.

After submitting his report, Grierson returned to London. Some months later, the Minister of Trade and Commerce cabled Grierson, asking him to return to Canada to help implement his recommendations.

Back in Canada, Grierson insisted that legislation be enacted to secure the mandate needed in order to achieve the objectives. As Grierson was working on the text of the legislation, he was also building support for it. He had to overcome the fears and vested interests of certain government departments and commercial film organizations. He enjoyed the support of the Canadian Prime Minister, William Lyon Mackenzie King, who "had an odd belief in what I was talking about."[5] King would eventually give Grierson "his personal backing and almost a blank cheque in support."[6] There was a special reason for thoughtful Canadians to be receptive to Grierson's ideas. Canada was a huge country, and sparsely populated. West of the Great Lakes, its long southern border had no natural basis. Geographically, and to some extent culturally, the west coast had more affinity with Washington and Oregon than with the rest of Canada. The prairies were an extension of the American prairies. Southern Ontario shared an affinity with the upper Midwest. The Maritimes resembled New England. And French Quebec was a cultural entity unto itself. Factionalism threatened the unity of Canada. "Has Canada got an identity — this everlasting, frustrating, humiliating question!"[7] — was no doubt on the minds of many Canadian leaders. It was apparently on King's mind; Grierson later recalled that the Prime Minister once remarked to him:

> Wouldn't it be a great pity if Canada were to lose her sense of dependence on the Mother Country only to fall into a sense of dependence on . . . "our good neighbour to the South"; and what in fact [are] we going to do about it?[8]

Grierson knew how to speak to such sentiments. As he recalled much later:

> And of course, being a Scotsman, I had always been sensitive to the particular movement under which . . . countries seek rather earnestly to find their identity.[9]

The legislation was drafted and sent to Parliament, which approved the National Film Act on May 2, 1939.[10] The Act specified that the National Film Board would consist of eight members: the Minister of Trade and Commerce as chairman, another Minister, three members from the Civil Service, and three members from outside the Civil Service. Parliament would appropriate funds annually for the Board. There would be a Government Film Commissioner responsible to the Board. He would not be subject to Civil Service regulations. Among other duties, the Commissioner would advise upon the production and distribution of Canadian films "designed to help Canadians in all parts of Canada to understand the ways of living and the problems of Canadians in other parts"; coordinate all government film activities; and advise on all government film production and distribution matters. The Director of the Motion Picture Bureau, "notwithstanding anything in the *Civil Service Act*," would be allowed to hire temporary personnel. Government film production and distribution would be centralized under the MPB director. Thus the Board's function was essentially supervisory; the MPB remained the actual production body.

His mission apparently accomplished, Grierson again left Canada. For some months, however, the National Film Board remained little more than a piece of legislative paper. Although the Board was staffed with its eight members, no Government Film Commissioner was appointed. Grierson had urged that a Canadian fill the position, but the Board found only one Canadian it considered suitably knowledgeable and experienced — E.A. Corbett — but he refused the job.

Had it not been for events in Europe, it is unlikely that the National Film Board would have developed into an exceptional organization. A Commissioner would have been found, with the Motion Picture Bureau remaining a distinct entity, under Captain Badgley's direction. The new

Act gave Badgley a more general mandate, he controlled all government film production, and he could hire temporary personnel, but he
lacked the vision or sense of purpose to do much with his new power.
When the Federal Government, shortly after the passage of the Film
Act, needed a pair of films about employment problems and opportunities, Badgley hired Stuart Legg, an accomplished filmmaker from
England, to make them, but Badgley did so on Grierson's suggestion.

If the passage of the Film Act is the most significant date in the Film
Board's history, then August 31, 1939 — just four months later — is
the second most significant date. That was the day Hitler's troops
marched into Poland. England and France immediately declared war.
Canada followed suit.

Grierson was in Hollywood at the time, stopping there en route to
Australia, from where he had received another invitation to help advise
on government film problems. He postponed his trip, and went instead
to Washington, where he conferred with the British Ambassador on
matters of propaganda film distribution in the United States. In October,
Grierson was still there, and there was still no Commissioner for the
Film Board. The Chairman of the Board wired Grierson. Grierson came
to Ottawa, intending to stay only a few days, but he was persuaded to
accept the job of Commissioner for six months, three of which he would
spend in Australia. His term of service eventually would span the length
of the war.

Grierson's acceptance of the Commissionership introduced a
charismatic force into a routine situation. The Grierson-inspired Act
itself had contained elements which attempted to correct this problem
— the separation of the Film Board (although not the Motion Picture
Bureau) from any other government department, the broader mandate,
and the right to hire temporary personnel — but the positive energy of
charisma was lacking until Grierson set to work, which was, in fact, a
few days before his appointment was made official.[11] Shock waves
started emanating from the Film Board and, although the Motion
Picture Bureau would feel them the hardest, they would soon wash over
all of Ottawa.

One of Grierson's very first acts illustrated both his sense of purpose
and his ability to improvise in its service. The act also precipitated a
major crisis, one that would inform the entire development of the Film
Board. Grierson felt that Canada needed a film on its war effort, but the
Film Board had very little production capability. Grierson talked Louis
de B. Rochemont, the producer of the American *March of Time* series,
into doing one of its monthly issues on Canada. Grierson then left for a

three-month consultancy in Australia. Soon after his departure, Ontario's Premier, Mitchell Hepburn, launched a bitter attack on Prime Minister King, accusing King of failing to meet vigorously Canada's war obligations. In response, King called a general election. Meanwhile, with the Film Board's connivance (but apparently not Grierson's, for he was 12,000 miles away), King got *March of Time* to show him in a favourable light. When the film was completed, Hepburn learned of its pro-King slant, and he banned the film in Ontario. The film and Hepburn's response sparked a lively political brouhaha, which died after King won the election easily. But the incident irrevocably had planted in the minds of informed Canadians the suspicion that the Film Board was little more than a propaganda machine for the party in power.[12] "Here comes a load of trouble," Legg muttered when Grierson arrived back from Australia.[13] For the next forty years, it would be a rare NFB film that included material about contemporary political figures.

Stuart Legg was hired immediately and set to work producing a monthly series of films on Canada's war effort, called *Canada Carries On*. McKay writes of this series:

> Month by month the films were finished in time for release to the theatres — but just. Often it meant editors and negative cutters working around the clock, but a theatrical release date was a sacred commitment.[14]

A large portion of Grierson's energy went into recruitment. In addition to Legg, he brought Raymond Spottiswoode, Stanley Hawes, and Evelyn Spice over from Britain. Norman McLaren, a Scot, was lured from New York. He recruited Irving Jacoby and Julian Roffman (a Canadian expatriate) from the United States. But most of his recruits were young Canadians who had never dreamed of a career in filmmaking. Grierson criss-crossed Canada in search of potential talent:

> Literature, in the broad sense of learning, and philosophy were the first prerequisites of the intelligent person; and then the person could become a filmmaker.[15]

If Grierson was suitably impressed

> he might say: "You want to be a director? You've got lots of imagination. Report for work on Monday."[16]

Learning and imagination apparently came in various guises:

> One day ... he returned ... from a recruiting foray out West. "Watch out," he warned, "the nuts are all coming." ... He had been out interviewing poets, designers, hot-eyed unionists, unfrocked school teachers, maverick journalists. Kids. Non-conformists. Nuts, in a word.[17]

Travelling about the country in search of talent was, during the war, illegal. Beth Bertram, who was in charge of personnel during the later war years, recalls:

> You were supposed to go to the Selective Service and place your order and they would see, in their own good time, whether you got somebody or not. So I was always coaching people to go to Selective Service and pretend they had just heard we had an opening, and not to appear and start working until they had that precious little slip of paper from Selective Services.[18]

Even that formality may have been ignored often. A former recruit recalls:

> Of course nobody got hired. You just got drawn in by a kind of osmosis.[19]

Grierson was not only recruiting, he was training, and his essential objective and effect in this regard appear to have been the opposite of what is normally associated with charisma. According to Weber's analysis, the charismatic movement comes first, and then is rationalized into a formal, routine structure, as followers — necessarily, if the movement is to continue — learn to "make a living out of their calling." Here, the organization existed first, and Grierson's task was to teach the new employees to make a *calling* out of their *living*. One such employee was Grierson's first secretary, whose story was probably typical:

> After two weeks she was determined to resign . . . she hadn't been home for dinner in all that time. Lunch was a hasty sandwich. Night after night it was seven or seven-thirty, or later, when she left the office, and she could have worked later if she hadn't been so hungry. After years of leaving work at five sharp, she was exhausted, injured, and hungry — hungry — hungry. A brief session with Grierson . . . [and] she was reassured that this was only temporary . . . [and] she decided to stay another month. By then she was so interested in the dynamic growth and the excitement engendered in the office that she got over being hungry, and didn't notice that it was still seven and even eight before she packed up her typewriter.[20]

One young $20-a-week apprentice had been at the Board only a week or so, but was already known for his correct, rather formal manner, and his orderly habits. He would arrive at work promptly at nine o'clock and leave promptly at five, never a minute late in either case. One day, on his way out at a few seconds after five o'clock, he passed Grierson in the corridor. The apprentice nodded a "good evening" to Grierson. Grierson stopped and asked him where he was going. The apprentice answered, "Home; it's five o'clock." "WHAT DO YOU MEAN YOU'RE GOING HOME!" thundered Grierson, "GODDAMMIT YOU'VE GOT TO *EAT, DRINK* AND *THINK FILM!!* YOU'RE NOT WATCHING THE CLOCK!" The apprentice took the admonition absolutely literally. Each day thereafter he'd work past midnight until about two in the morning, go home for a few hours' sleep, and rush back before "normal" starting time. After a week or so of such devotion, he was called into Grierson's office. Grierson told him, "Look, that's not what I meant. You're killing yourself." Grierson explained that he had meant to attack the nine-to-five mentality, not to set impossible demands.[21] The young apprentice eventually became one of the Film Board's most distinguished producers.

Stanley Jackson, who joined the Film Board very early and who has become well-known for his films and excellent commentaries, remembers that:

> There were virtually no positions, no compartments, no kind of stratification. We were a group of people he had *excited* into thinking this was an important thing to do.

Not everyone in Ottawa was impressed with Grierson's recruits. According to McKay, many civil servants resented

> their youth and vitality and eagerness to get to work ... their uninhibited conversation ... females in purple slacks ... males with long untidy hair and an air of Greenwich Village bohemianism ... [unmatched] socks ... young men with only a few months' service having their way paid all across the country ... the unbelievable items submitted on their expense accounts: carrots to feed a horse; face cream for makeup; rubber boots so they could shoot in a swamp.[22]

And not every government filmmaker was so excitable. Many didn't last long. The Film Board was the one government organization in which personnel turnover was constant. But Grierson had a more immediate problem. Captain Badgley and his staff were experienced bureaucrats, with guaranteed permanent employment. They were older. During the thirties, there had been little production money available, and they were not used to working at the pace Grierson expected. And because Badgley had managed to keep the Bureau and their jobs intact during the Depression, his staff felt very loyal to him.

The once pleasant and cooperative relationship between Badgley and Grierson deteriorated rapidly. It was a daily struggle between Badgley's priorities of administration and Grierson's priorities of production. Badgley was a careful administrator; Grierson's philosophy of administration was to "administer erratically." For Badgley, the important thing about making films was that it be done in the correct manner, at a leisurely pace, and according to rules and regulations. He suffered from the "neatness syndrome," the displacement of the importance of goals by the importance of means.[23] For Grierson, the important thing about making films during a war was to "bang them out and no misses." Grierson would have subscribed to the attitude voiced by Thomas Edison when asked about his rules of procedure: "Rules! Hell! There ain't no rules around here! We're tryin' to accomplish sump'n."

Not only did the MPB staff refuse to work past five o'clock, "they wouldn't even start a job if they didn't think they could finish it by five," even if the job was something like screening a forty-five minute film at four-thirty.[24]

As the organization grew larger, and the proportion of Grierson-recruited, promising, and motivated staff increased, the recalcitrance of Captain Badgley and his staff might not have caused much trouble — except that there was a structural flaw in the relationship between the Film Board and the MPB. The MPB, where actual production took place, had remained under the administration of the Department of Trade and Commerce. The Film Board itself was independent of any particular government department, but lacked direct authority over the MPB. The rapidly growing new staff were NFB employees, but performed most of their work at the MPB.

At least once, however, the tension between Badgley and Grierson yielded a valuable result. Tom Daly remembers that both Grierson and Badgley had to sign memos *jointly* if an NFB employee was to work at the Bureau or go back to the Board. Once, when Daly had finished a job at the Bureau, Badgley wouldn't sign the memorandum authorizing Daly to go back to the Board, even though there was nothing more for Daly to do at the Bureau. Stanley Hawes, who was in charge of Film Board personnel working at the Bureau, found work for Daly: cleaning up a room filled with film — films in cans, films in boxes, films just lying around, bits and pieces of films, negatives — all of it inflammable. Daly's job was to sort through the material, and to save and catalogue whatever might be useful. This turned out to be the beginning of the Film Board's outstanding stock-shot library, from which hundreds of Film Board films, including the *Canada Carries On* series and the more widely distributed *World in Action* series, would soon draw material.

Grierson's appointment had been extended until January 1941, and was likely to be extended beyond that, but in November 1940 he wrote to the Chairman of the Board, James A. MacKinnon, that he did not wish to remain beyond January. In this letter, Grierson argued that:

> ... the Bureau should be brought under the administration of the National Film Board and freed from the trammels which attend a section of a department primarily engaged in a different kind of work....

> I foresee one danger in the next phase of the Board's development . . . a tendency to associate the Board more and more closely with the administration of the Department of Trade and Commerce. This, presumably, is to ensure that the National Film Board, like other government departments, will jump through the hoop of Civil Service regulation. It is, I am sure, a mistake. . . .
>
> Today most governments are finding it necessary to use increasingly such media as radio and film, and everywhere one notices the same tug-of-war. On the one hand, the Civil Servants with their formalities of government regulation; on the other hand, the creative people protesting that Civil Service procedure weakens the vitality and paralyzes the initiative which are necessary for good work. One notices that wherever the weight of influence has lain with the Civil Service, the spark has gone out and the use of the creative media has not been remarkable. . . .
>
> It will be urged that making films is no different from any other government activity and may, therefore, be fitted into the normal machine. Films, however, are different from other articles of government activity in one fundamental. It is at this point that the traditional rites of nine to five break down. A routine average will not do. They must either achieve showmanship and distinction or they are not worth doing at all. . . .[25]

The letter created heated debate among the members of the Board. The three who belonged to the Civil Service opposed Grierson's views. The three from private life agreed with him. The Chairman invited Grierson to elaborate upon his letter. To the Chairman, Grierson presented his case even more strongly, summing it up with the argument that, if the MPB was to be the instrument of the Board's plans, the Board must be given authority "to determine style and manner and purpose of production" at the MPB.[26] In effect, Grierson was arguing that the Board should absorb the MPB.

The Board appeared to accept Grierson's recommendations, and they persuaded him to stay on for another six months on the understanding that his recommendations would be acted upon. But as time passed without action, tensions grew worse:

> Protest meetings were held by the permanent civil servants in the Bureau demanding that the status quo be observed, and expressing complete support of Captain Badgley. Film work was held up unduly. Some of the new staff arrogantly ignored Captain Badgley in giving orders to his staff. The split between the old and the new regimes deepened.[27]

The conflict was finally resolved on June 11, 1941, when the Cabinet officially transferred, by an Order in Council, the MPB to the control of the Film Board. Grierson now had full control over the organization, which finally enjoyed the "central powers and central purpose" that he had spoken of in his initial visit to Canada three years earlier, and the need for which Ross McLean had sensed in 1936.

Captain Badgley was offered the directorship of the Stills Division, which remained for a while under the Department of Trade and Commerce. He rejected the offer, and secured a transfer to the Department of National Revenue.

Many years later, Grierson acknowledged that the creation of the National Film Board had required

> liquidating many vested interests. . . .[And there was] a great deal of cruelty in the liquidation of vested interests, so don't think it was an innocent affair.[28]

Grierson had won the personal struggle, but it would be inaccurate to generalize that charisma had driven out routine. For, on that level, there was a metaphorical sense in which the struggle lacked innocence. It had begun in seduction and ended in something like rape (albeit statutory), not combat, and the issue was an organization that, for the purposes of creativity in documentary film, inherited the best traits of both sides. The result was a peculiar hybrid vigour remarkably analogous to that possessed by the illegitimate child Pearl, of Nathaniel Hawthorne's *The Scarlet Letter*:

> Her nature appeared to possess depth, too, as well as variety; but . . . it lacked reference and adaptation to the world in which she was born. The child could not be made amenable to rules. In giving her existence, a great law had been broken; and the result was a being whose elements were perhaps beautiful and brilliant, but all in disorder; or with an order peculiar to themselves, amidst which the point of variety and arrangement was difficult or impossible to comprehend.

In the next few years following the NFB's absorption of the MPB, the source of the Film Board's creative energy would be predominantly charismatic, for in addition to the leadership of Grierson and the intrinsic interest of filmmaking, there was the war. But it was not until long after the war, when a fertile balance between routine and charisma developed, that the Film Board began to produce the kind of documentary that approached the standards Grierson had originally set. The spirit of Grierson would prove a major force in the emergence of these documentaries, but he did not have all the answers. The ghost of Captain Badgley, if often an irritant, would contribute something, too.

3
THE BIG BANG:
THE FILM BOARD AND THE
WAR

The National Film Board's absorption of the Motion Picture Bureau established a basic structure that the Film Board has retained, in its essentials, to this day. The legislation contained certain ambiguities, but it was clear enough for wartime, and clear enough for Grierson. The "central powers and central purposes" that Grierson had sought were now a structural reality. A single authority now controlled both policy and production, ends and means.

The next four years were a time of phenomenal expansion for the Film Board. In October 1941, four months after the absorption of the MPB, there were fifty-five people on the staff. By December 1942, there were 293. By January 1944, there were 458. In 1945, the number of staff reached a peak of 787. During the war, the Film Board produced approximately five hundred films. By the end of the war, a single series, *World In Action*, was reaching a monthly audience of 30 million in twenty-one countries.[1]

This growth was rapid and variegated, but it was not as haphazard as it might have seemed at the time. It had a common theme — wholeness — and a single agent — Grierson. In a CBC broadcast made in 1940, Grierson had said:

> The Act most duly says that [the Board's] function is to coordinate government film activities. But, when that sentence was drafted, I remembered one thing, why can't we say and be done with it, the National Film Board will be the *eyes of Canada*. It will, through a national use of cinema, see Canada and see it whole — its people and its purposes.[2]

The war provided the context for realizing this wholeness. On the very day that the NFB absorbed the MPB, another order-in-council was passed, this one designating the Minister of National War Services as the Minister to whom the Film Board was to report. And in 1943,

Grierson took on an additional job as Director of the Wartime Information Board. The dual role gave Grierson enormous power. By having complete control — subject to the two Boards — of all government propaganda, he enjoyed almost complete freedom over the appointment and development of creative staff and at the same time worked closely with the Cabinet on crucial policy matters. At one moment he might be viewing the rushes of a novice's first film; at the next moment, he might be conferring with government ministers.

It was Grierson's policy that he, and he alone, approach the government on film matters. He "didn't want the waters muddied." Grierson thus became a broker between the interests of government and the development of the Film Board and its staff. He milked the government of anything he could squeeze out of it. Jane Marsh Beveridge recalls that "if a government department didn't know they needed a film, Grierson persuaded them that they did." Judy Crawley remembers an example:

> Grierson called me up one day and said, "Judy, can you cook?" I'd been married only a couple of months and I wasn't sure. I said, "Why?" He said, "I think we can get some money from the Department of Agriculture [for] a film about cooking apples, because there is a surplus."[3]

That was the origin of a film called *Four New Apple Dishes*.

Grierson not only found money wherever he could, he also protected the interests of the filmmaker, declaring that even the worst film "had a right to six months of no criticism." He is said to have remarked, "Never give a sponsor an even break."[4] Once, a dispute arose between the Army and the Film Board about a recruiting film for women. Julian Roffman, the filmmaker assigned to the project, wanted to do a musical, complete with Busby Berkeley routines. The army officer in charge of the project responded coolly to the proposal. The idea was a bit irregular, and the cost would be higher than the Army wanted to incur. Grierson reportedly told the officer that although the officer might know the army, he didn't know films. "This small young man is an excellent filmmaker. Let him do what he wants." Grierson got his way. Roffman made *The Proudest Girl in the World*. And the Army liked the film.[5]

If Grierson seems to have been opportunistic, he was, as Evelyn Cherry has described him, an "opportunist in its finest sense ... a clever, far-seeing opportunist who saw an advantage and used it expertly."[6] Getting money to make *Four New Apple Dishes* or turning a recruiting film into a musical may seem far removed from the needs of a nation at war, but only when considered in isolation. Like most of

Grierson's minor coups, they also served the central purpose. It was the essence of his notion of wholeness that a seemingly infinite variety of films and activities, given the proper orientation, were relevant to the wartime effort. "Truth in its corporate conception," Grierson now was saying, "has many facets."[7]

This theme of wholeness revealed itself in three major areas: the Film Board's internal structure, the character of its production, and the forms of its distribution.

Internally, the Board had very little formal organization. Even its facilities lacked observable order, the Board's operations being dispersed among fourteen buildings scattered about Ottawa. The force holding the NFB together was charismatic, fluid, and goal-oriented, as in Grierson's old Empire Marketing Board unit. Evelyn Cherry remembers of her days as a young filmmaker that:

> there wasn't one single day, to my knowledge, that we weren't reminded, in one way or another, that we were serving the people of Canada, and that everything we were doing was with that object in mind.[8]

This sense of purposefulness helped build confidence. Marjorie McKay describes the attitude of the young recruits thus:

> Here was ... a sense of doing something which mattered. The writer of a script of a recruiting film was certain his film would bring so many recruits that the offices couldn't handle them. The cameraman on a film on first aid knew his film was going to save lives. The editor of a film about the need for farm labour believed he was saving the harvest. And behind them, the stenographers, the typists, the stores men and shipping clerks, the accountants and business managers, felt they were making these films possible and they in turn were helping their country.[9]

The spirit of teamwork and togetherness was deliberately promoted. In the early years of the Film Board, its films did not carry personal credits. Stuart Legg explained:

> All our people work strictly as teams in which the corporate effort is everything. Since films are essentially things contributively made, we reckon that their weight lies in the collective effort and that the individual who claims a solo performance tends to become a feather in a vacuum. We therefore don't put personal credits on our pictures.[10]

There was little interpersonal competitiveness:

> You were trying to make the best damn film you could. But you weren't trying to beat down somebody else's film.[11]

This sense of cooperation seems to have been pervasive. Evelyn Cherry recalls that

> this [togetherness] must sound very Polyanna, all this . . . about how . . .
> eveybody loved each other. . . . But it was true. We did love each other.
> We worked in groups. We recognized cinema as a group thing.

Red Burns, another wartime employee, remembers that

> everybody was concerned with the whole. And it wasn't that everyone
> said, "We're concerned with the whole." That's simply the way every-
> body worked.

Along with cooperation came a freedom from strict role definition. To Beth Bertram, the Film Board's first personnel director, Grierson seemed to believe

> that an organization shouldn't jell, or get into a firm position. About every
> six months he would say, "Well, a few people are going to be moved
> around now," and the whole thing would go up in the air and come down
> again, everybody in a different job.

This role freedom reached all across the Board, not just at the personal level but also at the branch level. Marjorie McKay recalls that

> it was a fabulous time to work at the Film Board. Production and
> Distribution overlapped at times. Technical departments overlapped. There
> wasn't the fragmentation. One day you'd be doing this. The next day you'd
> be doing something quite different. And the next day you'd try to merge
> the two together.

There were no committees, and, although Grierson had a core of experienced assistants, there was almost no stratification, no people standing between Grierson and the filmmaker. He was always accessible. Once, a young female assistant rushed up to Grierson and angrily asserted her desire to direct a film herself. Grierson calmly responded, "Why don't you?" The next day, she was working on a film.[12]

Stanley Jackson remembers that

> there was a girl called Margaret Ann Adamson . . . of whom Grierson
> joked, "The real function of Margaret Ann is that she has a large apartment
> near the Film Board." This apartment was our "club." That's the place
> you met. *Everybody* — neg-cutters, secretaries, too — met there. You had
> a drink, you talked about films, about the Board, about everything.
> Discussions and arguments. That's the kind of organization it was.

Thirty years after the end of the war, Tom Daly, with a wistful glaze in his eye, and with equal emphasis on each word, remembered the war years more simply as a time when "There were no memorandums."

In production, too, there was a theme of wholeness relating a series such as *World In Action*, which eventually reached a monthly international audience of 30 million, to a film such as *Four New Apple Dishes*, the audience figures for which are unknown.

The aim of *Canada Carries On* was to dramatize Canada's war effort. The films were composed of original footage to the extent possible, but the pressures of time, money, and transportation — this was during the Atlantic blockade — required that original footage be supplemented by stock footage from the rapidly growing stock-shot library. The first film in the series, *Atlantic Patrol*, released in April 1940, used some original footage, but the film was made mostly from stock footage from the Canadian Navy. The next two, *Letter from Aldershot* and *The Home Front*, used mostly original material, but also some stock footage.

But Grierson and Legg believed very strongly that Canada's war effort could not be dramatized meaningfully if it were seen in isolation from world events. In 1941, some films in the series dealt with Canada only tangentially. *Churchill's Island*, made in June 1941, was about the defence of Britain. The film was made up entirely of British film and captured German footage. Richard Griffith wrote of this film that what made it "seem an altogether new kind of film was that it dealt with the defence plan of Britain *as a whole*."[13] *Churchill's Island* won a special Academy Award in 1941.

Another notable *Canada Carries On* film with an international emphasis was *War Clouds in the Pacific*. A compilation from stock footage, the film predicted that war would break out between the United States and Japan. *War Clouds in the Pacific* was finished at a frenetic pace and released in Canadian theatres in late November 1941. Stuart Legg recalls that "everyone thought we were mad."[14] Ten days after the film's release, the Japanese attacked Pearl Harbor.

Suddenly there was a demand in the United States for background material. Seizing this opportunity, Grierson was in New York City the next day and sold the film to United Artists for immediate release. But some of the footage used in the film was from the American *March of Time* series. *March of Time* had known that the Film Board was using some of their footage for *Canada Carries On* films but hadn't cared, because the *Canada Carries On* series was not distributed in the United States. Now they cared. Claiming that their footage was being used improperly, *March of Time* sought an injunction on *War Clouds of the Pacific*. The injunction would keep the film out of the United States market at least until after *March of Time* could put together a release of their own.

Grierson immediately countered *March of Time*'s ploy by phoning newsreel companies and getting replacement footage. Then he let it be known that all the *March of Time* footage in *War Clouds in the Pacific* would be replaced within twenty-four hours. The top brass of *March of Time* quickly changed their attitude, and allowed the Film Board to use the footage in return for a credit line.

Perhaps to avoid a suggestion of parochialism in the series title, the Film Board released *War Clouds in the Pacific* in the United States not as a *Canada Carries On* film, but under a new series title, *World in Action*. After *War Clouds in the Pacific*, *World in Action* became a separate series, with Legg as writer and producer, and Tom Daly as editor. Grierson later turned *Canada Carries On* over to Sydney Newman and Guy Glover, who had complained about the dearth of Canadian content in *Canada Carries On*. Glover stayed with the series for two years; Newman continued to produce it for several years after the war.

Canada Carries On did not, however, turn parochial during the war. *Canada Carries On* emphasized Canada, but in relation to the world. *World in Action* emphasized the world, but in relation to Canada. This distinction was suggested even in the respective individual titles of the two series: for example, *Look to the North*, *Battle of the Harvest*, and *Women are Warriors* in *Canada Carries On*; *Food: Weapon of Conquest*, *Geopolitik: Hitler's Plan for Empire*, and *Pincers on Axis Europe* in *World in Action*. By the end of the war thirty films, including those that had originally been *Canada Carries On* films, had been released. *Canada Carries On* continued until April 1951.

But war was not the only subject of the Board's wartime films. The Film Board had been established as a peacetime organization. This meant that its mission was wider than just the production of war films. The timing of the war nicely accommodated Grierson's hope that the Film Board would show Canada "as a whole." In an early radio broadcast, he had said:

> It would be a poor information service . . . which kept harping on war to the exclusion of everything [else]. . . . War films, yes, but more films, too, about the everyday things of life, the values, the ideals which make life worth living.[15]

By 1942, the Film Board was producing non-war films, among them a series on Ukrainian, Icelandic, French, and Italian minorities, and a series on Canadian artists. By the end of the war, non-war topics included unemployment compensation (*A Man and his Job*), day nurseries (*Before They Are Six*), post-war farming (*Food As It Might Be*), coal-mining (*Getting Out The Coal*), forest conservation (*Trees for Tomorrow*), natural history (*Mites and Monsters*), prairie resettlement (*New Home in the West*), opportunities in the Northwest (*Land for*

Pioneers), weed control (*Just Weeds*), salmon (*Salmon Run*), West Coast Indians (*Totems*), and, of course, new apple dishes.

Even *Canada Carries On*, a series originally meant to dramatize Canada's war effort, began to broaden its scope before the war ended. Sydney Newman remembers that:

> When I took over the series, it had dropped in popularity down to about 190 bookings a month. It was clear that the war was being won, and my job was to begin converting the series to peace. The first thing I did was to ask Lorne Greene [the narrator] to leave. His voice was too strongly associated with the early war-oriented films. So I dropped him. He wouldn't speak to me for two years.

For the two major series, *Canada Carries On* and *World in Action*, Grierson sought theatrical distribution. Both series were *sold* to distributors, for two reasons: if they were given away, no one would think they were any good; and it also provided a yardstick for gauging the series' success. Ninety percent of Canadian theatres showed these films. Both series were distributed in Great Britain, New Zealand, and Australia, and *World in Action* went also to India, South Africa, Latin America, and the United States.[16]

But in a vast and sparsely populated country such as Canada, Grierson had a great opportunity to develop the kind of non-theatrical distribution he had merely experimented with in Britain. Under the direction of Donald Buchanan, NFB Distribution sought every available Canadian outlet. All major films were translated into French, which immediately increased the Canadian audience, but probably the most imaginative distribution mechanism was the "travelling theatre," or "rural circuit." This was eminently suited to Canada's geography. The Film Board hired projectionists, and gave them a salary, a mileage allowance, projection equipment, sometimes a generator, a monthly allotment of films, and a list of communities to visit. For many Canadians, the first visit of the travelling theatre to their community was the first time they'd seen a film of any kind. There are stories of groups coming forty miles by canoe to attend a screening, of an old man walking seven miles to see a show, and many others. One such story recalls a phenomenon associated with the invention of cinema a half a century earlier:

> In a far-northern Saskatchewan community the audience was seated on two-by-ten planks set on two-foot blocks of large cordwood down the length of the hall. One of the films showed a train coming straight down the track toward the audience, who had never seen a train before, let alone a movie of one. As the train came closer and closer, and loomed larger and larger on the screen, the audience leaned farther and farther backward. At

the climax of the scene every member of the audience tumbled backward, and they and the planks and the firewood slabs crashed resoundingly on the floor.[17]

By June 1942, there were forty-seven travelling theatres, and they reached an estimated 280,000 Canadians a year.

Shortly after the introduction of the travelling theatres, the Film Board organized a trade union circuit, through which films were shown in union halls, and an industrial circuit, through which films were shown in large factories. A volunteer projection service was developed, whereby local service groups could show films in their communities. The Film Board established regional libraries, from which individuals or groups could borrow films. By 1942, there were twenty regional libraries.[18]

Grierson was proud of this non-theatrical distribution system; he called it "one of the most exciting things I have seen — the swift development within a matter of about three years of a great new audience and a great new system of information."[19]

These three holistic systems — the organizational structure, the range of film production, and the variety of distribution — were themselves interrelated, at least in the ideal case. Evelyn Cherry remembers that:

Through our distribution system we had the most splendid flow of enthusiasm [for NFB films], and ideas for films kept coming back from the people. . . . The film ideas came in, and then we sat and talked about how we could do it. We'd say, "Now how can we get this done in order to send a film back to them?"[20]

Although this theme of "wholeness" pervaded the Film Board's wartime expansion, there were two key areas in the Board's work in which it was not realized: the Board's relationship with the Canadian government, and the aesthetics of the films themselves.

Early in 1943 Grierson confided to Sir Stephen Tallents, who a decade earlier had been the British documentary movement's "angel" in the civil service, that the Film Board will

operate . . . far closer to the political scene than informationists are expected to do. It is dangerous, of course, but personally I don't care a damn.[21]

Grierson didn't conceal his devil-may-care attitude. Exactly one month before he wrote to Tallents, a journalist reported in a generally favourable article that:

Grierson uses the speediest and most direct route to anything he wants, slashing red tape. . . . A lot of people in Ottawa gun for him. Some accuse

him of aiming for greater authority in the propaganda field, of wanting to
be a Canadian Dr. Goebbels.[22]

Ottawa had been suspicious of Grierson ever since the *March of Time*
incident in 1940. Two years later, Ontario banned a *Canada Carries On*
edition, *Inside Fighting Canada*, primarily because it contained a
favourable reference to the Prime Minister:

> Behind the spires of parliament and the leadership of William Lyon
> Mackenzie King stands a people disciplined for war.

Grierson's defence of the line of commentary referred to the international function of the film:

> It would be strange to Canadians if in a survey of Britain's war effort
> special care were taken to omit the name of Mr. Churchill.[23]

Criticism of a Film Board film became an annual affair, although each
year for a different reason. In 1943, the Board's *World in Action* film,
The Gates of Italy, was accused of being "soft on fascism."[24] In 1944,
Our Northern Neighbor — another *World in Action* edition — was
attacked for being pro-communist. A member of Parliament complained:

> There has been a growing suspicion that the Film Board has become a
> propagandist for a type of socialist and foreign philosophy.... My
> objection is that we have a national instrument of government that is
> obviously putting out soviet propaganda.[25]

In 1945, the Film Board got into yet another kind of political trouble,
again with a *World in Action* film, *The Balkan Powder Keg*. Apparently
the commentary included a leak concerning the Canadian Cabinet's
Balkan policy. King asked that the film be withdrawn. Grierson
resisted, insisting to his Board of Governors that the Film Board must
not become simply a spokesman for the government's point of view.[26]

Thus during the course of the war the Film Board was accused of
being a tool of the party in power, of softness toward fascism, of
pro-communism, and finally — to make the circle complete — of
exceeding its limits of independence from the aims of government. One
fact emerges from this carnival of suspicions: the Film Board kept its
own counsel, answering to no one ... except Grierson.

Ironically, those Canadians who suspected Grierson of wanting to
become the Canadian Dr. Goebbels were vaguely correct. The wartime
NFB films were terribly propagandistic — not for fascism, nor for
communism, nor for Mackenzie King, but for winning the war. The
films were done with flair, and they managed to cram a lot of
information into brief and snappy packages. A critic who has closely

analysed the wartime films has pointed out that the films masterfully employ Eisensteinian contrasts in order to create metaphoric images.[27] But techniques alone, however brilliantly employed, do not make art, especially if Grierson's early aesthetic theory is used as a standard. There is no intimate relationship with the material, no exploration of actuality. The sound tracks in *Canada Carries On* and *World in Action* overwhelm the images. The commentary is shouted, the music shrilly dramatic. Artful the films may have been; art, no. They were tracts. They drew only from the Russian half of Grierson's original synthesis.

The urgency of the war cannot be blamed for the excessiveness of the Film Board's wartime propaganda. The American *Why We Fight* series, produced by Frank Capra, was far less shrill than *World in Action*. And in England, from the Crown Film Unit, some wartime propaganda films emerged which still speak to an audience today: *Listen to Britain*, *London Can Take It*, *A Diary for Timothy*, and *Fires Were Started* — all by the same director, Humphrey Jennings. These were films which really did pursue something akin to "the creative treatment of actuality" as Grierson had once written of it. Whereas the Canadian war films were almost always compilation films, with an overbearing commentary carrying the burden of ordering the material, Jennings's films were made from original footage which he himself shot or directed. His method resembled Flaherty's. Like Flaherty, he took his time; *Fires Were Started* was a year in the making. In terms almost paraphrasing Grierson's earlier praise of Flaherty's method, an associate of Jennings remembers that he

> would interpret a situation in disconnected visuals and he wouldn't quite know why he was shooting them ... until he got them together. Then he created a pattern out of them.[28]

In *World in Action* films, the relationship between the order and the actuality was almost exactly the opposite. The filmmakers started with the message and then searched the stock-shot library for material to accompany the message and perhaps even support it. And whereas the Film Board's messages were heavy-handed, Jennings's films did not incite, proclaim, berate, or harangue, but simply affirmed the values of the culture threatened by the war. His films can be shown today without eliciting derisive laughter. The Film Board's wartime propaganda films cannot.

Grierson had known Jennings when the latter was just starting out at the GPO Film Unit. Grierson disliked Jennings; he considered him a dilettante. Grierson wasn't alone. Basil Wright, the director of *Song of Ceylon*, thought that Jennings had a patronizing, "almost sneering" attitude toward the lower classes. (Wright has since revised this opinion.[29]) During the war, Grierson was aware of Jennings's work and of the work of the Crown Film Unit as a whole, and he disapproved of it. In an article called "The Nature of Propaganda," Grierson wrote:

> *London Can Take It* was a beautiful film but it raises a very special issue of relativity in propaganda. That is the difference between primary and secondary effects. . . . *London Can Take It* created enormous sympathy for England and so far so good. The question is whether creating sympathy necessarily creates confidence.[30]

In the same article, Grierson, calling Hitler a great master of propaganda, asked for a more positive, aggressive propaganda:

> Propaganda on the offensive is, like every weapon of war, a cold-blooded one. Its only moral is that the confusion and defeat of the enemy are the supreme good. In that sense it is a black art.

Meanwhile, the British filmmakers, many of them former protégés of Grierson, thought that the Canadian films were "a bit over-direct, even to the point of vulgarity."[31] Grierson responded with a long article called "The Documentary Idea: 1942," in which he wrote that because propaganda

> is a question of giving people a pattern of thought and feeling about highly complex and urgent events, we give it as we know, with a minimum of dawdling over how some poor darling happens to react to something or other. This is one time, we say, when history doesn't give a good goddamn who is being the manly little fellow in adversity and is only concerned with the designs for living and dying that will actually and in fact shape the future. If our stuff pretends to be certain, it's because people need certainty. . . . If we bang them out one fortnight and no misses, instead of sitting six months on our fannies cuddling them to sweet smotheroo, it's because a lot of bravos in Russia and Japan and Germany are banging out things too and we'd better learn how, in time. If the manner is objective and hard, it's because we believe the next phase of human development needs that kind of mental approach. . . .
>
> . . . [These days] one has to chill the mind to so many emotional defences of the decadent and so many smooth rationalizations of the ineffective. One has to even chill the mind to what, in the vacuum of daydreams, one might normally admire. In our world it is specially necessary . . . to guard against the aesthetic argument.[32]

Grierson went on to stress his disapproval of what he regarded as parochialism in British wartime films, a failure to see Britain in the context of a larger whole.

Grierson was calling for propaganda that would "give" people "a pattern of thought and feeling about highly complex and urgent events," but Jennings seems to have done precisely that. As Erik

Barnouw has suggested, perhaps Jennings's films, by showing real human beings behaving in a civilized, calm way under conditions of great danger, "helped set a pattern for crisis behaviour." Jennings's films are "films of affirmation."[33] They are tough films, which, in Auden's phrase, "teach the free man how to praise." They do not lie. They present an honest picture of England under siege, and yet manage to achieve a positive tone, a sense of hopefulness.

These films apparently were very influential overseas, especially in America. They seem to have performed the propagandistic function without assuming "that being human could ... be postponed until some postwar era."[34]

This is an irresolvable issue, for there is no way to determine the comparative effectiveness of the two approaches to propaganda. Nevertheless, the evidence, slight as it may be, suggests that the burden of proof would lie with those who would agree with Grierson. Jennings's work was art — Grierson admitted it — and it seems to have been just as effective as propaganda.

There are, however, further points on which the issue is of interest. Jennings was apparently more interested in his own development than in the documentary movement as a whole. At least he struck some of his colleagues that way. When, during the war, other British documentary filmmakers shared the responsibility of producing, Jennings did not. "His whole approach," Sussex writes, "ran counter to Grierson's ideal of group collaboration in the interests of public service."[35] But it may have been impossible, or at least extremely difficult, for a large talent to work in a collaborative way, at least in a Grierson-run or Grierson-inspired organization. There was the case of Flaherty and the EMB in the early thirties, and in Canada there was another interesting case, although there is little information about it. Joris Ivens, an extremely accomplished Dutch filmmaker, did one free-lance assignment for the Film Board. The film, called *Action Stations*, was composed of original material, but lacked the feeling and vitality present in most of Ivens' better-known work. And never to this day has a distinguished visiting filmmaker produced an outstanding documentary film at the Film Board. "Truth in its corporate conception" was also a corporate endeavour.

One thing is certain. By the nineteen-forties, Grierson had drifted far from his early line of thinking. He had always called himself a "propagandist first and filmmaker second," and his aesthetic was always action-oriented, but it had been based on the principle that "it is in the hands of artists, and artists alone, that truth becomes a principle of action." Near the end of the thirties, his increasingly strident anti-aesthetic line seems to have been directed less against the ostensible target — artiness, or art-for-art's-sake — than against a hidden one: truth. He was wary of artists because they told the truth. Sometime in the late thirties, he off-handedly characterized his aim as being to "tell a lie today and make it come true tomorrow."[36] In 1939 or 1940, in a phrase that is still often quoted at the Film Board and elsewhere, he called for an art that was "not a mirror but a hammer," an art that

> is a weapon in our hands to see and to say what is right and good and beautiful, and hammer it out as the mold and pattern of men's actions.[37]

Films should be sermons, carrying messages illustrated by pictures, rather than creations of truth discovered in actuality. Grierson suggested that in times of great change "the only songs worth writing were marching songs," and he expressed admiration for Goering's famous, pithy remark, "When anyone mentions the word culture, I reach for my gun."[38] Much of this may have been rhetoric, designed to startle, and there is no doubt that Grierson was sincere in his desire to use propaganda for democratic purposes. But there is also little doubt that it was now out-and-out propaganda, not art, that he was talking about. He seems to have lost confidence in the very ideals he wanted to propagandize. He had "chilled his mind" to them. He mistrusted the *polis*. It would be a fair question to ask: which was more patronizing, the work of Humphrey Jennings, which did not try to hammer correct attitudes into people's heads, or the wartime philosophy of Grierson's, which did?

But Grierson was no longer a filmmaker himself. He was a man who made it possible for others to make films. He was systematic in his thinking, and he was far-seeing. The British documentary film movement, within a few years of the end of the war, exhausted itself. The Crown Film Unit dissolved in 1952. Jennings's post-war work did not match his wartime films. (He was killed in 1950, falling off a cliff while making a film.)

If no great films emerged from the wartime Film Board, a great *potential* did. Through the variety of production and the extended, imaginative distribution system, Grierson accomplished several feats crucial to the Film Board's future. One is that he built up a constituency for the Film Board. Millions of Canadians appreciated it. Foreigners began to notice it. He also developed a deep respect for craftsmanship and an almost universal competence among the large, young staff. Guy Glover has put this point well:

> Grierson knew that if the Film Board was going to work at all, it had to learn to work with people of modest talent. Its day-to-day work couldn't depend on genius or remarkable talent.... [His aim was] decent craftsmanship rather than wildly imaginative artists. If you look at the totality of the Film Board, *that's what it is.*

This totality of careful craftsmanship, rare and valuable in its own right, eventually would provide a context for the occasional documentary that had craftsmanship and more.

And if Grierson discouraged the pursuit of "the creative treatment of actuality" as he had once conceived of it, he implanted suggestions of it in his staff. Norman McLaren remembers that:

> He assessed the artistic value of a film through a whole structure and set of references to other human values —and especially to values of a specific human society at a given time.[39]

Margaret Ann Elton remembered that Grierson

> had the cadenced righteousness of the Old Testament, and most of the thunder. The Human Condition, as described for example by Dostoevski or Melville, occupied him a lot.[40]

But finally, as Grierson himself wrote, although documentary was an anti-aesthetic movement (which, as we have seen, it wasn't), "What confuses history is that we had always the good sense to use the aesthetes."[41] Stanley Jackson remembers that at one of those parties at Margaret Ann's, Grierson startled the group around him — in whom he had, of course, inculcated his utilitarian aesthetic — by remarking that Norman McLaren, who had recently joined the Film Board, was the most important man on the staff. Grierson had recruited McLaren with the promise that he would not be asked to do propaganda films,[42] but soon after his arrival in Ottawa McLaren was applying his experimental genius to such baldly utilitarian purposes as publicizing war savings (*V for Victory*), urging people to buy war bonds (*Hen Hop* and *Five for Four*), moving the mail (*Mail Early for Christmas*) and fighting inflation (*Dollar Dance*). In 1943, McLaren took on the responsibility of supervising and developing the Film Board's animation department. And yet McLaren eventually would prove Grierson's remark uncannily prophetic, not only by the fame his post-war masterpieces such as *Neighbors*, *Pas de deux*, and *A Chairy Tale* would win for the Film Board, but also for his indirect contribution to the development of the Film Board documentary.

If the aesthetics of the Film Board's wartime documentary were, in retrospect, disappointing, Grierson nevertheless had created an enormous potential for the production of films approaching his early standard. This potential would remain latent, however, until after the Film Board endured an almost fatal crisis and acquired some organizational characteristics and attitudes which ran directly counter to Grierson's thinking.

4
THE POST-WAR CRISIS

The war had meant a lot to the Film Board. The war brought Grierson there as Commissioner, and kept him at the helm until its end. The war gave the young organization an immediate function, an incontrovertible justification for its explosive growth. The war was uncontroversial; few could dissent from propagandizing for the enemy's defeat. The action was far away, which meant that Ottawa was a safe and logical place for a large-scale film operation.

Perhaps most of all, the war was timely. Had it broken out a year or two later, the Film Board might have lost the chance to get Grierson. The Board might have already established policies and procedures which it could not easily adapt to the opportunities the war offered. But had the war broken out several months earlier, the Film Board would not have been established as a peace-time organization. Because it was established as a peace-time organization, the end of the war did not imply the Film Board's automatic dissolution. (There were cutbacks after the war. For example, the staff, which had reached a wartime high of 787, was cut back to a low of about 589.[1] But it would seem extremely unlikely that, had there been no war, the staff of the Film Board would have grown, by the late forties, anywhere near that figure. Thus, despite the cutbacks, the war was clearly a net boon for the Film Board.) It would take a lot more than the end of the war to get rid of the Film Board.

And yet the Film Board barely survived peace. For although it had been conceived and established as a peacetime operation, during the war and under Grierson it developed into a wildly expanding, politically reckless, volatile organization. It functioned without visible structures or routines, and under an Act that was not entirely clear. The war and Grierson, by instilling purpose into the Film Board, gave coherence to its rapid growth. Remove Grierson and the war, and the growth would have seemed cancerous, without direction, form, purpose, or control.

As the end of the war drew near, Grierson sensed this problem. In May 1944, the "erratic" administrator established a formal Personnel Office. New employees were no longer immediately put to work, but were given lectures and tours. Annual programmes were drawn up in the hope of providing a rational basis for planning. And the era of memorandum-free functioning was coming to an end. In 1944, Grierson issued a long memorandum announcing the establishment of a formal structure for film production.[2] The memorandum formalized a system of production *units* that had developed, somewhat spontaneously, during the war. Grierson announced that there would be twelve specialized units: *World in Action* and *Canada Carries On*, Industrial Relations, Health and Rehabilitation, Newsreel and Armed Forces, Animation, Dominion-Provincial, Travel and Outdoors, Armed Services, Foreign Language Programme, French Language Programme, Agriculture, and Education. In addition, there would be one or two "roving" units, which would be responsible for films and projects not easily fitting into one of the more defined units. The roving units would "inevitably be in a position to plan out special fields for themselves as new and real growing points emerge."

Grierson explained that the size of the Board no longer allowed the personal control and leadership he and his assistants had provided during the early years of the war. The Film Board should prepare for a more permanent and productive ongoing execution of the Film Board's purpose, which, Grierson wrote, was that "a living and growing educational service might be created from the specific information needs of specific departments." This should not mean, Grierson went on, merely the quick and efficient response to immediate departmental needs, for "the execution of departmental requirements in piecemeal fashion, without a plan of our own, would reduce the Film Board to the status and quality of an advertising agency, which God forbid." The Board should make of each sponsored film "a constructive contribution to the total educational picture." This would require "a sense of educational plan on the part of each unit." And, Grierson added, the Film Board would "get nowhere unless this responsibility is understood for what it is."

Grierson was assigning to the units the *responsibility* for "a sense of plan" contributing to "the total educational picture." The plan and the picture themselves were left to the filmmakers in the units:

The central and key responsibility for relating films to a larger educational plan must fall on production units. It means that they must know more precisely what field of education they are developing. Necessarily they have to exercise imagination, both as filmmakers and educational planners. They have, in other words, to become leading experts and even pioneers in their field.

But the need for organizing the organization was greater than Grierson realized. Ironically, this need manifested itself most clearly in an increasingly burdensome amount of paperwork, caused not by emerging bureaucratic tendencies within the Board but by the Board's own radically anti-bureaucratic character.

For example, because Grierson believed job security hindered organizational creativity, every employee was on a three-month contract. Most employees stayed longer than three months, and many of them stayed for the duration of the war and beyond. Every three months, a new contract for each of these employees had to be drawn up. In 1945, an employee who had been hired in 1940 would have signed about twenty contracts.

The Board found it very difficult to conform to the demands of the Treasury Board, whose criterion of organizational success was not good films but balanced books. The young filmmakers Grierson hired received informal but intensive training and feedback. Their work, at all stages — script, rushes, rough-cut, fine-cut — was subject to the scrutiny of the British experts, including Grierson. Mistakes were visible immediately and could be corrected. But for the novices in the accounting area, supervision and training were lax. A mistake in accounting would go unnoticed until it created a large problem. There was the case of the woman in accounting who would tell people she didn't like that she had not received their pay claims. Apparently she disliked a lot of people. Finally a search was made, and the unprocessed claims were found in her desk. Then there was the time when the Board noticed that orders it had placed to certain commercial laboratories for film prints had not been filled for several months. When he called the labs to complain, Grierson was told by each that it had outstanding claims against the Board. After an intensive search, the unpaid invoices, amounting to hundreds of thousands of dollars, were found in the filing cabinet of a clerk who hadn't known what he was supposed to do with them. On another occasion, the Chief Accountant was pleased that a young clerk was able to complete, rapidly and efficiently, the balancing of an account which had always been difficult. Scanning the account, he asked what the final entry, termed "balancing entry," meant. The girl replied that that was the figure needed to make the account come out even.[3]

But these were small problems compared to those resulting from the peculiar nature of the Film Board, which was partly a government organization, and partly a business. The Film Board was simply unlike any other government department, and it was for the ordinary government departments that the Treasury Board had designed its accounting policies and procedures. The Film Board was different in both the way it obtained money and the way it spent it.

Except for the Film Board, all government departments received money from one source — their annual vote from Parliament — and the accounting procedures presupposed but one source of income. (Some departments might receive income from other sources, but such income was simply turned over to a general revenue fund.) The Film Board received, and could spend, money from several sources. Besides its annual allotment from Parliament, the Board would receive money from other government departments whenever they sponsored a film. And in addition to that, there was income whenever the Board sold its theatrical films to distributors. This variety of income sources was compounded by the nature of filmmaking, particularly the nature of filmmaking at the Film Board, where, during the war, it was "bang them out and no misses." The Board couldn't predict accurately the number, subject, or cost of all the films it would want to make during the coming year. Nor could it predict accurately the cost of any particular film. Costs were subject to weather, events, and other unpredictables — e.g., the availability of apples. Moreover, the accounting rules were such that any expenditure — pencils, paper clips, whatever — had to be charged to a particular film.

The Film Board tried to cope with this problem by keeping the accounts in two ways, i.e., two separate accounts, one that made sense to the Film Board, and one that made sense to the Treasury Department. McKay describes the resulting confusion vividly:

> One year is long remembered for the attempt to prepare the estimates in both ways . . . and a final decision, less than twenty-four hours before they were due, to prepare them in yet a third way. With the estimates due at the Treasury Board at 10:00 a.m., the main calculations were finished at 2:00 a.m., the typing started, the final pages written at 7:00 a.m. and the typing completed at 9:00 a.m. And this was all done after a week of working until midnight and later.[4]

But the real solution was apparently the use of various para-legal sleights of hand, "irregular" techniques. Happily, the accountants "closed their eyes to some of the less serious contraventions as long as the intent was right." Although periodic attempts would be made throughout the Board's history to solve the accounting dilemma, the problems still exist, as do some of the solutions.

When Grierson resigned shortly after the war and went to the United States to try to set up an independent, international filmmaking operation, Ross McLean — the man who in the mid-thirties had spurred Canada to invite Grierson to consult on the nation's film policy — inherited the problem of stabilizing the organization. McLean believed revising the Film Act would solve the problem, and soon he set to work designing new legislation. McLean's intention was not, however, to transform the Board into an innocuous peace-time bureaucracy. On the contrary, he wanted to get this apparently minor matter of administrative house-cleaning over with so that the Film Board could move into new areas of production, such as feature films and television. Even in documentary, its staple, the Board was not content to rest on its wartime laurels. Stuart Legg, who resigned shortly after Grierson, issued in his last days a memorandum exhorting filmmakers to a renewed commitment:

> The times are not ripe for sitting back and talking memories. . . . All that matters now is the present and the future. . . .
> [The Board] must constantly infer the future from the known facts of the present, and act boldly on the inference. . . . Production must forever be ferreting out the significant new facts [and] seeking new means of expressing their relationship to the whole pattern of progress. . . .
> [The] pressure of daily chores shall never be allowed to obscure the ultimate purpose of documentary. . . . It is the business of documentary to act as a compass in the midst of change. . . .
> [Documentary filmmakers] occupy a position of highest responsibility among the prophets and teachers. . . .
> And this in turn . . . demands an unremitting preoccupation with the meaning of events. It demands that everything which happens in the country and much which happens outside it be known, examined, and understood. [Thus] documentary can never be a matter of eight hours a day. It is everything that we can give, or it is nothing.
> [And it is] necessary that established styles should invariably be called in question. . . . It is always easier to save time and effort by falling back on routine treatments. . . . But the known, at best, is tedious; at worst, it leads to an obsession with unimportant detail. And the slick, when applied to matters in reality profound, will end by revealing only its own superficiality.[5]

Clearly the Film Board did not view the coming of peace as an opportunity to settle into a comfortable routine. But the Film Board, and perhaps especially McLean himself, had no inkling of just how uncomfortable peace could be.

The first important sign of post-war trouble occurred only three months after Grierson's departure. In September 1945, Igor Gouzenko, a clerk at the Soviet Embassy in Ottawa, defected. He brought with him a mass of documents implicating a number of Canadians in a Soviet spy ring. Among those named was one Freda Linton, who had been a secretary to Grierson for six months. Gouzenko's files on Linton included a note which read, "Freda to the Professor through Grierson."[6] The Royal Commission investigating Gouzenko's charges twice called Grierson from New York to Ottawa. In the course of the second hearing, Grierson was asked directly if he was a "communist or communistically inclined." Grierson replied:

> I have been a public servant now for a matter of eighteen years. I was trained in the classical Whitehall School. I have been first and last a public servant, that is, a civil servant. Now, that meant in the Whitehall sense that you have no party affiliations.

Pressed further, Grierson responded:

> I am entirely a person who is concerned with the establishment of good international understanding. Therefore I am concerned with the floating of all ideas. I mean, I get as much from Gobineau as I get from Marx.[7]

Although no evidence was produced to implicate Grierson, his image — and the Film Board's — was severely tarnished for Canadians, and he was eventually hounded out of the United States by the FBI.[8]

The Gouzenko affair crystallized the diverse resentments and suspicions of the Film Board that had developed during the war. A group of Conservative Members of Parliament, led by G.K. Fraser, launched a relentless attack on the Film Board.

The immediate casualty was the hoped-for international, prophetic scope of the Film Board documentary. Shortly after the war, the Film Board made two documentaries about the rehabilitation work of UNRRA and UNESCO, *Hungry Minds* and *Suffer Little Children*. The Board made *Guilty Men*, about the war crimes trials. In 1946, Grant McLean, Ross McLean's nephew, took a Film Board crew to China at UNRRA's request. His film, *The People Between*, portrayed the plight of a people caught between two opposing governments — one of them, of course, Mao's. After a requested screening, the Department of External Affairs asked that the film not be released. The film revealed that there were two governments in China, a fact that the Department — in deference to the United States, McLean believes — did not wish to recognize.[9]

The People Between was released a few years later, but almost two full decades would pass before the Film Board again dared to examine international issues in any serious way, and a full ten years would elapse before the Board would make a film exploring even a Canadian issue in any depth.

The Film Board's retreat into safe areas of documentary did not appease its enemies in Parliament, for they were representing an additional interest: the commercial film industry.

Private film producers had expected that after the war the Film Board's role would revert to the original advisory one, thus freeing all government film contracts for commercial bidding. When this didn't happen, they were disgruntled and resentful. Nevertheless, for a while after the war the commercial industry and the NFB appeared to be natural allies in a larger struggle in which the stakes were much higher. Canada suffered a post-war balance of payments problem with the United States. To alleviate the trade deficit, Canada followed the lead of European nations and imposed a wide range of import restrictions. Unlike most European nations, Canada stopped short of restricting film imports, but there was serious talk of such restrictions in the near future. Canada's loss from foreign film imports amounted to 20 million dollars a year, 17 million of it to the United States.

Anticipating government action of some sort, private producers offered a variety of suggestions for reinvesting some of that money in Canadian production. Meanwhile, Ross McLean proposed that the American film industry be required to reinvest about a quarter of its Canadian earnings in Canadian production, and that it distribute forty to fifty Canadian shorts in the United States.[10]

Learning of these proposals, the Motion Picture Association of America concocted something called the "Canadian Cooperation Project" and managed to sell it to key Canadian officials.[11] The project was ballyhooed as a means of developing the Canadian film industry, especially feature films. For a while, private producers and the NFB supported the project. They were disturbed, however, when the details of the plan were finally revealed. The plan called for little more than a few American-made tourist films about Canada and the insertion of an occasional reference to Canada in the occasional feature film. One of the project's few tangible results was the line, "red-winged orioles ... from Canada," which Jimmy Stewart struggles to say in *Bend of the River*.[12] By 1949, McLean was so disgusted that he asked that responsibility for the project be transferred to the NFB.[13]

As the hopes engendered by the Canadian Cooperation Project fizzled, Canadian private producers, instead of joining the Film Board in its resistance to Hollywood's continued predominance in Canada, turned against the NFB. Apparently they were willing to let the big fish of feature production get away, and settle for government-sponsored documentary. In their anti-NFB efforts, private producers were aided (if for very different purposes) by the distributors and exhibitors, which were predominantly American subsidiaries, and the Canadian Broadcasting Corporation, which wanted to thwart the Film Board's intended move into television. Private producers, however, remained in the forefront of the attacks.

Fraser's forces in Parliament now had three charges in their case against the NFB: that the Film Board couldn't be trusted politically, that it was fiscally wasteful and irresponsible, and that it was performing a function in Canadian life that rightly belonged to private industry, which could do the job better.

In 1949, the Film Board became the object of three major investigations, each addressed primarily to one of the three major charges against the Film Board. In April 1949, Canada appointed the Royal Commission on National Development in the Arts, Letters and Sciences. The Commission's purpose was to examine the state of various Canadian arts, with particular reference to the role of governmental assistance. On November 15, the government engaged a Toronto management-consultant firm, J.D. Woods & Gordon, to conduct a thorough examination of the Film Board's administrative structure and functioning. Four days later, the *Financial Post* ran a front page story headlined, "Film Board Monopoly Facing Major Test." The *Post* story revealed that the Film Board, despite the mounting criticisms against it, had had the nerve to submit a brief to the Massey Commission asking for an increased role in the Canadian film industry. The Board wanted more money, control over television, and independent, corporate status. The bombshell in the *Post* story, however, was the revelation that

> the Department of Defence no longer uses the Film Board on "classified" (i.e. secret) work for security reasons.
>
> As a result, films "classified" for security reasons are being placed by the Department of National Defence with outside commercial organizations.
>
> This is actually now happening.
>
> It is a terrific blow to NFB pride and prestige; shoots the Government movie monopoly full of holes so far as this department of government is concerned.

> Apparently there is no chance of this policy being reversed until RCMP authorities ''screen'' the NFB staff; declare them Okay so far as national security is concerned.[14]

Thus was revealed the third major investigation of the Film Board. It had begun in May, at McLean's request, as a result of pressure from the Department of National Defence.

The November 29 meeting of the Board of Governors proved to be McLean's last. Board members were irate over the *Post* story. McLean told the Board that he believed the leak came from none other than the chief liaison man for the Canadian Cooperation Project, his motive presumably being to shift heat from the CCP to the NFB.[15] Two months later, McLean's contract expired, and was not renewed.

The Film Board's future looked awfully bleak in the winter of 1949-50. After *The People Between*, the Board's documentary work had become cautious. The prospect of moving into feature production was crushed by the Canadian Cooperation Project. The Canadian Broadcasting Corporation had the inside track on control over television. The private film industry's briefs to the Massey Commission unanimously opposed the NFB. Film Board employees suspected the real mission of the Woods-Gordon investigators was to find administrative justifications for clipping the Board's wings. The RCMP investigation seemed to be a witch-hunt; every NFB employee was a suspected subversive until cleared. Evelyn Cherry, who has spoken so warmly of the wartime NFB, said of these times that there was an atmosphere

> of tremendous fear. There were these subtle things going on. We weren't accused of anything, but it was suggested that some of us were enemies of our country.[16]

And yet, as dire a future as these three investigations seemed to forbode, they turned out to be the Film Board's salvation.

The RCMP investigation produced a list of thirty-six employees who might be security risks. Arthur Irwin, McLean's replacement, whittled the list down to three. By March 1950, the three had been discharged,[17] and the Board was considered purged.

But was it competent, and did it have a legitimate role in the nation's cultural life? These were the questions the Woods-Gordon team and the Massey Commission, respectively, were to answer. The results of each study were summarized in lucid, unpretentious documents, known in short form as the Woods-Gordon Report[18] and the Massey Report.[19]

The Woods-Gordon Report surprised the Film Board by the sympathy with which the management team regarded the Board's problems. The report attributed the Board's organizational confusion to two

54

causes: the rapid wartime expansion and the unusual nature of the Board's work. In the consultants' view, these problems could never be completely solved:

> It is obvious that some of the difficulties ... are inherent in government film production and will continue to be problems.

Furthermore, the report stated that the Film Board could work with reasonable efficiency only if it were exempted from certain aspects of government control. One possibility would be to make the Film Board a Crown Corporation — which is what the Film Board itself desired — but the report recommended against this, because it would mean losing the Board's important close ties to the government. The report expressed the opinion that:

> It should be possible to establish the National Film Board within the regular government organization plan and yet give it the flexibility which it must have to operate effectively.

This would require "a tightening up of [the Board's] administrative practices, particularly with respect to planning, organization, and control." But it would also require amendments to the Film Act.

The report noted a certain haphazard quality to the Board's production methods. There was no regular procedure for approving projects; sometimes films would be started before detailed scripts or budgets were prepared. Budgets, when prepared, were often incomplete, unrealistic, and unreliable. Appointments would be made without checking to see if funds were available. Purchases would be arranged, and invoices received, before requisitions had been submitted to the purchasing agent.

To solve these problems, the Board would need a Director of Planning. Written authorization would be required for script preparation and film production. The Board's work would need closer administrative supervision, so that no purchase would be allowed without the written authorization of the Director of Administration. More importantly, the Board would need to strengthen its business management section, which suffered from the lack of sufficient authority over expenditures, the necessity to adapt the Board's unusual work to government accounting practices, and the dispersal of the Film Board's operations among fourteen different buildings in Ottawa. Another problem was that the Film Board had no working capital.

The report found that there wasn't a lack of accounting at the Film Board, but rather there was too much of it. There were over five thousand individual accounts. Further:

> The greatest source of additional accounting has, however, arisen from breaking down costs and expenditures by the so-called "objects of expenditure" usual to government departments. . . . [This] serves no useful purpose.

Without losing any control, the number of accounts could be reduced by seventy-five percent. This would require new provisions in the Film Act ensuring that the Film Board would have adequate working capital, that accounts would be kept on an accrual basis rather than a cash basis, and that the Board would have greater flexibility in entering contracts. The Board also needed central accommodation.

But of all the recommendations made by the team of management consultants, the most interesting one challenged a principle that had been central to Grierson's thinking:

> It is said that creative work benefits from fairly frequent turnover of staff. It is a fact nevertheless that the Board suffers as an employer in not being able to offer greater security of employment and superannuation benefits.

It would appear that the team from J.D. Woods & Gordon had read Grierson's critique of the Motion Picture Bureau, wherein Grierson had written that the Bureau "suffers from the permanence of its staff." The wording that Woods & Gordon used was almost a perfect parody. The management consultants had considered the words of the master and disputed them.

If the Film Board had reason to fear the Woods-Gordon Report — which turned out to be so highly favourable — it had reason to expect sympathy from the Massey Report. The chairman of the Commission, Vincent Massey, was the man who in 1936, in London, had asked Ross McLean to express his recommendations regarding government film production in a formal memorandum. And in 1948, a year before the establishment of the Massey Commission, Massey had published a book called *On Being Canadian*, wherein he had written:

> But there is one department of film production in which [Canada has] achieved distinction. . . . An examination of [the Film Board's] work shows that it has well served the purpose for which it was funded [*viz.*, to help promote national unity]. . . . [The films] illustrate every aspect of Canadian life, and in quality, they are of recognized excellence.[20]

The Massey Commission looked into a wide range of media, but a quotation from St. Augustine on the flyleaf of the report suggested an all-embracing frame of reference for the study:

> A nation is an association of reasonable beings, united in a peaceful sharing of the things they cherish; therefore, to determine the quality of a nation, you must consider what those things are.

National identity, particularly in the cultural sense, was the basic theme of the report. On the subject of films, the Commission noted that

> the cinema at present is not only the most potent but also the most alien of the influences shaping our Canadian life. Nearly all Canadians go to the movies; and most movies come from Hollywood. . . . For the last fifteen years, however, Canada has been experimenting with something different from Hollywood's entertainment feature, [namely] the documentary film. . . .

After acknowledging the preponderance of militarist themes in the Board's wartime production, the Commission noted that the Film Board also produced, during the war, a number of films "equally acceptable in peacetime." The Commission noted the Film Board's uniquely penetrating distribution system. Many of the organizations submitting briefs to the Commission knew the Film Board through that distribution system, and of the briefs the Commission noted:

> Most of them approved of [the Board's] work, and asked that the work be extended. They went further. Many Canadians expressed pride in the work of the Film Board . . . [regarding it as] a valuable and distinctive Canadian achievement. . . .
> Films on the Canadian landscape, on Canadian communities, on Canadian painters and on Canadian songs have been mentioned by name over and over again. . . . Films on social problems have also received much praise. . . . Films on Canadian history and folklore are appreciated.

The Commission noted also that many of the groups submitting briefs, especially voluntary groups, were "convinced that the truly and typically Canadian films they want can be given them only by the Film Board."

The report also noted that the fact "that these films when sent abroad are received with enthusiasm was a further cause of pride to Canadians." The Commission had "on file warm tributes from many parts of the world to the artistic and technical excellence and to the integrity of National Film Board films."

The Massey Report concluded with various recommendations, among them the expansion of distribution, more support for technical research and development, more French-Canadian films, and the establishment "without delay" of "safe and efficient premises."

But despite its almost total endorsement of the Film Board, the Commission did summarize accurately the limitations to the Film Board's achievement in the *art* of documentary. The Commission did this very simply and straightforwardly, by reporting criticisms — from the public — of the Board's films:

Criticisms both general and expert have been offered to us. Some voluntary societies have been very severe about certain films ... which they consider vague, incoherent and technically poor. Others complain of a succession of subjects treated in too general a manner, with nothing to follow up and "take you right into" the theme. One group demands fewer films to advertise Canada and more "to raise the intellectual level of the masses." Some, with special knowledge, criticize certain films on painting as being more dramatic than informative. The same criticism would apply, we are told, to supposedly factual films in various fields, produced by individuals relatively ignorant of the subject matter, who cannot resist the temptation to sacrifice reality to dramatic effect.

Of the two reports, the Woods-Gordon Report was more immediately relevant to the designing of the new legislation. A bill was submitted to Parliament and assented to, with very little debate, on October 4, 1950. The Massey Commission was still conducting its inquiry, and its report would not be published until 1951.

In general, the new Film Act[21] gave the Film Board more strength and flexibility. Two important category headings alluded to Grierson's early insistence on "central powers and central purposes." Under "Purposes of the Board," the Act assigned the Film Board the mandate to "produce and distribute and to promote the production and distribution of films designed to interpret Canada to Canadians and to other nations." The Board would represent the government on all film matters and "engage in research into film activity." Under the heading "Powers of the Board," the Act allowed the Board to make and distribute films, to "determine the manner in which monies available to the Board for the production of a film may best be spent," and to "do other acts and things as are necessary or incidental for the purposes for which the Board is established." In addition, the Act provided the Film Board with an operating account. And Film Board personnel, although remaining outside the Civil Service, would be eligible for permanent employment and for Civil Service benefits.

In order to reduce the Board's vulnerability to political interference, the Act specified that the Film Commissioner would serve as the Board's Chairman and that cabinet ministers would be excluded from membership of the Board.

Although the recommendations of the Woods-Gordon Report are predominantly evident in the text of the new Act, there are, under the "Purposes of the Board," at least two items suggesting that the Massey Report, although not yet completed, was influential, too: the reference to making films not only interpreting Canada to Canadians (which was in the original Act) but also *to other nations*; and the mandate to engage in research activities. These were not management issues, but policy issues, and the Massey Report, when published, stressed both the international aspect of the Board's work and the need for ongoing research activity.

Thus, five years after the war and Grierson's departure, the Film Board was given, in the formal, legislative sense, a stronger and clearer set of "central powers and central purpose" than Grierson had enjoyed. The Board earned its new stability through the recognized goal-orientation of its work and its holistic approach to propaganda, whereby all aspects of Canadian life were covered. It had worked hard and done well, and both achievements had owed much to Grierson's leadership. But, with the passage of the new Act, there were two additional inputs, each of which countered Grierson's thinking. The new Act, incorporating the recommendation of the Woods-Gordon Report, introduced job security, along with other forms of routine. And the Massey Report, although praising the overall work of the Film Board, tactfully had called attention to the often overbearing, propagandistic tone of its films.

And the new Act couldn't immediately erase the effect of the severe chastening the Film Board had received since the end of the war. The ghost of Captain Badgley had got its revenge. But although the Film Board would remain quiet for a while, the elements of routine introduced by the new legislation would encourage the eventual production of documentaries which rose far above the wartime films in depth, subtlety, and honesty. Perhaps the Film Board's post-war ordeal was a rite of passage, preparing the Film Board for maturer work.

5
UNIT B AND "AN ATTITUDE TOWARD THE CRAFT"

In 1950, the Film Board was eleven years old. Canadians appreciated its work and it had begun to achieve foreign recognition. Because its work was perceived as valuable and distinctive, the Film Board not only survived, but emerged from its crisis with greater legislative strength than before. The Film Board now enjoyed a wider mandate, and more potential power to carry out the mandate as it saw fit.

And yet, in eleven years, the Film Board did not produce a single documentary that speaks to a modern audience. The strength of the Film Board documentary lay in its quantity and variety, not in the excellence of individual films. The quality was high, but not exceptional. The Board's best educational films were probably the *Mental Mechanism* series of the late forties, films explaining psychological disorders, such as depression and shyness, in narrated, scripted scenes performed by actors. They were good films, but only in the loosest sense were they documentaries.

It is possible to describe the deficiencies of the early Film Board documentary in terms of Grierson's original definition of documentary as "the creative treatment of actuality." The Film Board documentary typically did not probe deeply into its subject. It did not explore the reality being filmed. Instead, the Film Board documentary tended to start from certain didactic premises and then collect material useful for illustrating them. Often, the illustrative material was sought in the stock-shot library. The live-action documentaries usually were pre-scripted, and the action rehearsed. The "actuality" in these documentaries thus tended to be superficial and largely contrived. The "creative" side was not highly developed, either. Omniscient commentary was the main organizational device, and it tended to overwhelm the visual aspect of the film rather than draw structure from it or interact with it.

In part, this was Grierson's doing. By the time he had become Commissioner in 1939, Grierson had retreated from his early-thirties view of documentary, in which propaganda and truth were considered inseparable. During the war, propaganda had become the dominant value. Grierson no longer spoke of "the creative treatment of actuality," but of "banging them out and no misses." When he attacked the British, but especially Humphrey Jennings, for "cuddling [their films] to sweet smotheroo," he had, in effect, abandoned the two terms of his early standard, which required patience in the filming (Flaherty) and patience in the editing (the Russians). He no longer cared so much for either "creativity" or "actuality." He wanted to win the war.

In the relative quiet of the nineteen-fifties, the Film Board — or, more precisely, a small group of filmmakers within it — began to reach toward "the creative treatment of actuality," although they wouldn't have put it that way. This development occurred in the context of security, stability, and order that had emerged with the passage of the new Act in 1950.

By 1950, the Unit System had evolved into something simpler than the wide array of specialized units that Grierson had formalized in 1944. By 1950, there were only four units. The units were now given a simple letter designation — A, B, C, and D — rather than a name suggesting a particular subject or style. Each unit made more than one kind of film. Unit A was responsible for agricultural, French-language, foreign-language, and "interpretative" films. Unit B had sponsored, scientific, cultural, and animated films. Unit C did theatrical films, the *Canada Carries On* series (until its demise in 1952), newsreels, and tourist and travel films. Unit D had international affairs and special projects. Each unit had its own staff of writers, producers, directors, and editors. The units would draw cameramen and other technical help from technical departments. Each unit was headed by an executive producer, who in turn was responsible to the Director of Production.

The Unit System retained its basic form until 1964, when the system was abolished. But there were fluctuations over the years. In 1953, in response to growing demands from television, a special television unit was created. Television became so insatiable, however, that soon all units were involved in producing some films for television, so the specialized unit was disbanded. A special unit for original French-language production was created, and then a second one. By 1964, the last year of the Unit System, there were seven units. Five were English-language production units, and two were French-language.

In addition to fluctuations in the number of units, there were shifts of areas of responsibility among the units. French production, in the early sixties, became the sole province of the two French units. Among the English-language units, the distinctions came to be less strictly by subject, and more by orientation and source of money. Units A and B each had a large measure of "free" money — money which could be spent on non-sponsored films originating within the Board. Unit C had mostly sponsored work near the end of the unit era. Unit D became known as the military unit, and as a former member of Unit D remembers it, "'military' describes its structure, function, and content." Unit E did a lot of sponsored work and a lot of "films we had to do out of political reasons, like films about the Queen's visit."

The most important distinction among the units, however, was an informal one, a difference in values. After the war and partly as a result of the post-war attacks on the Film Board, most units and filmmakers at the Film Board had quietly adapted a fairly routine approach to production. The aim was to produce good, solid films in response to specific problems, usually identified by a sponsoring government department. The important thing was to turn out a professional product according to a fixed schedule and a reasonable budget. Professionalism was the prevailing value, and reasonably good, solid work was produced. However, no significant advances in the Film Board documentary were made by the professional school. But in one unit, Unit B, professionalism became subordinate to a different value, aesthetic quality.

Stanley Jackson, a member of Unit B, remembers that the typical unit was run by an executive producer

> who'd say, "Here's the budget, here's the schedule," which had to be adhered to strictly. Filmmaking was a kind of machine process. The films were always within budget, always on time ... but, except for a fluke, they weren't very good films.
>
> Now Unit B — it was a different bunch of people, and a different style. It didn't have the preoccupation with schedules and budgets ... and if it was going to take an extra couple of weeks to get "quality," well, you took it.

The first two distinctive documentaries made in Unit B emerged from an unlikely project. *Faces of Canada* was a series of short, low-budget films designed to do two things: contribute to fulfilling the mandate of "interpreting Canada to Canadians" and get young filmmakers to search out and find the "Canadian character" in their home towns. Each filmmaker was to find a person who was typically Canadian and yet an individual in his own right. The films were to be short vignettes.

One of the resulting films was *Corral*(1954), directed by Colin Low and filmed on the Alberta ranch where he had grown up. Another was *Paul Tomkowicz: Street Railway Switchman* (1954), directed by Roman Kroitor — his first Film Board film — and shot in his home town of Winnipeg. The making of each of the films involved departures from what was either customary or condoned at the Film Board.

Kroitor returned from Winnipeg with outstanding footage, shot by Lorne Batchelor of the Camera Department. The black-and-white images were startlingly crisp, and evocative of the prairie winter. The character of Paul Tomkowicz, a well-travelled immigrant from Poland, was engaging, both visually and in the conversations Kroitor had taped. The picture showed Tomkowicz at work and in relaxation; the tapes contained reminiscences about his past. Talking about his life, he would say intriguing things in a thick Slavic accent. He was witty. For example, when Kroitor asked him how he liked living in Winnipeg, Tomkowicz replied, "Winnipeg? After *Paris*?"

There was one problem. To get Tomkowicz to open up about his life, Kroitor had hidden the microphone. During the recording, Tomkowicz had walked around a bit, often moving too far away from the microphone. The tapes were unusable.

For its size and scope, *Paul Tomkowicz* was already an expensive film, already over budget. Kroitor went to New York, where he recorded an actor reading a transcript of Tomkowicz's monologue. When he returned to Ottawa and started laying the tracks, he and Stanley Jackson, who was helping Kroitor edit the soundtrack, realized that it wasn't very good. It was technically fine, but it had lost its believability. The voice was obviously an actor's.

Kroitor and Jackson decided not to tell Unit B's Executive Producer, Tom Daly, that they had to re-record. Either Daly would be unable to authorize it, or he would be put into a difficult position vis-à-vis the Director of Production (Donald Mulholland). As Jackson recalls, "If some people were going to be naughty, it would be us."

Someone recommended an actor in Toronto. Without telling Daly, Kroitor and Jackson brought the actor to Ottawa. After recording him, they realized that once again they had made a mistake. His was the wrong voice. He sounded totally false. Jackson recalls:

Now the situation was that if we didn't get it right, we'd wasted a lot of money. Then I remembered a friend I had in Winnipeg, a marvellous mimic. He had worked in the Depression as a ditchdigger with a gang of Poles and Ukrainians. His name was Tom Tweed, the only Anglo-Saxon on the crew. One day, some rich friends and I were out driving in a large car. We passed this group of ditchdiggers. One of the riders said, "Hey, that's Tom Tweed." Tom put down his shovel and said, in a most convincing Slavic accent, "Ruskie government *good* government. Canadski government *bad* government."

Jackson was convinced that Tweed, who was now living in Toronto, could mimic the voice of Paul Tomkowicz. Jackson and Kroitor borrowed Colin Low's car and drove to Toronto, where they met Tweed at a radio station. They played a short bit of the original tape, and Tweed almost immediately said he could do the voice. Kroitor and Jackson recorded him. It took about fifteen minutes. Tweed used the exact words Tomkowicz had spoken. The tapes sounded exactly alike — except that the new one was technically perfect. Kroitor and Jackson arrived back in Ottawa in the early hours of the next morning, knowing that they could now finish the film without compromising its aesthetic promise, but somewhat concerned about the deception and the budget-breaking they had committed. Jackson recalls:

When Tom (Daly) found out ... he was very unhappy, because he'd already been bugged by the Director of Production about this film being so far over budget. So we said, "Look, let's *us* [Kroitor and Jackson] go to the Director of Production and tell him we've done this illegal thing, but that we think it was worth it, and that Tom had nothing to do with it." Tom said no. In effect, he said that he'd take care of it. He was clearly impressed that we'd do this outrageous thing, that we'd be so tenacious, to get the film right.

When the film was completed, a print was sent to Germany, where it won the 1956 Oberhausen Prize as the best short documentary of the year. The film is still in distribution — and crucially for the development of the Film Board documentary, so is the persistence and patience with which its aesthetic potential was realized. *Corral*, the other distinctive film from the series, was from the beginning a departure from the Film Board's usual approach to filmmaking. Colin Low wanted Wolf Koenig, a member of Unit B and not a member of the Camera Department, to shoot the film. This was revolutionary for the bureaucratic post-war Film Board. In protest, the Camera Department sent deputations to the Commissioner. But perhaps because the *Faces of Canada* series was small, low-budget, and exploratory, Low and Koenig prevailed.

As had Kroitor, Low returned with visually exciting material, in this case of a cowboy gathering horses into a corral. Low and Tom Daly completed the picture editing but, as the end of the fiscal year approached, the film still lacked a commentary. Jackson had the job of putting on the commentary, over the week-end, if the film was to be completed within the fiscal year. Jackson recalls:

> There was a great rush about this. . . . I went to work on Saturday morning . . . and I ran it . . . I studied the film . . . and studied it . . . and tried a few tentative goes at a commentary. This was very difficult. It began to feel like an intrusion. By the end of the morning, I had decided that it didn't *want* a commentary. A commentary would be a fifth wheel. All it needed was a simple statement — a creeper title or something, just to orient you. . . .

On Monday, Low and Koenig, worried about the deadline, asked Jackson how the commentary was going. Jackson said, "It's done." They gathered around the moviola and looked at the film. About halfway through, someone asked, "Where's the commentary?" When the film had ended, Jackson asked "What would a commentary do for that?" They agreed that the film didn't need a commentary and probably would suffer from one. They went even further, deciding that the film didn't need a sound-effects track, either. The musical score, composed by Eldon Rathburn, would be sufficient. *Corral* became the first Film Board documentary without a commentary or sound-effects. Tom Daly remembers that *Corral* received some severe criticism from within the Film Board; people "expected to be told what to think about pictures."

Rathburn's score was a remarkable example of film music. It was not "memorable," which — considering the absence of commentary and effects — is an indication of its strength. There were no other sounds for the composer to hide under. Tom Daly remembers receiving a letter from a person who had seen the film (for the second time) on television. The viewer complained that "they had changed the narrator and he wasn't as good."

And so, out of the modest *Faces of Canada* series emerged the Film Board's first two documentary classics. A "classic" has been described as something that "implies continuity and consistency, a tradition that forms a whole, is handed down, and endures."[1] Each film became a prototype. The influence of *Paul Tomkowicz*, a portrait film using the subject's voice — or, as in this case, a facsimile of it — in lieu of a written commentary, is pervasive in documentary today. So is the influence of *Corral*, which uses music but no commentary or sound effects. Each film — now a quarter-century old — is still a delight to see. Each has its own beauty: the stark, crisp beauty of *Paul Tomkowicz*, and the lyrical beauty of *Corral*.

And each film recalled (if modestly), in the manner of its making, aspects of the early Griersonian aesthetic. In each case, the filmmaker, like the Flaherty that Grierson had once so admired, knew intimately the area in which he was filming. And in each case the structure of the material was allowed to arise from the demands of the material itself. Both films required perseverance and patience. Neither was made to order, nor could have been.

Another prototype that emerged from Unit B was *City of Gold* (1957). Colin Low had discovered in the Dominion Archives a collection of old photographs of Dawson City, the Klondike gold-rush town of 1898. With Roman Kroitor and Wolf Koenig, Low planned a film about Dawson City using these still photographs. The team then came up with the idea of using actuality footage of present-day Dawson City to bracket the still-photograph content. In Dawson City — where they discovered even more photographs — they filmed quiet scenes of old men sitting in front of dilapidated stores and young boys playing baseball. For filming the still photographs, Kroitor invented a camera-plotting device that enhanced the filming by alleviating the appearance of "flatness" normally associated with filmed still photographs.

Two years after the filming of the live-action footage in Dawson City, the editing of *City of Gold* was almost complete. The music was being composed. All that remained was to write and record a commentary. Unlike *Corral*, this was a film which absolutely needed commentary. But it needed an *outstanding* commentary, one that would work together with the pictures and the music to evoke the nostalgic mood that the filmmakers were after. Wolf Koenig came up with the idea of using the Canadian author Pierre Berton, who had grown up in the Yukon. Low and Kroitor agreed to try out Berton, but they feared that he would want to change everything around. To their surprise, Berton loved the film. Berton set to work on a commentary, with Stanley Jackson helping him adapt it to the needs of film time and pacing. Berton also spoke the commentary. Despite one or two lapses into forced spontaneity, the commentary as a whole was unpretentious, informative, personal, and elegant. It enhanced the film's nostalgic effect immensely. *City of Gold* won seventeen international awards and remains today the best film of its kind, and much imitated.

As the ability of Unit B — particularly the informal group composed of Kroitor, Koenig, Low, Jackson, and the unit's executive producer,

66

Tom Daly — became recognized by the management of the Film Board, the unit achieved a status that would allow them, occasionally, to break the rules beforehand, i.e., with permission, instead of having to quietly exceed the budget or projected completion date and then justify the transgression with an outstanding film. An example is another prototype, *Universe* (1960), one of the Film Board's most famous and successful films.

Low and Kroitor had had a long-time fascination with cosmology. The project began as a proposed classroom film about five years before Sputnik. Discussions about the project drew in several other interested persons, and the scope of the film grew. The aim of the film, they agreed, would be not so much to convey facts about the universe as to invoke a sense of wonder about it. The film would be an adventuresome project, because there was insufficient knowledge of the techniques that would be required in order to create the images that were desired. As one member of the team remembers, "We couldn't say, 'To shoot these solar prominences we'll have to do this and this and this'; we just didn't know yet how to achieve the images we wanted." Because so much technical experimentation would be required, the team knew that they would need a lot of money to make the film they had in mind.

The team prepared an outline, a rough storyboard, and a budget estimate of about $60,000, which in the nineteen-fifties was an enormous sum for a single Film Board film. Tom Daly remembers that Donald Mulholland, the Director of Production, suggested that the film be divided into three parts, three classroom films. That would make it easier for him to defend the cost of the project. The team argued persuasively that the film should remain a single film, a unity, for among other reasons, "unity" was in a large part the very theme that they wanted the film to suggest. Jackson recalls that Mulholland said something like:

> "As a responsible Director of Production, I absolutely cannot authorize putting that much money into a single production. It would knock out other worthy projects. However, I am not the ultimate authority. The Commissioner is the ultimate authority. Go see him and tell him your story, and ask him to phone me."

The Commissioner, Albert Trueman, responded enthusiastically. He called Mulholland and told him that some way should be found to proceed with the project. Mulholland was, Jackson remembers, delighted, but still concerned about the costs.

> "But," he said, "there's no deadline, no hurry. If I give you $60,000 and say 'go ahead,' that isn't fair [to you or to other filmmakers]. So we'll do it

this way: I'll give you $20,000 this year. Get going. When you've spent it,
put the film on the shelf until the next fiscal year." This meant that the next
time Low and Kroitor could get at the money, they'd be more sure of
where they were going.

After the end of the third fiscal year, the film was still not done. More
money was required. The money was provided, but with the stipulation
that the film must be finished by the end of that — the fourth — fiscal
year. The team finished the film on March 31, the last day of the fiscal
year.

The film had taken four years, but not four whole years, because
after the first few months of each fiscal year, the $20,000 allocated for
the year had been spent, and the film had to be placed on the shelf. This
on-again-off-again process may have worked to the film's advantage.
William James once remarked that "We learn to swim in the winter and
skate in the summer." With *Universe*, this principle was incorporated,
intentionally or not, into the Board's battery of production strategies.

A filmmaker from outside Unit B remembers that when *Universe*
was finished, and test-screened, its general reception was summed up in
the reaction of one filmmaker, who exclaimed, "You spent $60,000 for
. . . *that*!?" But *Universe* became one of the most widely distributed
educational films ever made, earning much more than its total production cost in revenues. NASA ordered at least 300 prints of the film,
which they used for training and for public information. By 1976, the
Film Board had sold over 3,100 prints of *Universe*. Stanley Kubrick,
when he started work on his *2001: A Space Odyssey*, discussed the
project with Colin Low and hired Wally Gentleman, the wizard who
had achieved the optical effects for *Universe*, to do the same for
Kubrick's film. And Kubrick used the voice of Douglas Rain, who
spoke the commentary (which Stanley Jackson had written) for *Universe*, as the voice of Hal, the computer.

The culmination of the documentary work of Unit B was a series
called *Candid Eye*, half-hour documentaries made for television. The
series began in 1958 and ran for about three years. Koenig and Kroitor,
the series' main instigators, believed that television, with its voracious
appetite for material, offered far greater opportunities for experimentation than had been recognized. Most of the documentaries on television
— many of them, in Canada, Film Board documentaries — were
boring, shallow and unimaginative. Kroitor and Koenig had seen
Thursday's Children, a documentary by Lindsay Anderson and the
British "Free Cinema" group of the mid-fifties, and believed that the
scriptless approach of films like *Thursday's Children* could be adapted

favourably to a series of Canadian documentaries. The two filmmakers were equally enchanted by the work of the photographer Henri Cartier-Bresson, who seemed capable of combining the spontaneity of candid photography with an acute sensitivity to form.

When the Unit B team proposed a series of films for which there would be no script at all, the Board's management, and many filmmakers within the Board, were puzzled. They didn't think films could be made without a script and without rehearsals of the action. Management was hesitant to approve the project, because it had no way of knowing what the results might be. Daly has summarized both the problem of getting the project approved and the solution:

> The most you could give for each film in the series was a subject, and perhaps a list of sequences you were likely to cover. It was known that the shaping and structuring would occur in the editing room. In order to get the proposal accepted — and to be able to drop a subject that later proved unsatisfactory — we gave the programme commmittee [about] thirty-two subjects, and asked them to agree on a priority fifteen, from which we would do seven. So they had an input.

The cost of the films would not be any more than the cost of the typical Film Board documentary. Although the lack of scripts meant that more footage would have to be shot, and that editing would take a lot longer, money would be saved by skipping the script stage and by using small crews, with new lightweight equipment.

Terence Macartney-Filgate joined Koenig and Kroitor for *Candid Eye*, Stanley Jackson wrote the commentaries, and Tom Daly served as executive producer. Several French-Canadians also worked on the series. They included Georges Dufaux, Gilles Gascon, Michel Brault, Claude Pelletier and Marcel Carrière. Roles interchanged considerably. Stanley Jackson directed one of the films. Tom Daly edited sequences of at least one film. Several of the French-Canadians did some directing.

Among the more remembered titles in the *Candid Eye* series are *The Days Before Christmas* (1958), *The Back-Breaking Leaf* (1959), and *Blood and Fire* (1958). *The Days Before Christmas*, a survey of the rush of activities that precede the holiday, was the pilot film for the series, and at least six filmmakers directed sequences of it: Roman Kroitor, Wolf Koenig, Stanley Jackson, Terence Macartney-Filgate, John Feeney, and Michel Brault. Macartney-Filgate directed *The Back-Breaking Leaf*, a film about the gruelling work of tobacco pickers in the annual southern Ontario harvest, and *Blood and Fire*, a film about the Salvation Army.

These films did not solve fully the formal problem presented by the scriptless, high-ratio approach to reality: how to fashion this wider and less contrived range of actuality into some meaningful, aesthetically satisfying whole. But *Lonely Boy* (1962), filmed after the end of the regular *Candid Eye* series as a kind of grand finale, did. More money was spent on *Lonely Boy*, and more editing time, than on any of the regular *Candid Eye* films. More effort, too. Koenig and Kroitor shot and co-directed the film; John Spotton and Guy Coté worked on it as editors.

A totally engrossing portrait of Paul Anka, the popular Canadian entertainer who excited tears and screams in worshipping North American teen-age girls in the early nineteen-sixties, *Lonely Boy* was, for the Film Board and for documentary in general, an advance in "the creative treatment of actuality." The film is a fascinating mixture of the formal and the formless. Raw, vigorous, often spontaneous content is organized into a rigorous structure.

On the one hand, much of the material in the film seems to consist of random shots — snaps, almost — of the Atlantic City environment in which much of the film is set. In one tracking shot, the camera and crew follow Anka hurriedly as he moves down a street. In another scene, the crew surprises Anka by waiting in his dressing room. In some ways, the film is almost arrogantly — for its time — sloppy-*looking*. The microphone appears in the tracking shot of Anka walking down the street. As Anka bursts into the dressing room, he stares at the camera in a brief moment of surprise. Jump-cuts abound in the interview sequences. A question from the filmmaker is heard in one scene. In one of the film's most engrossing scenes, in which Anka presents a gift to the owner of the Copacabana night-club in New York, the filmmaking team becomes involved in the action. The owner rather insincerely kisses Anka to thank him for the gift. We hear a voice asking him to do the kiss again. Anka and the manager break into laughter. "The camera moved," the filmmaker, off-camera, explains. They kiss again, and then Anka, still laughing, asks if the film crew wants them to do it *again*. The filmmaker tells them no, just keep talking. The entire uncut sequence appears in the film.

On the other hand, *Lonely Boy* is tightly structured. The film opens with Anka singing the song of that title. "I'm just a lonely boy," he intones, as we see billboards (with Anka's name on them in huge letters), the centre of the highway, et al, from the point of view of the car in which Anka is riding. The loneliness of an entertainer who has become an idol, worshipped by hordes of silly young girls, is the theme, and this theme is relentlessly held to. At a concert, a human barrier of policemen and security guards protects Anka from the screaming mob. When Anka presents his gift — a huge portrait of himself — to the night-club owner, the gift is received with no real warmth. Rehearsing a new composition on the piano, Anka looks scared and insecure. He is surrounded by sycophants. At one point near the end, the film becomes highly stylized for a documentary. The shrieking audience, which in an earlier scene had drowned out the words of the singer, is now faded out *in the editing*, so that we hear the song, and only the song, over a series of silent shots of agonized, idolatrous fans. The film ends with more shots down the highway. Anka, inside the car, appears bored with, and alienated from, his crew of managers and agents. A woman in a passing car stares at him. On the soundtrack, we hear, again, ''I'm just a lonely boy....''

Paul Tomkowicz, *Corral*, *City of Gold*, *Universe*, and the *Candid Eye* series, each a prototype in its own right, could be taken as benchmarks in the evolution of a distinctly Unit B style of *working* that was to affect the Board deeply, if not universally or unambiguously. With *Paul Tomkowicz* and *Corral*, perfection became regarded as a criterion far more important than the budget, the schedule, or the norm, i.e., professionalism. Grierson had urged that films must ''achieve distinction or they're not worth doing at all,'' and, for their time, the wartime films were distinctive, or at least technically well-made. But there had always been the urgencies of the war, the theatrical release date, and Grierson's Calvinistic strain to keep rein on any one project's pursuit of its full potential. It took several years of peace, and the introduction of a measure of routine, before the Film Board began to free itself from wartime constraints. The beginning does not seem to have been a planned or conscious one. The concept of what *Paul Tomkowicz* should be, and the means to make it that, were both discovered largely by trial-and-error. The discovery that *Corral* did not need a commentary, and that it would be a far better film without one, occurred while struggling with the material itself, and did not follow from some theory.

With *City of Gold*, the notion of using Pierre Berton as the narrator arose from difficulty with the commentary, but in the filming of the still photos, there had been an image of what the film ought to look like, and then a problem-solving effort — Kroitor's camera-plotting device — to achieve the image. With *Universe*, there was the imagination and the planned-for exploration and experimentation, and even the budget and scheduling problems were anticipated, so that if the manner of the production departed radically from the professional norm, it did so purposely, with management's prior approval. In the case of *Candid Eye*, the right to experiment on a grand documentary scale was negotiated beforehand, with a minimum of compromise, with management. The Film Board professional norm was no longer the rule, if you belonged to Unit B, and if you could convince management by the merit of your proposal and your track record.

This striving for perfection, which invariably involved the odious (to Grierson) "cuddling to sweet smotheroo," was nevertheless associated with characteristics Grierson had promoted. The team approach to filmmaking was one such characteristic. The names Kroitor, Koenig, Low, Daly, and Jackson occur again and again in the best Unit B films, although others were involved, too — especially Eldon Rathburn, who did the music for *Corral*, *Universe*, and other Unit B films, and Terence Macartney-Filgate in *Candid Eye*. In several ways, the group's style of working recalled the old Empire Marketing Board in England, and aspects of the early wartime Film Board. There was in this team and in Unit B as a whole a degree of "role freedom." A filmmaker might produce one film, direct the next, and edit a third. John Spotton, trained as a cameraman, took a pay-cut to work as an editor on *The Back-Breaking Leaf* and *Lonely Boy*. Tom Daly, the unit's Executive Producer, would sometimes edit a film. And in any one production, the roles of producer, director, camera, and editor would often overlap. As a film critic wrote in the mid-sixties, the Unit B films "are so thoroughly the product of a group that their names do not matter."[2] Unlike the early EMB and early Film Board films, the Unit B films, like all contemporary NFB films, did carry credits, but the credits did not reflect clearly defined roles. Credits, Tom Daly recalls, were "apportioned at the end of the filming according to where we felt the centre of gravity lay." Another kind of reward — pay raises — were also somewhat communally awarded. When there were pay raises, everyone in the Unit deserving one got one, whether he had asked for it or not.

The cooperative approach of the Unit B team of Kroitor, Koenig, Low, Jackson, and Daly did not involve simple self-effacement, but something quite different. Tom Daly remembers Unit B as a group which, at its best, combined aspects of communality and individuality:

> There was a desire not to be separate. Each person, confident of his ability in one or two areas, would recognize his lacks in other areas, and other persons' abilities in those areas. Each person had a sense that his own fulfilment could not be fully achieved on his own, but only in connection with a project to which he and others contributed where they could ... to

achieve something greater than the sum of the various contributions. . . .
To achieve this harmony, filmmakers don't have to be geniuses, but they
do have to be first-rate in *something*. And if they are, they will also be
aware of not being first-rate in other things, and will therefore *enjoy*
cooperating with people who *are* first-rate in those things.

But the day-to-day process by which such creative collaboration was
achieved was anything but harmonious. Wolf Koenig remembers that

for all the rosy light cast on old Unit B by the haze of memory and
nostalgia it should be remembered that it had a very tough strand running
through it. It's this strand, in my opinion, which made it functional (like
the wires inside Michelins). And what it consisted of was opposition and
conflict! What made the unit function under such apparently self-destruc-
tive impulses was that Tom Daly, our Executive Producer, accepted this
conflict and, intuitively, used it as a source of energy for the group.

The polarities within Unit B were best expressed by the two major
personalities within it: Tom Daly and Roman Kroitor. The personalities of
these two men were almost diametrically opposed to each other. Tom, the
conservative, pragmatic, technically and artistically accomplished, apparently unemotional administrator; raised in the traditions of Upper Canada
College; apprenticed to film aristocrats like Grierson and Legg; always
conscious of his obligations to pass on tradition and to serve the public's
needs. In other words, truly Anglo and the nearest thing we have in Canada
to an aristocrat.

Roman, on the other hand, was a rebel (in his way); an accurate but
devastating critic; a Saskatchewan Ukrainian — therefore highly emotional; a brilliant student at University (a gold medal winner); a highly creative
filmmaker without (at that time) a full technical knowledge, but learning
fast; very nervy and, at times, disrespectful of the opinions of "older and
wiser" heads; with long hair when it was unfashionable and a life style
which bordered on the "Bohemian". He was the object of envious ridicule
by some but, like Tom Daly, he was dedicated to the public good (although
he saw it from another angle).

Well, these two personalities clashed, mostly in discreet ways, sometimes not so discreetly. Tom certainly could have gotten rid of this Kroitor
guy in about five minutes and he would have been applauded for doing so.
But he didn't. Instead he helped to train him and supported him in films
which were, to many, very far out. At times he fought against management
even though this went entirely against his own traditional upbring-
ing. . . . So . . . it was between the polarities of these two men that the
strand I mentioned earlier was stretched, and to such fine tautness that all
the rest of us could balance on it.

The group-dynamic of this team resembled that of the smaller
two-person and thus simpler team that discovered the structure of DNA.
Both James Watson and Francis Crick were expert in something —
Watson in biology, Crick in crystallography — but, as in Unit B, there
was a "role-freedom" in the relationship that encouraged each to probe
the other's area of expertise. Watson and Crick had a similar generosity

toward credits; they decided senior authorship by the toss of a coin. And finally, they could criticize each other, bluntly.[3]

The work of the Unit B team and the work of the DNA scientists resembled each other in one more respect. A sociologist has noted that the motivation of scientists cannot be explained solely by desire for fame or reward, and has argued that there is a "charisma" in science which must be adduced as a complementary motivation. Among scientists, "charismatic things are those which bring order out of chaos and which guide, direct, and make meaningful human action."[4] Although there were the usual egoistic motivations in the race for the structure of the double helix, awe of the elusive structure itself was a motivation, as is evident, if not explicit, in Watson's account of the discovery.[5]

But to colleagues of Watson and Crick their pursuit of the structure seemed at times zealous or obsessive. Similarly, to many NFB employees outside of Unit B, there seemed to be a touch of messianic zeal in the team's pursuit of aesthetic perfection. Sometimes it seemed to others that Unit B filmmakers lived only to make brilliant films, subjugating all other aspects of life and living to that single purpose. For Unit B, the pursuit of perfection had apparently become "the sacred commitment" that the theatrical release date had been during the war. It was as if it were holy to seek perfection and sinful to compromise.

On this point, Stanley Jackson comments that

> it did *look* like, at times, a kind of crazy dedication ... but it was an attitude toward the craft. There was a filmmaker who had produced a number of mediocre films, and if you asked him how the film was, he would say, and I quote,"We got away with it." For *us*, though, it had to be as good as you could make it. You had to get as much out of the material, through structuring, through the use of sound, the orchestration of all the materials, so that it would be as good as possible. It wasn't a holy crusade. It was an attitude toward the craft.

If it wasn't a holy crusade, the "attitude toward the craft" certainly had charismatic aspects. But there was now no war, and no Grierson, to inspire this charismatic devotion. Its sole source was an ideal of aesthetic fulfilment.

Unit B's aesthetic ideal involved an idea of *wholeness*. A similar idea had pervaded the wartime NFB work. But Grierson's idea of wholeness was such that each film, insignificant in itself, contributed to the "whole" picture of Canada that the Film Board was attempting to produce. An individual film might contain a *thematic* wholeness, in the sense that a *World in Action* or a *Canada Carries On* film would show single events or local situations in relation to world events. Wholeness also referred, for Grierson, to the overall *system* of production and distribution which established a dynamic relationship between production and constituency.

Unit B modified this "wholeness" in a significant way. Unit B emphasized wholeness in the *individual* films, but in none of the Unit B prototypes is the subject related, in an explicit or thematic way, to the rest of the world. The "wholeness" of *Paul Tomkowicz*, *Corral*, *City of Gold*, *Universe*, and *Lonely Boy* lies in the coherent fullness with which the subject is presented. The films contain an organic wholeness, a certain aesthetic integrity that avoids the imposition of forced connections to some larger issue, some greater relevance. But the avoidance of explicit relevance does not mean that these films were esoteric or trivial. Their popularity was enormous, and still is. These films did not *refer* to a wider world, but *spoke to* the wider world through their integrity of structure and material, or style and content. Perhaps their aim and effect were to find the universal in the particular — the lyricism of ranch-hands rounding up horses, the occasionally tremulous inflection in Berton's nostalgic commentary, the moment at the piano when Paul Anka looks so tentative and alone — and to communicate with their audience not intellectually but emotionally. With reference to the *Candid Eye* films, Wolf Koenig wrote that the aim was to "show them on television to millions of people and make them see that life is true, fine, and full of meaning."[6]

Although in part a modification of Grierson's sense of the whole, the aesthetic "wholeness" in the Unit B films was rooted in the work of the Grierson-led wartime Film Board. Two members of the team, Jackson and Daly, had joined the Board very early. Daly had developed the stock-shot library. Partly because he was the one "who knew where everything was," he became the editor of the *World in Action* series. This meant that Legg and Daly, between them, had to edit a film a month. Jackson directed and edited films, but increasingly he was called on to write commentaries.

From working in these capacities and under Grierson, Daly and Jackson developed a keen sense of structure. In the nineteen-fifties, Daly would often edit a film, but his structural sense was expressed mainly in a kind of informal teaching that was part of his approach to producing. Jackson's structural sense was brought into the work of the unit mainly through writing commentaries, an art which in documentary requires a sense of structure as much as a facility with words. Once, however, it was brought in by *not* writing a commentary, for it was precisely this structural capacity that allowed Jackson to recognize, finally, that *Corral did not need* a commentary. A less confident talent might have tried to force a commentary onto the film.

If documentary is thought of as "the creative treatment of actuality," which means giving form to disparate pieces of reality, then the importance of editorial skill in documentary is obvious, especially as the introduction of lightweight equipment opened up a wider and less contrived range of reality to the filmmaker. But there was also a non-obvious input to the team's sense of structure: Norman McLaren and the Film Board's work in animation.

During the war, McLaren, whom Grierson had called "the most important man at the Film Board," a remark that puzzled those who heard it, developed an Animation Unit and trained young animators. After the war, as the Unit System became simplified, Unit B absorbed the Animation Unit. Colin Low joined the Film Board as an animator in 1945, and Wolf Koenig in 1948.

In 1952, McLaren made *Neighbors*, an eight-minute experimental film with a pacifist theme. Guy Glover has called *Neighbors* a kind of half-way house between animation and live-action film. McLaren used live actors, but shot the film one frame at a time. Wolf Koenig was one of McLaren's cameramen on the film. *Neighbors* won an Academy Award in 1952, and even today — unlike many early Oscar-winning films — is in distribution and is popular.

McLaren, however, was a "loner" in his art. Although quite capable of working with others and generous with his talent, he really didn't need others. Yet, in the development of animation in the late forties and early fifties, "McLaren's presence as a great artist," Low remembers, "was not inconsequential." His abstract work inspired an attempt to develop the cartoon form of animation, which, as it existed in Hollywood and elsewhere at the time, was too expensive for the Film Board. But cartoon animation necessarily involved a partial break from McLaren's approach. Low comments that "cartoon animation demands a very close team collaboration. It is essential." And it was in 1953, on a cartoon film, *The Romance of Transportation in Canada*, that Low, Koenig, Kroitor, and Daly collaborated for the first time as a team.

Thus it was in cartoon animation, not documentary, that the individual talents of the team began to merge into a group-based aesthetic. This was significant for the later development of the Unit B documentary. Low remarks:

> The patient, detailed single-frame work generated a working discipline
> quite different from the [contemporary] live-action documentary school.

Guy Glover has specified in detail what the experience of animation gives to the documentary filmmaker:

What the animator learns about film he learns early and fast:

1. That film is made up of 24 still pictures per second and that these still pictures can be drawn or painted. When an animator comes to live action and has shots on his editing apparatus he tends to look at them *as if* he had drawn them — especially the *frames* leading up to and away from the cutting point. He observes the frame as keenly as the non-animator observes the shot.

2. From drawing frames for animation he learns a lot about the nature of cinematographically synthesized motion and therefore also about relative speeds, pacing, rhythms and about what the camera does to the material it "captures."

3. How compositional emphasis *in motion* works and the relation between foreground, mid-ground and background elements in motion.

4. He learns to be concise because he has to and, having learnt that, it is carried unforgettably with him into situations where strictly speaking he does not "have to."

5. Animation forces the animator to give life to his film organism; later, if he comes to live action, he is aware that the life "out there," of some fleeting moments on which he has trained his camera, does not guarantee the life of his film. The subject is not the content.

6. He is haunted by thoughts of artifice knowing better than most, however, that in documentary he is dealing with the most treacherous artifice of all — the artifice which maintains that to "bring 'em back alive" is gospel truth.

But the image to which the animator is trying simultaneously to give form and content originates inside his head; the images for the documentary filmmaker — especially if he is not working from a script — originate outside his head. The animator can integrate the form and content of his single-frame image on his work-bench, in the quiet of his studio. The documentary filmmaker who wants to give form to the single image must do so in the rush of life, in social activity. This is a more trying and complicated task.

The work of the still-photographer Henri Cartier-Bresson, and the aesthetic notions he had offered in his preface to his photographic collection *The Decisive Moment*, suggested to the Unit B team a way to get from animation to live-action motion-picture photography without losing their sensitivity to single-image form. The whole preface to *The Decisive Moment* is of interest, but perhaps one sentence is the key:

[Photography] is the simultaneous recognition, in a fraction of a second, of the significance of an event as well as of the precise organization of forms which give that event its proper expression.[7]

Thus when the Unit B team came to experiment with scriptless documentary in *Candid Eye*, the loss of formative input which the increasingly old, tired, and restrictive approach of shooting according to a script had provided was compensated for by the formative input of "the decisive moment," in addition to the increased after-the-fact inputs of editorial skill. Guy Glover has pointed out that

> besides the vérité aspects of *Candid Eye* films, there was always a fairly strong preoccupation with the medium itself (or with the elements of which it is composed). The results of that preoccupation were what . . . set those films apart from the run-of-the-mill documentaries being produced at that time at the Board. I would label those preoccupations "formalistic" if the word were not so loaded.

And so Unit B's aesthetic ideal was a unique formulation of "the creative treatment of actuality," a finely honed tension between the ultimately inseparable qualities of form and content. The ideal drew upon the Film Board's own tradition — Grierson's sense of the whole and McLaren's sense of detail — but it was not entirely inbred. The example of scriptless filmmaking of the British "Free Cinema" school and the form-sensitive photography of Cartier-Bresson were essential inspirations. The ideal reached perhaps its fullest expression in *Lonely Boy*, a film that contains more raw "actuality" than others, and more form — much of it inherent in "the decisive moments," the individual shots themselves. Observation of life and the reformulation of it into life-enhancing aesthetic expressions were at the heart of "the attitude towards the craft" that inspired round-the-clock work, the invention of new techniques in order to achieve an effect, exceeding the budget in order to realize a potential, and, to puzzled colleagues, the appearance of messianic zeal.

It was charisma in the context of routine. Unlike the lives of the EMB filmmakers, the lives of Unit B filmmakers were not subject to bans against marriage. Nor did Unit B filmmakers have to make do on the $20-a-week paid to wartime apprentices. There were even pay raises for the diligent. Some had families, some owned houses, all had security. The self was not fully effaced, but expressed in often strenuous cooperation with others. If film credits did not reflect clearly defined roles, they did reflect "centres of gravity," and were, at any rate, credits. Unit B filmmakers, to an extent probably unequalled earlier or later in the Film Board's history, were at one and the same time making "a calling out of their living" and "a living out of their calling." Stanley Jackson remembers Wolf Koenig, in the middle of some piece of work, suddenly exclaiming, "Imagine — being paid for doing what you want to do most in the world!"

The enthusiasm that Unit B felt for its work — and perhaps for itself — was not shared by everyone else at the Film Board. There was a tendency for Unit B filmmakers to regard themselves as a bit superior to the "drones" in the other units. There was in Unit B an insufficient appreciation of the Film Board's routine, mainstream documentary work, the variety, utility, and professional excellence of which provided the context for Unit B's adventures. This snobbery seems to have been innocent, but it grated on outsiders. Once, a special programme of Unit B films was screened, causing some to mutter that the screened films should be thought of as Film Board films, not Unit B films. Not long thereafter, there appeared on the notice boards a satirical document called "How to Make a Festival Film," and soon the joke of the place was to say, "I'm making a festival film," while striking a snobbish attitude or describing a project of dubious relevance to the Canadian scene. At the root of the dissension was the difference in criteria between Unit B and the rest of the Film Board. One old-timer from a different unit remembers bitterly that

> in the early sixties [the high point of the Unit System] we used to hit budgets right on the nose. We used to *make* money from them. But there were no laurels for that.

Indeed there weren't. Another filmmaker remembers an incident in which

> an Executive Producer of one of the other units rushed out into the hall and shouted triumphantly, "We did it again: *under budget!*" The Director of Production [then Grant McLean] walked out into the hall and bellowed, "I don't give a damn. I want good films."

Even within Unit B, there was a measure of dissent that could not be harmonized. There was community but not necessarily equality. The team of Kroitor, Koenig, Jackson, Daly, and Low was only the central core. One person outside the unit remembers Unit B as somewhat priestly in structure:

> There was an Inner Circle and an Outer Circle. The Outer Circle was delighted to be part of Unit B, to be associated with its successes. The Outer Circle in turn was patronized by the Inner Circle. The Inner Circle were the Gods, and the Outer Circle was allowed to sit at the feet of the Gods.

Some Outer Circle members would regard such a characterization as unfair. One says of the Inner Circle that "they were a lot smarter than I was, that's all." But fair or not, that is the way many outsiders perceived the social structure of the unit, and some disgruntled Outer Circle members felt that way, too. Two or three talented filmmakers had an extremely difficult time getting along with the Inner Circle.

That there were within Unit B severe personality clashes that could not be brought into harmony is not startling. They occurred in other units, too, and perhaps they occur in any intensely creative (or even intensely sterile) situation. Surrounding Watson and Crick, for example, were other scientists interested in the structure of DNA or in similar problems, and clashes among some of these people were sometimes acute.[8] The personal friction that existed in Unit B would therefore lack special interest were it not in some way associated, if mainly in retrospect, with an aesthetic problem.

It is no denigration of the work of Unit B at its best to note that in terms of Grierson's early aesthetic, a standard which demanded as much from documentary as Picasso demanded of painting or Auden of poetry, there was one significant shortcoming. The Unit B sense of wholeness was cautious, exclusive, and elitist. When Grierson, in his aesthetically bold years, had written that "in art there must be praise," he did so in a context that implied that this praise must be forged from the ugliest and most depressing realities, which in England included — for Grierson — "brutality" and "starvation," political bankruptcy, sapped public confidence, and troubled beliefs. It was this perspective that made Grierson's aesthetic ideal sophisticated, interesting, and demanding. There was certainly "praise" in the Unit B classics, but it was of a kind that avoided grappling with "unsuccess" (Auden's phrase), a praise that avoided "the bottom of the night" (again, Auden's phrase). *Paul Tomkowicz* was simply a portrait of an engaging immigrant. *Corral* pictures a process that is beautiful in itself. *City of Gold* looked at the past, and through still-photographs taken by others, for a primarily nostalgic effect. *Universe* may have been about "the whole universe," but as such it was a film about something subject to awe-inspiring, natural physical laws, already possessed of an order far more coherent than that of human affairs. And the bias of the *Candid Eye* series was slanted toward individuals who themselves had *already* achieved a kind of "wholeness," or positive response to life. (Several of the forgotten *Candid Eye* films were about successful performers, such as Glenn Gould and Igor Stravinsky.)

In other words, Unit B tended to *report* success, to *report* the existence or achievement of unity or wholeness. That this is so is not contradicted by the unity, or aesthetic wholeness, of the films themselves. Many films are about wholeness, or beauty, but are ugly, or at best boring. But to make a beautiful film about something beautiful, or a coherent film about coherence, is not as difficult as making a beautiful film which explores the ugly as well.

Of the classic Unit B films, *Lonely Boy* came closest to a beautiful film about something not so beautiful, but it did this in part by skirting what was most intriguing and perplexing about the Anka phenomenon. The centre of the film's attention is almost always Paul Anka. The filmmakers are evidently ambivalent about him. On the one hand, they are impressed by his diligence, discipline, talent, and effect. On the other hand, they poke fun at his success, defining it in terms of screaming teenagers (invariably pimply or homely or silly) or by revealing that Anka has had a "nose job." But while the film brings us close to Anka, it distances us from the idolatrous fans. When the police and security guards form a barrier protecting Anka from the audience, the film crew is on Anka's side of the barrier. The film crew comes close to resembling the writer of articles for movie fan magazines, whose mention of human flaws in his subject serves mainly to spice up an overall ga-ga portrait. In *Lonely Boy*, the filmmakers focused on the easier subject, Paul Anka, and only gingerly touched upon the real problem. The emptiness of the teenagers' lives — their unsuccess — is not explored. It is *shown*, often, but in cold, distant shots that generally deride or mock the girls.

It might seem that the tendency of the Unit B classic films to praise life in part by avoiding its darker aspects could perhaps be attributed to the age. The fifties and early sixties were perhaps a more optimistic time than the late sixties and the seventies. In Tom Daly's view:

> The world outlook was very different in those days. It was a period of centralizing and integrating. During World War II, Canadian politics moved rapidly from what had been largely a sleepy and local provincial level to a centralizing federal level with a view looking outward on the world. After the war, this tendency to look at the parts not separately, but as related to each other in a wholeness, was active on a still larger scale in the concept "One World or None," and in the optimistic developments of that time in relation to the United Nations. Economically, the situation was expansive: problems might be big, but mankind might be equal to solving them.... In Canada, things headed to a peak in this respect up to 1967 with the Centennial and Expo '67.

But the Inner Circle's avoidance of themes that included the sick, the horrible, or the ugly cannot be attributed solely to an atmosphere of optimistic internationalism. There were people at the Film Board, inside Unit B and outside it, who were not so optimistic, whatever the atmosphere.

One such person was McLaren. His *Neighbors*, made in 1952, before the emergence of Unit B's documentary prototypes, had an internationalist theme, plenty of horror, and a mildly optimistic concluding note. In *Neighbors*, a flower blooms between two houses. The men of the two families both become euphoric from the flower's scent. Then the desire to own the flower overcomes each man, and each starts to build a fence which will enclose the flower within his property. A fight ensues. The flower is trampled. Each man drags the other's wife and children outside and kills them. Finally, the men kill each other. The film ends with a new flower sprouting from the ground.

This is the original version, and the version that has been in distribution since the late nineteen-sixties. When *Neighbors* was made, the American distributor and some Film Board distribution representatives insisted that the sequence in which the women and children are killed be cut out, so that the film could be shown in schools. McLaren had formal reservations about the scene anyway, and so he assented. But by the late sixties, when the Vietnam War was raging, McLaren attended a festival in Europe, where several filmmakers argued against the cut. (An account of the excision of the scene had appeared in a book about pacifist films.[9]) Additionally, an American distributor for a package of NFB shorts refused to include *Neighbors* unless the sequence was restored. The sequence was reconstituted from original prints. The original version is now the only one in distribution.

Thus the Board *had* made a film which managed to achieve an aesthetic unity out of a vision that did not turn its eye from the ugly, even in the milder version. The film had an internationalist theme, but not a soft one. Although not a documentary, *Neighbors* was the toughest film of the Unit System era, and perhaps the truest.

After *Neighbors*, McLaren did not make another film with so urgent a theme. His work became more abstract. But he did not lose his awareness that the nineteen-fifties did not invite optimism. In 1960, at the height of Unit B's success, and well before the full emergence of the Vietnam War, McLaren expressed regret that he had not done more films with a larger social purpose than his experimental work after *Neighbors*, and he suggested that

> perhaps it is more important at the moment for a creative artist to turn his mind to the problems that are menacing our contemporary society, if he is at all inclined by instinct and temperament to do so. At a time when our whole civilization is in danger of being destroyed, we are perhaps fiddling away our energy on a host of pretty and beautiful things which the world has a surfeit of already.[10]

But it is perhaps one thing to achieve a full aesthetic unity, one that embraces the ugly and the horrifying, in experimental animation, and another thing to do it in documentary, particularly in the high-ratio, non-scripted approach that emerged in the late fifties. The gap between the material and the form in animation is far narrower, at least in some important respects, than in documentary. The animator does not have to cope with uncontrollable reality in order to collect his material, and the editing problems are far less demanding. Nor does he incur responsibilities to living subjects. The gap between order and disorder in animation is not so treacherous as in documentary.

McLaren, however, wasn't the only NFB filmmaker who in 1960 was concerned about menacing contemporary problems. David Bairstow, in the same year, produced a two-part documentary, *Poisons, Pests and People*, which explored an issue that at the time was not in the forefront of public consciousness. In 1961, Bairstow produced *River with a Problem*, a film about the pollution of the Ottawa River. These films were not particularly interesting as documentary art. They were journalistic and unengaged. Nevertheless, they were films which did explore something important and not itself inspiring.

Undoubtedly, there were other serious documentaries made outside Unit B which have been forgotten, but even within Unit B there were some filmmakers who tried not to ignore the more difficult aspects of contemporary life.

One such filmmaker was Terence Macartney-Filgate. His *Candid Eye* films were concerned more with the unsuccessful than with the celebrated. And just as the *Candid Eye* films made primarily by the Inner Circle team tended to select individuals as subjects, Macartney-Filgate, an individualist, tended to make films about groups. In *The Back-Breaking Leaf* (1960), Macartney-Filgate, working with several French-Canadians, explored the harsh life of tobacco pickers in southern Ontario. In his *Blood and Fire*, which examined the work of the Salvation Army, there is one scene in which a weeping, deeply troubled person, a genuine down-and-out, responds to the Call to the Mercy Seat. This scene was, during the editing, the subject of heated debates. Some believed that because the scene showed a recognizable man in a state of emotional nakedness, it should be cut out. It seemed raw and — worse — unethical. *Cinéma vérité* was in its early stages, and some filmmakers had qualms about using such material. But because there had been no attempt to hide the camera, and because the scene was so dramatic, it was kept.

Neither of these films had the coherent richness or energy of *Lonely Boy*. They were aesthetically flat. But neither of them was made under the special conditions and with the grand-finale purpose and licence of *Lonely Boy*. And if they failed to achieve a tone of "praise," i.e., a life-enhancing structure or perspective, they dealt in an area that the Inner Circle team generally avoided — unsuccess.

Arthur Lipsett was another member of Unit B who tried to deal in his work with the less cheery side of life. In 1962, he made *Very Nice, Very Nice*, an eight-minute film containing perhaps as many individual shots as an average hour-long documentary. Many of the shots were stills. The sound track was composed from pieces of sound tape discarded from other films. This was several years before Jean-Luc Godard made *Weekend*, a film introduced by the title, "A Film Found on the Scrap Heap." The vision in *Very Nice, Very Nice* was as dour as that of *Weekend* and a lot more succinctly (if far less richly) expressed. The bomb, international politics, materialism, pollution, noise, and alienation are among the pathologies covered in the film.

If the Unit B classics leaned toward an easy praise, in *Very Nice, Very Nice* there was no praise at all. It was a completely sour list of complaints against society as it existed at the time. *Very Nice, Very Nice* was to the Unit B aesthetic as Dostoevski's underground man was to the optimistic, rational positivism of Dostoevski's time. Even the title could be taken as a sarcastic comment on the Unit B aesthetic, a sardonic response to the easy optimism that saw life as "true, fine, and full of meaning" by seeing only half of life.

Unfortunately, Lipsett saw only that other half. *Very Nice, Very Nice* was like the underground man, but it was not like *Notes from the Underground*. It was the phenomenon without the form. It stands as a rather gross example of what in literary criticism is sometimes called "the expressive fallacy," the notion that the effect of an artwork should reproduce its subject — e.g., that a novel about boredom should itself be boring. *Very Nice, Very Nice* was a disordered film about disorder, a confused film on confusion. Its effect was accomplished by chopping up random pieces of actuality footage and sound-tape found in the Film Board's waste baskets. Almost any pieces would do. With *Very Nice, Very Nice*, the filmmaker was like a poet who attempts to show the decline of language and culture by writing an incomprehensible poem out of bifurcated, misspelled cuss-words randomly strung together.

Very Nice, Very Nice was, however, something of a *tour de force*, and was very popular among underground film persons and members of the counter-culture in North America. The film achieved an influential niche in the history of experimental film. It became a prototype. The film was influential at the Film Board, too. Several filmmakers regarded Lipsett as the Board's first resident genius since McLaren. The extreme positive response to Lipsett's extreme negativism suggests that there was, within the Film Board and outside it, a severe hunger for recognition of the negative side of contemporary life. If the film fails to survive aesthetically, perhaps it was at the time a refreshing challenge to the easy optimism that dominated the screens of the early sixties. *Very Nice, Very Nice* was a filmic restatement of McLaren's milder suggestion that perhaps creative artists shouldn't be frittering their talent away on pretty things when the world was menaced with the possibility of total destruction.

Lipsett, Macartney-Filgate, Bairstow, and McLaren were at various degrees removed from the Inner Circle, the Unit B team responsible for the Board's first classic documentaries. Bairstow belonged to another unit and had little to do with Unit B. McLaren was part of Unit B for a while, but only technically. In Daly's words, McLaren was always "an original, special person, available to all, and ready to help all." Macartney-Filgate joined the Unit B team for Candid Eye, but he did not get along well with them. The Inner Circle encouraged Lipsett at first, and actually supported and defended his work on *Very Nice, Very Nice*. Only later, as Lipsett continued to dwell on the same theme, was there a falling out.

It was as if Unit B had a group personality which could not absorb the negative into its aesthetic vision, even though it tried. Unit B's best films were made by the Inner Circle and avoided the negative; the unit's socially critical films were made by others and weren't so good. Unit B did, however, make one outstanding documentary which did not ignore the unsettling aspects of its subject. This film was *Circle of the Sun* (1961), directed by Colin Low. The film's specific subject is the Blood Indian Sun Dance, performed at a gathering in Alberta (Low's home province). This was the first time that the Indians had allowed the Sun Dance to be filmed; the reason for allowing it was that the Indians feared that the tradition might be dying. This possibility suggested the film's larger theme — the possible demise of the whole Blood Indian culture. The Sun Dance and its larger subject are explored through a portrait (and voice-over) of a young Blood Indian, who moves between two worlds, modern industrial civilization (he works as an oil rigger) and what's left of the Blood culture. This theme was not a new one, and the film did not develop new techniques, but it is a reasonably sensitive, honest, and beautiful film, its "praise" consisting in the aesthetic intensity with which the theme is rendered.

But *Circle of the Sun* does not necessarily belie the characterization of the Unit B aesthetic as overly positive. For one thing, as good as the film was, it was not a prototype. For another, it was perhaps aesthetically *too* intense. The film tends to aestheti*cize* its subject. As if the Sun Dance weren't itself sufficiently engrossing, a heavy-handed, overbearing musical score dominates the film in its most dramatic moments.

Additionally, *Circle of the Sun* was less of a team effort than the prototypal documentaries, and more the work of an individual. And its director, Colin Low, would eventually, when the team disbanded, pursue socially relevant filmmaking with a vengeance.

In sum, it does appear that the aesthetic ideal's difficulty with the negative was in some important way related to the personality of the group, a personality not reducible to those of the individual members of the group. The team had an aversion to rawness. It liked its reality precooked. It preferred to make films about subjects already somewhat coherent, somewhat whole, than to create that wholeness entirely itself.

The team's inability to absorb the raw into its aesthetic triumphs was a limitation to its "attitude toward the craft," but perhaps it was also an indication of aesthetic integrity. To expand the range of the aesthetic may have meant destroying it. For the Film Board of the time, the aesthetic was an indisputable advance in the art of documentary. Unit B represented the apex of the development of certain Film Board values and characteristics. It was the height of combining one's living with one's calling. It was the epitome of group filmmaking. And it was the strongest expression of a consciously considered, home-grown film aesthetic.

The Unit System came to an end less than two years after *Very Nice, Very Nice*. Therefore, it is hazardous to speculate upon the possibility that the Unit B aesthetic eventually might have widened its scope. But after *Lonely Boy*, The Unit B Inner Circle (and Unit B as a whole) produced no further existent documentaries of note. Possibly the Unit B aesthetic had spent itself with *Lonely Boy*.

But possibly it hadn't. In 1963, the group's attention turned toward planning a multi-screen extravaganza, *Labyrinth*, for Expo '67, Canada's centennial celebration. One of the requirements of Expo '67 was that whatever was shown had to be something that could not be seen anywhere else. It is impossible to see the original *Labyrinth* now [11] — which is unfortunate, because in Daly's view, *Labyrinth* "was perhaps the most complete embodiment of the Unit B philosophy." Daly recalls that

> the theme was the whole development of life, dark and light sides, through innocent childhood, confident youth, disillusion and depression, the search for something more, the meeting with the Minotaur (the dark side of

oneself), new directions of life, the facing of death, and the mysteries beyond. This theme was embodied in architecture, in personal movement of the audience through a "structure" of events and experiences including films as *part* of it.

If the Unit B aesthetic hadn't exhausted itself with *Lonely Boy*, it surely had with *Labyrinth*. This single project held most of the team together after the Unit System's demise, but by the time *Labyrinth* was over, Koenig had returned to animation, Kroitor had left the Film Board, and Low had begun to pursue a different kind of filmmaking in Challenge for Change. And some of their younger disciples had tired of documentary, and become interested in dramatic features.

But the contribution of Unit B to the Film Board documentary did not lie solely in the classics that it put into the Board's catalogue. That Unit B *had* an aesthetic ideal, that they made films which did not compromise the ideal, and that their commitment to achieving it was unswerving influenced filmmakers of various sensibilities. In addition, the success of Unit B earned for all Film Board filmmakers a greater authority over the purpose and process of filmmaking; the unusual freedoms that Unit B won for itself were transmitted to all the filmmakers in the form of structural changes that would occur in 1964. And three members of the Inner Circle — Tom Daly, Colin Low, and Stanley Jackson — would, as individuals, give generously to the Film Board documentary even into the eighties. Most of the Board's later achievements in documentary owed much to the work of Unit B.

Even now, Unit B is remembered vividly. Some of its severest critics remember it with nostalgia or at least respect. One who had been an unhappy fringe member of the unit laments that

> the *discipline* of the unit system — and in their own informal way Unit B was the most disciplined — was a good thing. Everything I know now is because of the discipline I learned in Unit B. I'm trying to develop discipline in these new guys, but it's not possible. Young filmmakers nowadays want to do just what they want. They don't listen.

A filmmaker who had belonged to a different unit remarks:

> They were snobs. . . . I couldn't stand them. . . . And yet, you've got to be a bit of a snob to do something of quality. If you're not a snob, you might be sloppy.

And a sound-mixer remembers:

> It was ... *trying* to work with them. Quite often they'd work by committee, in endless sessions, in the mixing studio. They were very meticulous. But they were always after a *good film*. It was a challenge and a joy to mix their films.

But the Unit B phenomenon was not the only important development during the Unit System. In the late fifties, a development was afoot that was less spectacular, but which marked the beginnings of an exploration of the harsh and dreary aspects of Canadian life, the side of Canada that the Unit B classics had avoided.

6

THE WORM IN THE APPLE: FROM FRENCH-CANADIAN VERSIONS TO QUEBECOIS ORIGINALS

The Unit B prototypal documentaries were made under the Board's broad mandate of interpreting Canada to Canadians. The geographic range of the films was equally broad. Paul Tomkowicz was an immigrant living in Manitoba; the cowboy in *Corral* was an Albertan; Dawson City, the "city of gold," was in the Yukon; the observatory in *Universe* was in Ontario; and Paul Anka was from Ontario.

The films were English-Canadian, and they were positive and optimistic. Geographically, they avoided the province of Quebec; aesthetically, they shunned the negative. Could there have been a relationship between the two omissions? Developments in French-language production in the late fifties and early sixties would lend weight to such an hypothesis. The best French-language films of the period were about Quebec, and they explored the negative. They were critical of the national dream.

The filmmakers who made these films had a different relationship to the Film Board from the one the Unit B team had had. Of the latter, two — Daly and Jackson — had joined the Film Board early in the war, when Grierson was Commissioner, and they retained much of Grierson's sense of structure and sense of purpose. Low joined the Film Board in 1945, Koenig in 1948. They were long-term employees. The filmmakers who were to make the noteworthy French-language films of the late fifties and early sixties were younger and more recent employees. Some of them had no idea who Grierson was.

It was Grierson, though, who brought a French-Canadian presence to Canadian government film production. The staff of the old Motion Picture Bureau included not a single French-Canadian. In December 1941, the Film Board took on its first French-Canadian, and within the next two years hired ten more.[1] (In the same period, though, the Board employed hundreds of English-Canadians.) The French-Canadians were hired in much the same irregular way as were the English-Canadians. Paul Thériault, one of the early French-Canadian employees, recalls that some English-Canadian friends had asked him why he didn't come join them at the Board. Thériault went to meet Grierson. "Two days later," Thériault recalled, "I received a message: 'You are hired; come begin your work.'"[2]

The Film Board, and perhaps Grierson himself, assumed that the French-Canadians wanted the same things as the English-Canadians did: victory in Europe, unity in Canada, and economic progress. Soon, however, an incident occurred (according to one old-timer still at the Board) that cast doubt on the assumption. The Board had almost completed a pro-conscription film aimed at Quebec. When the film was ready for printing, the negatives disappeared. An intense search of the Film Board premises failed to yield the negative. Perhaps, as the English-Canadian veteran who tells this story suggests, the film is "still lying somewhere on the bottom of the Ottawa River." Perhaps, too, the story is apocryphal.

The unity, or wholeness, that Grierson promoted did not apply to Quebec in the way it did to English-Canada. In practice, Grierson had modified the 1939 mandate of helping "Canadians in all parts of Canada to understand the ways of living and the problems of Canadians in other parts" such that the "other parts" included only superficial reference to Quebec. For the first two years of the war, French-Canadian production consisted solely in making French-language sound tracks for English-Canadian films. French-Canadian employees worked on original films, but these were English-language films. In 1943, the Board initiated a bi-monthly series of newsreel films called *Les Reportages*, most of which were original French-language material about the war effort in Quebec. In 1944, under Norman McLaren's supervision, a series of animated sing-along films, *Chants populaires*, was produced. These were film adaptations of French-Canadian folk songs. The *Canada Carries On* series, which lasted for several years beyond the end of the war, included several French-Canadian film-makers on its staff. In 1945, Jean Palardy, now an authority on French-Canadian arts and crafts, made *Le vent qui chante*, a documentary about the organ-building craft of the Casavant Frères. In 1947, Pierre Pétel made *Au Parc Lafontaine*, a view of the daily activities in a famous park in French Montreal. The soundtrack was a French-Canadian song.

But the major French-Canadian work in the wartime Film Board was the versioning of English-language films into French, and this kind of production continued to constitute a large portion of French-Canadian production for several years after the war. Jacques Bobet, now a producer at the Film Board, notes that although making French-language versions of English-Canadian films was not the most exciting kind of production, at least

> the effort kept us working. It gave us a continuity. It established us at the Board. They knew there was a French Canada somewhere, and we gave them something to *distribute*.

Nor was versioning completely lacking in satisfaction. Bobet recalls that the French-Canadians had a slogan to the effect that "the version is better that the original."

In 1951, Bernard Devlin became producer of all original French-language films. This was the beginning of a French production unit under the Unit System. In the next ten years, the size of French production nearly tripled, and a second French production unit was established.

The catalyst for the rapid expansion of French production was television. The CBC was unable to fill by itself the daily demand for hours of original French-language material. Suddenly there was room to manoeuvre, to experiment, to try out ideas. And in 1956, as per the recommendation of the Massey Report, the Film Board was given new premises, a single, huge building — but in Montreal, the centre of French-Canadian culture. In 1958, the Film Board would have a French-Canadian Commissioner, Guy Roberge. Biculturalism began to develop within the Film Board, as some of the French-Canadian filmmakers grew seriously dissatisfied with the established Film Board documentary style. Raymond Garceau remembers that just before the move to Montreal, he had

> made a film with the stuffy title, *Horizons of Quebec* (1952). They [management] wanted this to be in true NFB style, noisy enough for theatres but with the solid English documentary treatment like Stuart Legg at his best. Lots of action, machines, racket and clouds, with a narration that sounded big, dramatic, cavernous, with music to match, of the kind that has long haunted the depths of this noble institution.[3]

Ironically, just as the concern for a Canadian identity vis-à-vis the United States had helped motivate the establishment of the National Film Board, the French-Canadians were concerned — increasingly so — about their identity vis-à-vis English Canada. Garceau complained that the Film Board reflection of the national tendency to trivialize or patronize Quebec had hardly progressed:

> As specified by NFB principles, a French-Canadian was no longer as in the early fifties a sort of folksy curiosity but:
>
> 1. an English-Canadian who spoke French;
> 2. a French-Canadian who spoke English;
> 3. a French-Canadian who could correctly interpret the English ideas.[4]

In the early fifties, as Jacques Bobet remembers, versioning became less frequent. French-Canadians became choosy about which English-Canadian films deserved translation. There was some original production. The *Faces of Canada* series (1953-54), which yielded *Corral* and *Paul Tomkowicz*, also yielded three original French-language films with a French-Canadian flavour: Raymond Garceau's *Le bedeau*, about a minor church official whose dignified image is tainted when he chases a pig out of a church; Pierre Arbour's *Le notaire*, about a notary (an important position in the small towns of Quebec); and *Le photographe*, about a small-town photographer who makes his living photographing families at births, marriages, and anniversaries. But much of the so-called "original" French-language production in the early fifties were series films *reproducing* English-language series. One reasonably popular television reportage series, *Sur le vif*, was not a reproduction, but it was produced simultaneously with an English series, *On the Spot*, and in an English production unit.

In 1955, the French unit started its own original, large-scale series, *Passe partout*, which used both documentary and dramatic formats. *Passe partout* was a conscious attempt to depart from the English-Canadian approach. In a memorandum regarding the series, Guy Coté argued that communication and understanding between the two cultures were possible only at an "international intellectual" level, where the values of the respective cultures were being expressed as authentically as possible. But Coté was not advocating a filmic Esperanto. On the contrary:

> [it] is in the [popularization] of these ideas that the roads diverge. An English-Canadian mind cannot [popularize] for French Canada.[5]

Coté gave an example of how Canada appears, in NFB films, to French-Canadians:

> The concept of the "small town" and its community pride is one long dear to our film programme. In N.F.B. films, the citizens of the community all buy the local newspaper (because it has editorials about civil liberties) and dutifully support the Town Council in its welfare work. . . . They are full of admiration for the suburban supermarket and will vote for the new

> recreational centre at the next elections. They recognize the place of the
> Postman in their community and may even wave at him as he gaily goes
> down the street.... They never write Justice with a small "j" and they
> settle brawls by democratic discussion. They go to church at Easter, give
> the occasional dollar to the Salvation Army and plan to buy a split-level
> bungalow and a new Buick next year.

Coté concluded that although "no one can quarrel" with such social
values, they simply cannot register in the minds of most French-Canadians, whose "thinking remains traditional and non-Americanized."

Thus from the French-Canadian perspective the distinctly Canadian
production of the Film Board, the "whole picture" of Canada's
"people and purposes," looked like an uninspired imitation of the
culture south of the border. And the "whole picture" was not whole;
the interpretation of "Canada to Canadians" (as the 1950 Act phrased
it) was too largely the interpretation of only *English*-Canada to
Canadians. From about 1955 on, French-Canadians — who were
beginning to think of themselves as Québécois — would attempt to fill
that gap in the execution of the Film Board's mandate. In helping the
Film Board carry out the job that Parliament had asked it to do, the
Québécois eventually would help turn the government documentary into
a far stronger truth-telling instrument than it had ever been, anywhere.

Neither Parliament nor the Québécois necessarily had had this aim in
mind. When Parliament defined the Board's mission as the interpretation of Canada to Canadians, it had in mind traditional government
propaganda, if a liberalized version of it. Unwittingly, Parliament had
given the Board a mandate that resembled the right of free speech.
Quebec was part of Canada, and if a filmmaker was to interpret that part
of Canada, he could hardly do so in "vulgarized" English-Canadian
terms — not if he wanted to be honest and truthful. Of course, the
mandate by itself did not necessarily mean much; the Board's post-war
experience proved that. But the Film Board had survived, and had
emerged with more independence than it had before. And the Film
Board was now located in the centre of Québécois culture.

Nor were the Québécois motivated by a desire to help fulfil a
government mandate. They were concerned about their political and
cultural identity, which by definition involved dissension from government mandates. The Film Board's mandate, in effect, gave the
Québécois the right to dissent from all other mandates.

Perhaps the first significant step in the Québécois adventure at the
Film Board was *Panoramique*, a series of half-hour dramatic programmes produced from 1957 to 1959. These films were released first

on non-theatrical circuits and then combined in packages of two or three as one-shot features for television. In a low-key way, the films departed from the standard Film Board pro-industry stance and glorification of Canada's role in World War II.

Some English-Canadians were unhappy with the attitudes expressed in *Panoramique*, but English-Canadians at the Film Board were irritated by more than just the attitudes expressed in the films. McKay writes:

> [Ignoring the advice of the English-Canadian technical and production staff, the new French-Canadian filmmakers] made terrible mistakes in shooting, but they also achieved some new and unusual effects. They upset the routine of the sound department in their trial and error methods. They broke the rules of editing and every other rule. They were the despair of many ... experienced filmmakers. ... When six or eight [French-Canadian filmmakers] crowded around a table for four in the cafeteria and argued vociferously in their own language, they were glared at in the same way the youngsters of 1942 had been.[6]

One topic of conversation at these gatherings was the Film Board's idea of craftsmanship. To the Québécois there was something oppressive, boring, and stifling about the emphasis on clarity, coherence, and neatness. To begin filming with a detailed script was to blind yourself to what reality offered. Shooting from a script ensured that nothing was discovered, that the filmmaker merely selected from reality that which conformed to one's preconceived notion of it. Scripting prevented exploration. To then package what was filmed into a given structure was to compound the offence against reality. To attach a didactic commentary was still worse. The Film Board documentary gave an illusion of objectivity, but in fact presented an extremely biased, closed view of reality — no matter how "impersonal" the film might be in tone. This was a heavy style, one that suited the days of heavy equipment, when shooting a film was so awkward an operation that reality often had to be distorted for the convenience of the clumsy work of filmmaking.

That the Québécois complaint against the traditional Film Board documentary resembled that of the Unit B *Candid Eye* team is not surprising. Several of them had worked on some of the *Candid Eye* films. And both groups were attuned to what was developing in film outside the Film Board, and both were responsive to the possibilities offered by lightweight equipment.

But if both the *Candid Eye* team and the Québécois filmmakers were seeking a more authentic and vigorous style of documentary, the latter's quest was wider in scope. For the English-Canadian members of the *Candid Eye* team, the series was primarily an aesthetic adventure, almost a spiritual one. For the Québécois, direct cinema was tied to the theory and practice of defining a cultural identity, and it had political ramifications as well. The intellectual context of their documentary work was more intense than that of the Unit B work, and they were in closer touch with documentary developments outside Canada. Michel Brault, a cameraman associated with several of the new, interesting films, had worked with Richard Leacock in the United States. Brault, Georges Dufaux, and Claude Jutra worked with the Frenchman Jean Rouch briefly in the late fifties. Brault shot Rouch's famous *Chronique d'un été*. Rouch was to become known as one of the leading practitioners and theorists of *"cinéma-vérité"* or "direct cinema," but Rouch apparently learned as much from the Québécois as they learned from him. Rouch has said that:

> All that we've done in France in the area of *cinéma-vérité* came from the National Film Board. It was Brault who brought a new technique of shooting that we hadn't known and that we have copied ever since.[7]

Rouch himself was invited, in 1963, to make a film at the Film Board.

In the summer of 1958, at the Robert Flaherty Seminar, held that year in Santa Barbara, Brault had shown Rouch *Les raquetteurs*, a film that Brault, as cameraman, and Gilles Groulx, as director and editor, had just finished. The film was about an amateur snowshoeing event taking place in a Quebec village. The film had been shot in one weekend. When the English-Canadian Director of Production saw the rushes, he was appalled. He refused to allocate money for editing the film, and ordered that the material be sent to the stock-shot library. Unofficially, in his spare time — late at night and on weekends — Groulx edited the film. With the help of Tom Daly and his Unit B team, who saw merit in the film, Groulx and Brault were finally able to get money to complete it.[8]

One observer later described *Les raquetteurs* as "the first Canadian example of galloping reportage, grabbing images on the wing."[9] Gilles Marsolais, in his book, *Le cinéma canadien*, gave four-fold credit to the film for ignoring the rules of "clarity," "neatness," "lucidity," *et al.*; for launching direct cinema in Canada; as an early victory of the Québécois filmmakers' quest for "spontaneity, personality, and *authenticity*"; and as the film that "showed the way of liberation."[10]

Just as *Les raquetteurs* ignored the standard Film Board conception of form and style, Groulx's next film ignored the post-war Film Board's avoidance of touchy political issues. The film, *Normétal*, was a study of a mining town in Quebec, and had as its theme the domination of the villagers by this economic enterprise. This point of view amounted to a complete reversal of the Film Board's normal attitude toward economic development. The Film Board, in its mainstream documentary work, had always promoted industry and resource development as a means of furthering the general welfare. In *Normétal*, the mine does not serve the people. The people serve the mine. The entire lives of several generations are subordinate to the needs of the mining operation. Because the typical Canadian mine is owned by English-Canadians or Americans, the film implies that the villagers are the slaves of foreigners.

Management ordered that about half the film be cut out. In protest, Groulx and the others who worked on the original film demanded that their names be withdrawn from the credits.[11]

If the name Gilles Groulx seems particularly prominent in this departure from the traditional style and point of view of the Film Board documentary, Groulx himself would correct that impression:

> At first, at the NFB, nothing was possible. Then, little by little, things became more and more possible. We were a group, and we worked communally.... Call it, if you like, a common front, a conspiracy. We conspired together and forced the doors to open.[12]

Once again the team approach to documentary filmmaking had figured importantly in a development of the art. But whereas the advances in English-Canadian documentary of the time were the work of one unconventional unit, the leadership of the Québécois development cut across the two French-language production units. The boundaries of the two French units were not so rigid as those of the English units. But in this group — which included Groulx, Brault, Jutra, Claude Fournier, and others — there was interchange of roles similar to that which characterized the Empire Marketing Board and Unit B. There was the same excitement of developing, or trying to develop, a new kind of documentary film. There was the same attitude toward credits; several of the films of this group were signed as a team. In short, there was a charismatic aspect to the group's structure. A decade later, Claude Jutra was to recall:

> We were all there and we were all close. It was like a communion of spirits.[13]

To some Québécois, however, the team approach seemed ultimately inhibiting. In criticizing some of the best films of this period, such as *Les raquetteurs*, *Québec USA*, *A Saint-Henri le cinq septembre*, Gilles Marsolais (writing in the mid-sixties) noted in them a tendency to ''seek self-expression at the expense of the subject observed . . . to emphasize curious or ridiculous details'' of the people being filmed.[14] There was, at the same time, a cool detachment from the subject, a distance. Marsolais blamed this partly on the team approach to filmmaking, a system

> repugnant to our mentality or to our latin temperament.... Our best films are profoundly individualistic.[15]

The English-Canadian *Candid Eye* films had committed the same errors; *Lonely Boy* was cool towards the female fans of Anka, and tended to ridicule them. In Claude Jutra's view, the *Candid Eye* team "sought to describe events without taking part"; they made their films with an "anglo-saxon objectivity" with which the Québécois felt uncomfortable.[16] The Québécois sought to make of direct cinema "something truly and distinctly Québécois," something "much more personal," because — as they saw it — merely by the choice of subjects, by the choice of angles, and so forth, filmmakers already were personalizing the view of reality presented in their films. Michel Brault described the difference between the *Candid Eye* approach (as he perceived it) and what the Québécois were attempting as follows:

> One could say that there are two techniques: there is the tele-photo style and the wide-angle style.... I belong more to the wide-angle style, that is to say that the style consists simply in approaching the people and filming them, in participating in their lives and not in observing them in secret, inside a box, or from high up in a window with a tele-photo lens.[17]

Thus there were three elements in the aesthetic that the Québécois were attempting to build: the openness to reality that direct cinema offered, and which the *Candid Eye* team was with some success pursuing; the question of Québécois identity, which implied not only cultural but political content; and an individual, or personal, "participation" in, and interpretation of, the reality that direct cinema was capable of exploring.[18]

These elements figured in the development of Québécois documentary, not just at the airy level of theory, but also at the most practical level of making films and advancing one's career. Because direct cinema and scriptwriting were mutually exclusive, a filmmaker proposing a direct cinema project did not have to submit a script to the English-Canadian Director of Production. The filmmaker, by working in direct cinema, avoided the dreary task of writing a script and then translating it so that English-Canadian management could read it. He could avoid the revisions that would be demanded, and the misunderstandings that would occur from the loss of subtlety or precision in the translation. And he could by-pass an early hurdle of censorship. Fernand Dansereau, a Québécois director, has remarked, only partly in jest, that direct cinema caught on partly

> not because one was interested in direct cinema as such ... but because one knew that if he used direct cinema, he could get $20,000 with one piece of paper.[19]

One of the most successful examples of the integration of values that the Québécois were seeking was *Jour après jour* (1962), directed by Clément Perron and edited by Anne-Claire Poirier. The film's political orientation was much like that intended in *Normétal*, but in *Jour après jour* it was less explicitly put, at least in the verbal aspect of the film. In the film, the employees of a paper mill are seen to be the slaves of the dreary factory in which they work. The machine is an agent of oppression. The machine is also irrational: in the film's climactic scene, a machine runs amok, spewing huge spools of paper onto the floor. The paper almost buries the men who are frantically trying to regain "control" of the machine. It is a chilling scene, not at all dramatic in the conventional sense, but simply observed. The editing, which took about a year, and the mournful, bitter commentary ensure that we see the machine as only an agent of the oppression, not the source. After reading the Ten Commandments, the narrator concludes, " ... but you'll pay the union dues and Canada, too."

Another successful combination of the three elements in the new aesthetic was Arthur Lamothe's *Bûcherons de la Manouane* (1963), a film about the timber industry in Quebec. To the methods of direct cinema Lamothe added, in Marsolais' view, "a human dimension, a quality of feeling that was cruelly lacking in the earlier films," and the result was a film of "felt and *personalized* reality."[20] The film had political content as well, although not as much as Lamothe would have liked. Anticipating problems in gaining the film's release, Lamothe had written a commentary that was strictly factual, and shorn of all adjectival taint. The original commentary thus consisted of bald statements like:

> This land is part of Quebec.... The owners of the company are American.... The directors are Anglo-Saxon.... English is their language....[21]

This self-censorship was not sufficient; one by one, many of these lines were forced out.

Perhaps Gilles Groulx's most enduring film of the era was his *Golden Gloves* (1964), a documentary portrait of a black boxer, Ronald

Jones. Jones is bilingual: because his family is poor and lives in the French-Canadian part of Montreal, he speaks French; in the boxing world, he speaks English. The film suggests that French is the language of poverty, English the language for "making it." The film is quick-moving and visually rich. There is a stunning shot of Jones's brother jogging and shadow-boxing alongside a train as it passes through a depressed area of Montreal. There is an overall balance, or tension, between images of vulgarity and images of grace.

Another intriguing film from this group of filmmakers was *A Saint-Henri le cinq septembre*. The commentary makes explicit the French-Canadian insistence on the inescapable fact of personal interpretation of reality:

> We have chosen this day ... to invade Saint-Henri, a working-class district in Montreal....
>
> The most difficult task will be to adjust the image we had of reality to the one we discover....
>
> We took this particular shot because the girl was pretty....
>
> We have not brought back pictures of ... flies, filth. It is there. That is all you need to know. It should not be there. That is all we want you to know.

In addition, the commentary contains direct references to Marker, Resnais, Hitchcock, Truffaut, and Rouch. *A Saint-Henri* was one of the earliest, and remains today one of the most baldly self-reflexive examples of what has developed into a new genre of documentary film.

Ironically, an English-Canadian critic was to complain of the Québécois films of the period that

> while certainly moving social documents, most lovingly observed, [they] lack any reference outwards to the larger world beyond Quebec, so that even while admiring them, it is difficult not to be bored.[22]

How one can be bored by moving social documents is a puzzling question. And to the extent that these films were inward-looking, reflecting only Quebec, they were analogues to the Film Board tradition of taking only English Canada seriously. But on the social and political levels, there was certainly a "reference outwards," even after the exercise of censorship. The "reference outwards" was precisely the reason for the censorship.

Parochialism could have been cited legitimately as a minor flaw in a beautiful but largely apolitical film of the era, Pierre Perrault's *Pour la suite du monde* (1963). This film was a feature-length documentary, filmed by Michel Brault, about a community living on Ile-aux-Coudres in the St. Lawrence River. Until very recently, the community had escaped the influence of mainstream Canada, and had even continued a tradition of capturing beluga (a relative of the whale) as part of their economy. For the film, the islanders recalled legends about the beluga and also attempted to catch them in the old manner. (They manage to catch just one.) Perrault's film was reminiscent of Flaherty's *Man of Aran*, not just for its restaging of an economic activity that had a few years earlier been abandoned, but also for the depth to which the film explores the culture, and the sympathy it evokes for it.

There was a parochial tone to another fine film of the era, Guy Coté's *Têtes blanches* (1961), called "Cattle Country" in English. This film was made within Unit B and was shot in Alberta — where *Corral* had been shot. Made seven years after *Corral*, *Têtes blanches* is in colour, not black-and-white. Although the film is considered to have a very "French-Canadian flavor," it seems somewhat derivative of *Corral*, a sort of bovine *Corral*.

But of *Jour après jour*, there was no accusation of parochialism. The reasons were probably stylistic as well as thematic. Because the verbal component of the sound track in *Jour après jour* was almost entirely voice-over, the film could easily be versioned into English. An English sound track was constructed, and although no one has claimed in this case that "the version is better than the original," the film quickly joined the best Unit B films in their classic status. *Jour après jour* became known by documentary buffs throughout the English-speaking world. There was no mistaking the film's theme: the exploitation of men by machines, and by other men. The theme was an old one; it had flowed through the Western world at least since Wordsworth. What was intriguing about the film was the artfulness with which the theme was rendered — which may have helped the film gain release — and also the fact that such a critical, negative film could be made and distributed by a government filmmaking organization.

Nevertheless, the restrictions — mild as they were compared to those of any other government filmmaking organization — on political content were felt as shackles by the Québécois filmmakers. Whatever freedom they had — and they probably had more than their English-Canadian counterparts — there was still the irritating necessity of having to answer to an anglophone Director of Production. There was the feeling that the Film Board itself reflected the relationship of Quebec to the rest of Canada. Even the documentary form itself, a primarily English-Canadian heritage, was beginning to feel oppressive. There was, in sum, the feeling that Québécois filmmakers were colonized.

7
LIKE THE MUSK OX, MADDENED BY ITS OWN PERFUME: THE FILM BOARD AFTER A QUARTER-CENTURY

On the second of May 1964, the National Film Board celebrated its twenty-fifth anniversary. Work was suspended for the day. The many distinguished guests included a number of high-ranking government officials and each of the Film Board's past Commissioners. Drinks were served. Speeches were delivered. A film crew roamed the halls and mixed with the celebrants, for it was an historic occasion if not a particularly cinematic one.

Merely to have survived for a quarter of a century was remarkable in itself, reason enough to celebrate. In England, the Empire Marketing Board Film Unit had a life of less than five years. Its successor, the General Post Office Film Unit, had lasted for six years. The Crown Film Unit, had ceased to exist in 1952. Congress dissolved the United States Film Service in 1939, after only three years. "It's a miracle," John Grierson had remarked to an old-timer, "a bloody miracle, believe me, that the place ever survived."

Not only had the Film Board survived. It had excelled. Its excellent work had in fact contributed to its survival, for when the Board's right to exist was challenged in the late forties, public and expert approval of its films had much to do with the Board's gaining not only a renewed Act, but a stronger one.

The excellence of the Board's work had lain in its variety — the "whole picture" that Grierson had spoken of. The Board's films were well-crafted, professional, succinct, clear — and *numerous*. They ranged, in the Board's first decade, from McLaren's hand-drawn propagandistic messages for war bonds, to Legg's didactic compilation documentaries, to educational films like *Four New Apple Dishes*, to a musical for the military recruitment of women, to films about art and cultures, to films probing psychological disorders. There was something for everybody.

But only after the passage of the new and stronger Act of 1950, which gave the Film Board as an organization more independence, and its employees security, did the Film Board begin to explore the possibilities of "the creative treatment of actuality." While the main current of the Board's work continued the tradition of professional, but routine and unadventurous, craftsmanship instilled during the war years, Unit B demonstrated the untapped possibilities for the "creative," or form-giving, aspect of documentary, and a group of Québécois showed how the range of the "actuality," or content, aspect of government documentary could be expanded. In terms of another early phrase of Grierson's, Unit B had shown that government documentary film could achieve something like "poetry," and the Québécois had brought government documentary near to the level of "prophecy." And both of these developments in the aesthetics of the Film Board documentary had been achieved "as a by-product of a job of work done" — another early phrase of Grierson's. The two achievements were "by-products of work" in two senses: they were possible only because of the years of ordinary, but solid, well-crafted, and utilitarian work that still formed the mainstream of the Board's output; and the making of each of the distinguished films seems to have required an unusual degree of patience, perseverance, and hard work.

The varied work of the Film Board was gaining increasing recognition world-wide, not only from film festivals but also from teachers and other kinds of professionals who might have occasion to seek a useful film on a relevant subject. The films, in turn, reflected on Canada as a whole, contributing to its image of creative liberalism, the kind that would spend money on a *City of Gold* or a *Very Nice, Very Nice*, a *Neighbors* or a *Romance of Transportation in Canada*, a *Jour après jour* or a *Pour la suite du monde*.

Perhaps the most remarkable fact of all was that the Film Board's achievements had been won not at the price of organizational or personal security, but along with it — in part, indeed, because of it. The outstanding films were not the work of the occasional visiting documentary stars, such as Ivens or Rouch. Nor were they the work of the hundreds of lesser known free-lancers who had worked at the Board since the early years. The films that achieved the most recognition — including the non-documentary work — were almost invariably the work of *employees*, permanent personnel, as secure in their jobs as a tenured college professor. They were persons who were making a good living out of their calling, and they could all look forward to invitations abroad, speaking engagements, and ultimately even a government pension. The Film Board was not the proverbial garret; in all but a technical sense, it was the Civil Service, and a rather glorified one.

Thus there were plenty of reasons to celebrate on this balmy spring day in Montreal. The fact of success, of inordinate success, was apparent to everyone. Or just about everyone. There was one man among the distinguished guests who looked as if he felt out of place, as if he weren't especially happy with the atmosphere of the party. This man was the "gin-drinking terror," the "fire-eating Scot," the "tornado-cum-thunderstorm," the "oxy-acetylene firebrand." He was John Grierson, the man who started it all, who brought a standard and a strategy to the Film Board, who nursed it from a tiny baby into the terror of Ottawa in only a few years.

Something seemed to be bothering Grierson that day. Perhaps he was perplexed by the presence of the film crew. At one point, he turned to them and asked, "Why are you filming here? There's nothing here. Just a lot of friendliness. You can't make a film out of it."[1] Perhaps for him the presence of a film crew filming the Film Board was a symptom of a larger malady. He complained to one old-timer present that the Film Board seemed to be "like the musk-ox, maddened by its own perfume." And when, at the official part of the celebration, it was his turn to speak, he said something like:

> I have come to remind you that you are all employees of the government of Canada — you are all civil servants using the tax money of and working for the benefit of the people of Canada. This is not a playground. . . .
>
> It has come to my attention recently that the Film Board more and more is becoming infiltrated with "arty-tarty" types who intend to use the facilities which it offers for their own private purposes. There will come a time, and mark my words, it will come, when the limit of public tolerance will be transgressed and the activities of the Board will be severely curtailed. . . .
>
> The National Film Board of Canada is a public utility almost the same as is the Electric Company or the Gas Board. If it fails to do its service as a public function, it will no longer have any reason for existing and will be destroyed. . . .[2]

And rumour even had it that "he went charging up and down the halls shouting, 'I'd fire them all!'"[3]

The celebrants could perhaps dismiss Grierson's chastisement. He was, after all, getting older, and he hadn't had a large success since leaving the Film Board twenty years earlier. He was known to drink too much. Perhaps some disappointment remained from the cool good-bye Canada had given him, the failure of the Film Board staff to give this holder of impromptu parties to whom all were invited a farewell party of his own. And there was that reported dark corner of Grierson's personality that resented creative people — an ambivalence perhaps reflected in his aesthetic theory. Finally, there was that sermonizing streak in Grierson, who admitted he had come to film to "use it as a pulpit." Grierson could act the role of a preacher, a kind of preacher who would try to convince the most innocent congregation of its sinfulness.

This congregation, however, was not without sin — at least what Grierson regarded as sin. He had identified a trend in the Film Board which would in the late sixties and early seventies become, in various manifestations, an enormous problem for the Film Board: a growing difficulty in maintaining the "central powers and central purpose" which Grierson had from the beginning held to be the key to the Film Board's survival and success. For Grierson, there were at least two cardinal virtues required for the maintenance of "central powers and purpose": a sense of "wholeness," not of oneself but of the larger operation; and self-effacement. Grierson perceived a budding disunity in the organization, a tendency toward separation and individualization, a tendency that eventually would lead to a lack of consensus about the role of the filmmaker in the public service, an inability to find common grounds for agreement, criteria for selecting projects, or reasons for doing one thing and not another. It would, in the seventies, culminate in a severe crisis of purpose — a situation that was the polar opposite of that of the young, ebullient, selfless wartime NFB.

An irony in the Film Board's history is that as employment became more and more like the Civil Service in terms of security and benefits, it became less like the Civil Service in that personal anonymity gave way, over the years, to the possibility of worldwide recognition and fame. One small manifestation of this was in the area of film credits. In the early war years, the Film Board discouraged personal credits on films. "We don't put personal credits on our pictures," Stuart Legg had explained, because "the individual who claims a solo performance tends to become a feather in a vacuum."[4] This stance soon yielded to practical pressures, and later to egoistic ones. After the war, technicians often moonlighted on outside jobs. They needed credits for their résumés. Free-lancers needed credits for the same reason. Some films were produced jointly with outside film companies, whose employees needed credits. The people working in Distribution found that members of the audience frequently wished to know who made what film. Festivals and other honours increased the desirability of credits. Film reviewers and critics wrote about individual films and filmmakers. The *coup de grâce*, according to some, was the arrival of the "auteur" theory in one of its distorted forms — the concept that the individual artist should be in total control. Today, a filmmaker wryly remarks:

> You look in the back of an NFB catalogue . . . and you'll see that all the good films have four or five names on them. They're all claiming the same films.

The individualization developing in the Film Board had a cultural dimension as well. The attitudes and appearance of some of the younger members of the Film Board may have disturbed Grierson. The nonconformity of the wartime filmmakers was one of eccentricity, and one suspects that it was largely affected — a kind of studied Bohemia. In the sixties, long hair, blue jeans, and a flip attitude toward conventions and traditions were not eccentricities, but the common trappings of a "youth" movement that would grow to include hundreds of thousands of persons — not all of them young — all across the globe, representatives of a "counter-culture" which, in general, despised authority, ridiculed convention, and thought that discipline, government, structure, skill, purpose, duty, and order were ideological values promulgated by the powerful, the corrupt, and the boring to repress individual fulfilment and social change. The Film Board, which had always responded to cultural trends, absorbed this one as it had the strongly anti-fascist mood of the late thirties and early forties, and the internationalism of the decade following the end of the war. This new mood, however, was by definition divisive. In short, there was the beginning of a "generation gap" at the Film Board.

A third suggestion of the problem of the individual's role in the public service of filmmaking lay in the Board's aesthetic achievements themselves. Both the Unit B poets — the form-givers — and the Québécois prophets — the social critics — were equally opposed to the routine mainstream of Film Board production even though this work was far superior to that being done by other government filmmaking organizations. But there was an aesthetic dilemma posed by the success and limitations of their two approaches. Unit B's achievements in form were marked by a shortage of significant actuality, an avoidance of the socially relevant; the French-Canadian widening of the social and political scope of the Film Board documentary was short on order or coherence. To Grierson, both of these achievements would have seemed limited. In the imbalance of the achievement of each, Grierson might have perceived a drift from the pursuit of public purpose toward the pursuit of private purpose. There was a sense in which the Unit B films, although made by teams and not by individuals, were, if not self-indulgent, then group-indulgent. The preacher of social change in Grierson, if certainly not the whole man (who loved *Corral* and *City of Gold*), must have been suspicious of the Unit B classics. None of them got "their noses into public issues." Conversely, the aesthete in Grierson, the lover of order and meaning, must have worried about the achievements of the Québécois filmmakers. The Québécois, recognizing the disorderliness of their early explorations, had, of course, seized upon an ordering principle: the personal interpretation. In doing so, however, they risked — for Grierson — turning public issues into parochial concerns, of addressing not the whole of Canada but only a small part of it, of becoming politically deviant rather than leading or prophetic, of distorting social issues into opportunities for private gripes. For the taskmaster Grierson, a film like *Jour après jour* might have seemed a case of reducing an amenable social problem into a mere complaint, a whine.

There was not, at the time of Grierson's visit, any easily visible attempt to synthesize these two imbalanced advances in the art of the Film Board documentary. What would have been most evident to Grierson were two new developments that marked an apparent abandonment of the social documentary: an attraction to feature-length fiction films (dramatic features) and the emergence of self-expressive documentary.

Grierson condemned self-expression, calling it "the pursuit of disorder."[5] Stuart Legg, in that memorandum concerning the Board's future he wrote just before his departure, warned that documentary "cannot spin out of its own belly like the silkworm . . . for reality lies outside the filmmaker, not inside him."

The "personal interpretation" that the Québécois filmmakers had attempted in the late fifties and early sixties did not represent a "pursuit of disorder." They had tried to personalize documentary in order to give coherence and meaning to the broader range of "actuality" that the new light-weight equipment had allowed them to explore. For them, the interest was still objective. The reality outside the filmmaker was the important thing; the personal interpretation was meant to help make sense of the reality.

In a certain sense, the Unit B *Candid Eye* team had personalized documentary in *Lonely Boy*. The film included several references to the filmmakers or the filmmaking: a microphone in the shot, Anka looking at the camera in surprise, and a scene in which the filmmakers' off-camera comments become integral to the action. Here, too, the aim was to help order and clarify the content of the film.

But Arthur Lipsett's *Very Nice, Very Nice*, which from one perspective was an attempt to inject a pessimistic note into the rosy Unit B aesthetic, was from another point of view a reversal of the traditional relationship between the filmmaker and his subject. In *Very Nice, Very Nice*, there is a sense in which the filmmaker becomes the subject, and the material — the pieces of film — a means of self-interpretation. The film expresses the filmmaker's disgust with the state of the world more than it demonstrates the world to be disgusting. The film asserts that modern life is meaningless but does not succeed in *showing* it to be. Instead of leading the viewer to insights into a perplexing world, the film illustrates the filmmaker's own confusion.

The feature-length dramatic film had, by 1964, enchanted several documentary filmmakers at the Film Board. In the thirties, documentary had been seen as an alternative to a crassly commercial cinema of entertainment fiction. The post-war Film Board had flirted briefly and unsuccessfully with the idea of features, but documentary remained its central concern. Now, for many inside the Film Board, documentary was beginning to seem like dreary hack-work itself — at least compared to the exciting European developments in dramatic film. Neo-realism in postwar Italy had impressed the world with its use of documentary styles in making fiction films about social issues, and the New Wave in France a decade later demonstrated a variety of ways to make interesting, serious fiction films on comparatively low budgets. Films such as *Bicycle Thieves* and *Umberto D* from Italy, and Truffaut's *Les quatre cent coups* and Godard's *A bout de souffle* from France examined important social problems and yet were interesting, entertaining, and far more widely shown than any Film Board documentary — perhaps any documentary — about social issues. Additionally, they were more fun to make. One didn't have to struggle with genuine documentary material, but could make it up. In fiction, one could echo Godard who said, "I don't prove, I assert." And finally, fiction could make one famous. Most critics were interested in fiction, not documentary, and the audience for fiction was far greater. The names of Godard, Truffaut,

De Sica, and Rossellini were as widely known as those of many major novelists.

In 1963 and 1964, the Film Board produced its first three features. Each of them grew out of one of the three main trends of documentary work being done at the time: the mainstream of routine, mostly sponsored work; the experimentation of Unit B; and the cultural preoccupations of the Québécois.

The first of three features, *Drylanders* (1963), arose from a series of films on Canadian frontiers. One of the films planned for the series was to be about a dam in Saskatchewan, and part of the film was to portray a family who, long before the dam was built, had settled in the area and had survived the Depression and the droughts. This element of the story mushroomed into a project of its own, and became a feature.

Drylanders came from neither Unit B nor French production, but from an English-Canadian unit whose documentary work had not achieved special distinction. *Drylanders* reflected the controlled, routine approach of the mainstream of the Film Board work. The film was made from a detailed script, a story that was thoroughly worked out in advance. Professional actors with theatrical backgrounds were used. Scenes were carefully set up and filmed.

The feature from Unit B, *Nobody Waved Good-bye* (1964), directed by Don Owen, had an origin analogous to that of *Drylanders*, but a very different realization. Owen had been asked to do a half-hour documentary about a probation officer and a juvenile delinquent. In response, Owen proposed a half-hour dramatic film, which would be made from a story outline without detailed scripted scenes or dialogue. His proposal was accepted. He was given a three-week schedule and a budget of $30,000. He wound up shooting for five weeks at a cost of $75,000. Owen recalls that in the first three days of filming

> we shot almost half our budget and I was already into deep trouble because we were doing something that hadn't been done before, certainly not at the Film Board, anyway.... The cameraman [kept shooting] and I kept ordering more film. It so happened that all the people were away so that ... there was nobody at the NFB to say don't send any more film. They kept on sending film and I kept on shooting and the story kept on getting more elaborate and more elaborate, and I added some scenes — the great thing about improvising is that you're writing the script while you're shooting — so the thing grew. And when I came back to Montreal ... I said: "I shot a feature."[6]

The Québécois feature, *Le chat dans le sac* (1964), was directed by Gilles Groulx. Groulx's film, too, had started out as an approved half-hour documentary. In the shooting, Groulx converted the project into a politicized feature film about an alienated Québécois youth suffering from a lack of strong cultural identity. Like *Nobody Waved Good-bye*, *Le chat dans le sac* was largely improvised as the shooting occurred, and each film had youthful alienation as its theme. The main difference was that, in Groulx's film, alienation had cultural and political dimensions.

The most interesting thing about the three features is that each of them began as a short film and then was stretched into a feature. It shows. *Drylanders* is probably the least tedious of the three. It is stiff and contrived, and completely traditional in story and execution. But it has a plot and tells a story. Part of its modest appeal is that it looks like an old film, much older than it is. By contrast, *Le chat dans le sac* and *Nobody Waved Good-bye* are free in form and execution, the stories and dialogue largely having been improvised. But because their techniques are no longer fresh, their lack of vitality and plot development is now starkly apparent.

Drylanders, however, led nowhere. The other two films have come to be regarded as seminal influences in Canadian fiction cinema. Although baldly cynical attempts at getting box-office results have dominated Canadian fictional film for the past few years, there has been a struggling subtrend of socially relevant docudrama (such as Don Shebib's *Goin' Down the Road*) traceable in part to *Le chat dans le sac* and *Nobody Waved Good-bye*.

At the time, though, each film received a reasonably favourable critical response, and each eventually earned back all or most of its production cost. Apparently, features had arrived at the Film Board.

These two departures — self-expressive documentary and feature films — from "the creative treatment of actuality" were not escapist in aim, but were (at least in part) attempts to bring greater social relevance to the work of the Film Board. In one case, the attempt was announced in the film. *Le chat dans le sac* contained an explicit criticism of the Film Board documentary. At one point in the film, a character remarks, "Don't think the cinema is an immature art just because you've seen a Film Board film."

The growing dissent went much deeper than that. A filmmaker asked:

> Will it ever be possible for filmmakers within the structure of the Film Board to talk about love and sex and political aspirations and social change and all those things which man holds dear? Or will they be confined to talk about the history of paper-making and asbestos mining and Canadian wildlife and urban development with, as someone said, slow zooms on quiet seagulls?[7]

And in April 1964, the separatist Québécois journal *parti pris* carried an article in which five NFB filmmakers complained that there was very little freedom of expression at the Film Board. The editor, Pierre Maheu, concluded:

> The Film Board is an instrument of colonization. It is a gigantic propaganda machine whose role it is to put the public to sleep and to exhaust the creative drive of the filmmakers.[8]

In the decade following the Film Board's twenty-fifth anniversary, individualization and separation, expressed as dissent from either "the creative treatment of actuality" or "central powers and central purpose," would be the predominant themes of the Film Board's documentary development. This development would occur in the context of two radical structural changes in the organization of the Film Board, both of which had been accomplished shortly before Grierson's visit.

On January 1, 1964, just four months before the twenty-fifth anniversary celebration, a separate production branch for French-language films was established, and a French-Canadian was appointed Director of French Production. It was a move made in the spirit of bilingualism and biculturalism, but it also acknowledged the growing power of the politics of separatism embraced by Québécois artists and intellectuals. Only the creation of a completely separate National Film Board — a contradiction in terms — could have been more in tune with the political climate of Quebec. This horizontal strain on "central powers and central purpose" seemed an encouragement of two distinct and opposed sets of purposes — one for English Canada, and one for Quebec.

On February 28, 1964, just two months before the celebration, the Director of English-language Production announced the dissolution of what was left of the Unit System, and its replacement by a "pool" system. The Pool System freed individual filmmakers from attachment to any organizational unit smaller than the English-Canadian Production Branch itself.

If the establishment of the separate French Production Branch threatened to cut "central powers and central purposes" in half, the Pool System threatened to chop what was left in English-Canadian production into little pieces. At the time of his visit, Grierson's beloved "holism" was suffering from the entropic effects of time. During the war, "wholeness" characterized the entire organization, and even reached beyond it, to include the audience. During the reign of the Unit System, "wholeness" was reduced to the size of the units, or groups within the units. After 1964, "wholeness," to the extent that it remained an operative ideal, referred to the individual filmmaker.

Thus it is clear that when, in May 1964, Grierson expressed his concern about the apparent drift from public service to private purpose, there was ample evidence to merit such concern. But what is not at all clear is the extent to which Grierson was right to react so negatively to what he saw, to interpret it as direly as he did. The tendencies toward separation and individualization would lead to perplexing problems, but to have avoided them might have stifled the creative growth of the organization. The wartime Film Board, where everybody "loved each other," where all were "concerned with the whole," where "together-ness" pervaded, produced forgettable films. The art of the Film Board documentary improved under the Unit System. The divisive and disorganized Film Board of the late sixties and early seventies produced some terrible films, but it also produced some great ones, films which marked significant advances in "the creative treatment of actuality" as the *early* Grierson had once characterized it. From one point of view, the separation of English-Canadian and French-Canadian production and the establishment of a "pool" system for English production seemed to mark a further dissolution of the original unity of the Film Board. But from another point of view, they were bold adventures, courageous experiments, a kind of organizational brinkmanship testing the Film Board's capacity on another criterion reaching back to the Board's origins in Grierson's thinking: tolerance of ambiguity.

8
LET A HUNDRED FLOWERS BLOOM: THE DICTATORSHIP OF THE FILMMAKERS

If the development of Grierson's wartime Film Board was like a Big Bang, an explosion of energy and activity, outward in almost all directions, then the destruction of the Unit System and its replacement by the Pool System was like a secondary release. During the fifties, the Unit System resembled a small universe containing isolated enclaves hospitable to creative experiment. The Pool System was meant to liberate the Board's creative potential so that it could be tapped by any or all the Board's English-Canadian filmmakers, not just one small group in one unit.

The advent of the Pool System resembled a secondary explosion in another way. It resulted from a build-up of tensions which the Unit System could not contain. The success of the Unit System led to the tensions. Under the Unit System, the Film Board continued to produce a body of work remarkable for its professional quality and its variety. In addition, Unit B produced a body of films that represented genuine documentary art. But as Unit B gained an increasingly inordinate share of attention, achievement, and personal fulfilment, filmmakers in other units began to resent the restrictions under which they had to work. After watching yet another Unit B classic, many a filmmaker thought to himself, "I could make films like that if given a chance." For just as Grierson, largely via McLaren, had set a standard for Unit B to try to match, Unit B set a standard for the rest of the Film Board. And to the filmmakers not in Unit B, the standard seemed unreachable within their own restricted units. Within Unit B, filmmakers who found the Inner Circle uncongenial or its "attitude toward the craft" unresponsive to their own ideas or inclinations felt equally trapped.

The key flaw in the Unit System was rigidity. In most units, the structure had evolved in a somewhat bureaucratic and hierarchical manner. Some filmmakers found this to their liking, but most didn't. The boundaries separating the units were equally rigid. Filmmakers could not easily transfer from one unit or another, or work temporarily in other units on specific projects. And there was an insufficient variety of units. Unit B represented the grouping of congenial filmmakers who could work well and fruitfully together as a team, and who could develop a fertile aesthetic. What was lacking in the Unit System was not other Unit Bs, but similar opportunities for groupings of filmmakers of other outlooks. Such a grouping had developed in French production, where the boundaries between units were less rigid, but it was subject to the frustrations of representing a dissenting minority culture, and was not accessible to English-Canadian filmmakers.

The rigidity of the Unit System could frustrate even the Unit B Inner Circle. Stanley Jackson recalls:

> Units had the responsibility of keeping their people busy. Once the Film Board was given a subject that was of very great interest to me. But it was assigned to another unit, to a person who felt saddled with a *chore*, who wasn't enthusiastic about doing the film. He was a good filmmaker; it just wasn't his subject. I asked the Executive Producer of that unit why the film was assigned to that filmmaker. He told me, "Because there's nobody else." He meant nobody else *in that unit* who wasn't already busy. The filmmaker's salary had to be charged to something. There was a great to-do over this, and it went to the Director of Production. The issue was never resolved, and the film didn't get made.

In the autumn of 1963, it became common knowledge that the management was considering a radical reorganization of the English-language Branch after the imminent establishment of a separate French-language Branch. The Pool System was the new structure under consideration. With the approval of the Film Board management, Donald Brittain (a writer-director) and John Kemeny (a producer), who were not members of Unit B, conducted a survey of English-Canadian filmmakers. The aim of the survey was to elicit the frank opinions of the filmmakers themselves about the state and organization of English-Canadian production.

In the summary report of the survey,[1] Brittain and Kemeny acknowledged the peculiar situation of the government filmmaker in a creative organization:

> A production employee of the Board is asked to perform a very difficult dual-role. He must function both as a craftsman working in the realm of ideas, and as a public servant.
>
> If he neglects his public servant function he will soon [by executive decree] cease to make films. If he neglects his creative function, he will cease to make films of any value.

Unfortunately, the investigators asserted, the public-service role had become dominant. Creativity was being stifled. There was a lack of vitality and sense of purpose. There was no *esprit de corps*. And this was at a time when

> the motion picture industry is in a state of such ferment and high excitement. It will be tragic if the Board does not participate at this pivotal period in the history of the medium.

The report identified the Unit System as the cause of the organizational depression. A majority (eighty-seven percent) of filmmakers had expressed dissatisfaction with the Unit System. Some believed that minor changes in the structure would suffice to revitalize the Board; others believed that "only a dictatorship of creative artists will save the Board from mortal organic defects." In the investigators' view:

> The structure tends to make filmmaking more difficult, rather than the reverse. It is cumbersome and outmoded. It blocks the easy movement of ideas. [The many good films] often seem to be the triumphs of individual effort working against a system.... [The Unit System] is a negative force.... [It] throws up unnecessary and destructive barriers to lateral and vertical communication and movement.

The investigators focused on the role of the executive producer, at the head of each unit, as the key problem. If the filmmaker had a difficult dual role, the executive producer had an impossible multiple role. He had too many responsibilities, a burden which tended to "magnify his weaknessess, while neutralizing his potential strengths." To many filmmakers, the executive producer "seems to have little time to make his own films but just enough time to ensure that no one else gets to make theirs."

The investigators seem to have identified closely with those who desired a dictatorship of creative artists: "Too little cognizance is given to the concept of film as a personal expression." Often, as in the following paragraph, it is difficult to tell to what extent the investigators were reporting opinion and to what extent they were expressing their own:

> It is the majority opinion that [the Board] should rapidly become "director-oriented." By this we mean that the key creative personnel in any film should have the final creative responsibility.

The report concluded with an endorsement of the concept of the Pool System and an expression of hope that the Film Board would "confidently move again into the mainstream of modern cinema." The Director of English Production enacted the Pool System on February 28, 1964.

In one sense, the change from the Unit System to the Pool System was less a replacement of one structure by another than simply a partial abolition of structure. The very name of the new system was something of a contradiction in terms, in that the entropic connotations of "pool" opposed the meaning of "structure" or "system." With the establishment of the Pool System, the Director of Production moved all the executive producers, who under the Unit System had occupied different parts of the building with their units, into a row of six offices in a corridor near the Director of Production. (The corridor became known as the "Via Dolorosa.") The purpose was to increase communication and control, but as the executive producers now had no clear function or authority, there was little to communicate or to control. Without units to administer, executive producers became simply producers. And producers, as members of the Pool, suddenly had very little authority beyond what their reputation or personality could command. Once big fish in little ponds, they were now little fish in a big pond. A producer (then an executive producer) recalls:

> When the Pool System was invented ... there was ... a deliberate and total downgrading of the role of executive producer and even producer ... and the producer role has been questionable around here ever since then. No real authority, responsibility, or even dignity of office was accorded producers, who had to shop around, to cajole filmmakers into working with them.

The new locus of authority lay among the directors themselves, or at least the ones who knew what they wanted to do and were sufficiently aggressive to get it done. Programming — deciding which films to make — was now performed by a committee of executive producers and two directors. (The composition of the committee would within a few years include more filmmakers and fewer producers.) Filmmakers could bring their ideas directly to the committee, which might approve the project even if there were as yet no producer for it. The filmmaker with an approved project could choose from the pool of producers, who had to "seek popularity, to solicit work."

In the broad historical sweep of the National Film Board, the authoritative weight assumed by the filmmakers under the Pool System constituted a radical advance in a process of devolution of authority that had begun with Grierson's appointment as the Board's first Commissioner. Before Grierson, the Motion Picture Bureau was little more than an orderly functioning tool of the governmental department above it, the Department of Trade and Commerce. It was a classic bureaucracy. As Commissioner of the new National Film Board, Grierson wrested the centre of authority from outside the organization and, in his role as Commissioner and in his own person, brought it within the Film Board. After Grierson, the authoritative centre of gravity slid further downward, to the Director of Production. He, in the course of the twenty-year reign of the Unit System, lost much of his authority to the executive producers, who headed the units. The adoption of the Pool System pushed the centre of gravity in English Production further downward, dispersed among the seventy or eighty English-Canadian filmmakers.

The aim of this radical restructuring — or destructuring — was to release creative energy suppressed by the Unit System. During the transition to the Pool System, a film was being made which did suggest a further permutation in the aesthetic progress of the Film Board documentary. The film was *Bethune* (1964), and it was made by none other than Donald Brittain and John Kemeny, the authors of the survey report. The film also marked a mid-point in the transition from group filmmaking to filmmaking largely by individuals. Brittain would direct several outstanding films during the sixties. In each case he would work closely with others, but not always with the same people. And in each case he would be the dominant creative force.

After an early career as a journalist, Brittain joined the Film Board in 1954. For several years, he laboured on uninspiring sponsored work with, as Brittain admits, uninspiring results. In 1962, he completed a thirteen-part series (*Canada at War*) of half-hour historical compilation films about Canada's participation in World War II. From such work, he was rapidly acquiring expertise in a skill which had become institutionalized at the Film Board since the time Stuart Legg first introduced it: writing commentaries that made disparate images, particularly from archival footage, cohere meaningfully. He was also developing a dissatisfaction with his own work and his opportunities, especially when he thought about the Unit B team:

> Here were men I really respected. . . . But these guys, they worked! I think they used to sleep in the hallways at night. Maybe I started to feel guilty because in the early sixties I seemed to be spending most of my time playing football during working hours with the guys in Distribution. You see a film like *Lonely Boy*, and you say to yourself, "I would't mind making something half decent."[2]

In 1963, when not playing football or conducting surveys of staff opinion, Brittain was labouring on a film sponsored by the Department of Veterans' Affairs. The aim of the film was to demonstrate the Department's concern for Canada's war dead, a concern expressed in war memorials. It was an uninspiring and almost macabre subject, but

Brittain, learning from Unit B, refused to take the assignment lightly. He exceeded his budget and his schedule, and he came up with something more than "half-decent": *Fields of Sacrifice*. The film is one of the Board's few really outstanding sponsored documentaries. Despite its origin in a somewhat chauvinistic purpose, the film has elicited emotional responses from non-Canadians.

But it was in 1964 that Brittain, with Kemeny, brought fresh winds to the Film Board documentary in *Bethune*, an hour-long film about the Canadian physician, Norman Bethune. Hundreds of millions of Chinese knew and revered this man's name, but few Canadians had heard of him. In the thirties, Bethune, an intense man who lived life to the full, almost died from tuberculosis and consequent despair. After recovering, he abandoned a successful practice as a surgeon in Montreal, became a communist, and went to Spain, where he served with the Republican forces. In the late thirties, he went to China. There he organized a medical corps for Mao's forces. He died in China in 1939.

Because Bethune was dead, the film was largely a compilation job — for which Brittain's earlier Film Board career had well prepared him. The film relies heavily on still photos and old footage. Additionally, there are interviews with people who had known Bethune.

Bethune seems to owe its existence in part to the confusions that resulted during the organizational changes which Brittain and Kemeny had promoted. To Brittain's knowledge, the project was never formally approved. The Department of External Affairs was, Brittain remembers, afraid of "offending the Americans." (Apparently, the Department's attitudes hadn't evolved much in the eighteen years since *The People Between*.) But because "two of the people who were to be in the film were *dying*," Brittain and Kemeny obtained money to film a pair of interviews. There was another small advance for some filmmaking, and finally management said (as Brittain remembers), "You've gone this far, you might as well make a rough-cut, and then we'll see if we'll release it."

Bethune is not a smooth film, nor a pretty one. It is eclectic in its range of actuality material: live footage, stock footage, still photos, interviews, and voice-over. A powerful commentary ties the material together. The film lacks the refinement of *City of Gold* (which used only still photos, live footage, and commentary), but *Bethune* is about a man of more interest than the usual Unit B subject. It is about a man who, after early worldly success, is stricken by tuberculosis and then spiritual despair, yet endures to find a new life and a new mission in one of the great mass political movements of the era.

In the mid-sixties, Brittain directed two other fine films and one great one. In 1966, he took over a project that another filmmaker had begun and then abandoned. The resulting film, *Ladies and Gentlemen: Mr. Leonard Cohen*, was a light but insightful portrait of the Canadian poet and novelist. The film appears somewhat derivative of the Unit B *Candid Eye* series, perhaps in part because the filmmaker who had started the project was originally from Unit B. In 1967, with the help of Guy Glover's production, and Arthur Hammond's idea and research, Brittain directed *Never a Backward Step*, a film about Roy Herbert Thompson, a Canadian ex-patriot who, in England, built a newspaper and television empire, and achieved a title, "Lord Thompson of Fleet." The film is a study of the imperturbable vanity of self-satisfied power, a wry, gently mocking film.

The subject of each of these three documentaries was a strong and complex character who in some way participated in an important social movement of the age: an impetuous activist-saint, a hip poet, and a self-made media mogul. In that they were "successful" people they resembled the typical subject of a *Candid Eye* portrait, but their "success" was won in arenas of larger social interest. And in the case of Bethune, the "success" was not free of torment. But in 1966, Brittain, with John Spotton as cameraman and co-editor and Kemeny as producer, built a documentary film around an almost expressionless character who had been a *victim* of his age, and the film, *Memorandum*, is a genuine "song of human unsuccess."

The theme of *Memorandum* is large: that the civilized "normality" of those who perpetrated or silently tolerated the Nazi policy of exterminating the Jews undermines any confidence one might have in the episode's "pastness." The film suggests that a determined refusal to forget is the only possible defence against a recurrence. The film beautifully explores this theme despite its unpromising documentary premise: the brief journey of an inexpressive camp survivor, one Joseph Laufer, now a Toronto glass-cutter, to Germany, where he joins a reunion of fellow survivors on a pilgrimage to the camps. Interlaced with this visit are archival footage and contemporary live-action scenes. The live-action scenes include an interview with Simon Wiesenthal, the relentless tracker of ex-Nazis, an interview with a man whose entire family was killed, a trial in Nuremburg of ex-Nazi war criminals, and a modern beer-hall fest. From disparate scenes such as these, the editing and the commentary — one of the most powerful commentaries ever written for a film — weave an excruciating tension between the enormity of the atrocity and the temptation to forget it, to relegate it to

118

the unrepeatable past. The struggle between remembering and forgetting is given historical, cultural, political, personal, and even generational dimensions. The survivor's son accompanies Laufer on the pilgrimage, but he seems unmoved, unconcerned, somewhat bored — a typical teen-aged North American in personality — until the very end, at Bergen-Belsen, where he finally shows some emotion. The depth and durability of his outrage remain uncertain.

Memorandum represented a consolidation of the main advances of the Unit System era. On the one hand, Brittain and Spotton — the latter had once taken a cut in pay as a cameraman in order to work half-time in Unit B — inherited from Unit B an "attitude toward the craft," a respect for form, for coherence, for getting things right. On the other hand, this formalizing energy is applied in *Memorandum* to an exceedingly difficult subject. Both aspects of "actuality," as Grierson had originally written of it, constitute the material for the film: the social, or "relevance" aspect, and scriptless exploration. Brittain says that *Memorandum*

> started with two ideas, the banality of evil thing [*sic*] and the fact that some Jews from Canada were going back over there. That was all I had. We just went and shot anything that looked like it would work in any way, shape, or form. We started to make connections on the spot. *Memorandum* took nine months to cut and when we were finished we were left with ninety-two edited sequences we never used.[3]

This exploratory attitude toward the subject resembled Flaherty's, but instead of achieving depth by long acquaintance with the subject before and during filming, Brittain and Spotton got it by shooting intensely and profligately over a short period. Laufer himself was in Germany for only one day. The crew stayed a little longer, to get those other scenes. Of this brief shooting period, Spotton remembers that

> we were just *running*, literally, and I don't think the camera stopped while we were there. We were all absolutely zonked after the shooting. We slept for a week.

And just as Grierson, who revered Flaherty from a distance, could not as his producer endure Flaherty's working methods, Kemeny, the producer of *Memorandum*, worried considerably over the material that was being flown to Montreal. Kemeny had not worked with cameramen like Spotton, who was experienced in the *Candid Eye* approach. Spotton remembers that after viewing the rushes of the twenty-four-hour shoot in Germany, Kemeny wired Brittain and Spotton that the material was all unusable, that it didn't say anything, that the camera was jiggly.

The John Street premises of the National Film Board during the 1940s

An NFB rural circuit screening being held in a school house.

Sydney Newman (extreme right) holds a production meeting for the *Canada Carries On*
series in November 1946

Colin Low

Tom Daly

Roman Kroitor

Donald Brittain (in foreground)

Michael Rubbo (above)
Wolf Koenig (right)
Gilles Groulx (below)

Grierson scrutinizes a poster for one of his films

Logo for the *Canada Carries On* series

The Romance of Transportation in Canada (1952)

Neighbors (1952)

Corral (1954)

City of Gold (1957)

Les raquetteurs (1958)

The Back-Breaking Leaf (1959)

Colin Low working on *Universe* (1960)

Circle of the Sun (1961)

Lonely Boy (1962)

Jour après jour (1962)

Pour la suite du monde (1963)

Bûcherons de la Manouane (1963)

Drylanders (1963)

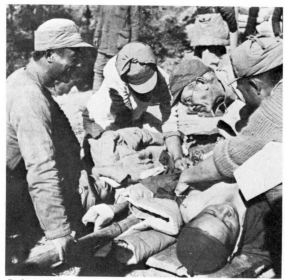

Bethune (1964)

Memorandum (1965)

Sad Song of Yellow Skin (1970)

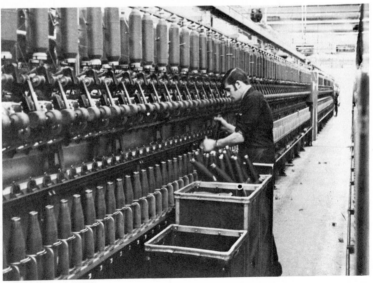

On est au coton (1970)

Action: The October Crisis of 1970 (1974)

Cree Hunters of Mistassini (1974)

Nobody Waved Good-Bye (1964)

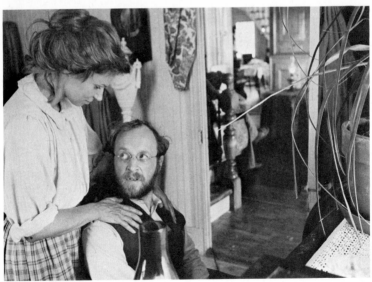

J.A. Martin photographe (1976)

There was a sense in which Kemeny, given his assumptions, was right. Direct cinema footage rarely does "say anything," or have much interest on its own, no matter how talented the cameraman. Although no great "direct cinema" film has been made from uninspired camerawork, the method presupposes a high shooting ratio and a long editing period. It was in the editing that Brittain and Spotton fashioned the mass of actuality material into an emotional but intellectually rigorous examination of modern civilization. Spotton remembers that the structuring of *Memorandum* was an agonizing affair and that "the fights that went on in the editing room were just *awful.*" Sometimes the fights, which were not personal disputes but simply heated arguments about the film, concerned large structural issues. Thirteen different structures were tried out. Sometimes the arguments were over apparently trivial matters — over things like what to call the film. (Brittain suggested "Memorandum '65" for the title; Spotton fought for just "Memorandum.") But it was ultimately the commentary that brought order to the material, and at that Brittain was expert. Writing commentary is an aspect of editing, and by the time the film was finished, Spotton and Brittain were exhausted. As a young filmmaker who has worked with Brittain has observed, "When Brittain gets finished with a film, there is practically blood dripping off the Steenbeck."[4]

A synthesis of the Unit System's advances in the "creative" and "actual" dimensions of documentary, *Memorandum* was an hour long, the first Film Board classic of such length. Perhaps the synthesis required this greater length. Thomas Mann once remarked that "only the exhaustive is really interesting," and subsequent development in the Film Board documentary would corroborate this view.

Television contributed to this development. Just as television had created a demand for original French-language material, and just as television had prompted the Unit B *Candid Eye* team to demonstrate that television documentaries didn't have to be dull and unadventurous, television, by its increasing tendency to programme by the hour rather than the half-hour, stimulated the production of longer documentaries, which in turn created the film-time needed for the adequate treatment of more difficult, complex subjects.

As a result, however, of the synthesis of the "creative" and the "actual" achieved in *Memorandum*, something was lost from each of the elements synthesized. The power of *Memorandum* results in part from the agonized axing of those ninety-two fully edited sequences. The scenes that Brittain and Spotton kept are very tightly structured, and the perspective from which an audience can view them is tightly controlled by the commentary. As a result, many of the scenes are not as engrossing as they perhaps could have been, and it is only the overall structure of the film, its compelling flow, directed by the commentary, that sweeps the viewer along. But if the complex structuring and the commentary prevent the film from slipping into superficiality, the film lacks the formal grace of the Unit B classics (which were, however, narrower in scope). As opposed to Unit B's documentaries, *Memorandum*, like *Bethune*, was eclectic in the kind of material it used. And the brilliant commentary itself has its rough spots. In one instance, its tone is momentarily disrupted when the narrator quotes a murky aphorism of the playwright Peter Weiss (who at the time of the filming was preparing *The Investigation*): "Once a crime has been committed, it remains for all times a potentiality," an unnecessary conundrum that interferes with the sophisticated train of thought that the commentary is developing. In another instance, the commentator suddenly "points" at a squad of West German police by exclaiming, "Look at all the white mice!"

But such flaws in *Memorandum* are trivial when compared to the film's overall achievement. Perhaps they illustrate another principle in the advance of the Board's documentary art: that just as a film treating seriously a difficult subject may need to be longer than usual, perhaps it needs to be a bit rougher, too, containing the kinds of flaws that are found in the great novels.

It seems unlikely that the achievement of Brittain and his changing team would have occurred without the switch from the Unit System to the Pool System. The films thus seemed to augur well for the fertility of the new structure. But if the Pool System allowed the emergence of these films, it was under the Unit System that the potential for them had developed. It was from the immense experience and discipline of making compilation films from old footage that Brittain acquired the structural sense and the commentary-writing wizardry that made *Bethune* and, especially, *Memorandum* the outstanding films that they are, and it was the example of Unit B that suggested to Brittain a standard of excellence — of something "half-decent" as he self-deprecatingly put it — for which to strive. And it was in Unit B that Spotton, who filmed the best of Brittain's documentaries, developed from a cameraman who was a technician into a cameraman who was an artist (and who could direct and edit as well). It was not, therefore, the Pool System alone which allowed for these films; it was the *switch* from the Unit System to the Pool System that seems to have made the films possible. The Unit System fostered the potential and the Pool System released it.

But *Memorandum*'s synthesis of the creative and the actual was as atypical a result of the first years of the Pool System as it was a promising one.

The report that Brittain and Kemeny had written urged that the Film Board move into the "mainstream" of the modern cinema. In the sixties, the mainstream of modern cinema included two strong currents: dramatic features and "experimental" films, the latter embracing self-expressive films of various kinds. Although the Brittain-Kemeny report specifically endorsed "personal expression," the report did not mention features. Later, though, in 1966, Brittain would participate in a report which asserted that the Film Board should "be making features on an extensive and regular basis — at least four in English every year."[5]

During the Pool System, an increasing proportion of the filmmaking staff were young people whose maturity, and entry into the Film Board, roughly coincided with the sudden burst of popularity and cultural respectability that the two currents of cinema were enjoying in North America. But if the attraction to these two kinds of filmmaking was therefore understandable, the phenomenon was not without ironies. The origin of the documentary film movement had been in part a reaction against the mainstream of the fictional cinema of the twenties and thirties, and during the thirties Grierson also combatted the tendency of young filmmakers to use documentary film as a means of self-expression. The movement arose and developed as an innovation, a new kind of cinema, consciously intended as something distinct from the mainstream. And the Board's own brightest achievements had, up to 1964, lain in work that — had documentary been regarded as an art — could have been called "avant-garde" in one way or another. *Memorandum*, in 1966, was a further forward thrust for documentary. Without realizing it, the filmmakers who wanted to enter the "mainstream" were attempting to abandon their position in an innovative tradition and to become followers in older ones.

Another irony was that Brittain, who had co-authored the two reports that endorsed and abetted the Film Board's entry into the "mainstream," himself remained aloof from it, continuing in documentary. He never attempted a dramatic feature at the Board. And his documentaries were anything but self-expressive. Of the five documentaries discussed here, only *Memorandum* was from an idea of his own. *Fields of Sacrifice* was an assignment for the Department of Veterans' Affairs. *Bethune* was Kemeny's idea. Arthur Hammond suggested the idea for *Never a Backward Step*. Another filmmaker had started the project that became *Ladies and Gentlemen: Mr. Leonard Cohen*. And although the idea for *Memorandum* (his best film) was his own, Hannah Arendt's *Eichmann in Jerusalem* had suggested the theme. Brittain's contribution to the advancement of the documentary art was directly in line not only with Grierson's early aesthetic, but also with Grierson's conception of documentary art as "a by-product of a job of work done." Brittain, who has called himself a "hired gun,"[6] was a very different kind of filmmaker from the kind the two reports had seemed to endorse.

If *Very Nice, Very Nice* revealed the filmmaker instead of the world, it did so without visual or aural reference to the filmmaker, but solely with pieces of "actuality," pieces of film (or stills) of external reality. The kind of self-reference that appeared in *Lonely Boy* was simply a requirement for retaining the integrity of a scene, and this is the kind of self-reference that began, initially, to appear with increasing frequency in Film Board documentaries of the Pool System era. Even *Memorandum* contained such self-reference. (In one scene, an accused war criminal, just before entering the court building, shoves his briefcase into the camera; in an interview, an off-camera question of Brittain's is kept.) Self-reference was gaining enough legitimacy, however, that the explicit subject of a film could become the filmmaker's relatives, his friends, filmmaking, or the filmmaker himself. Arthur Lipsett's *Free Fall* (1964) included scenes of himself. *Christopher's Movie Matinee* (1969) is a feature-length documentary about the filmmakers and a group of children making *Christopher's Movie Matinee*. *A Film For Max* is an impressionistic, feature-length documentary about the filmmaker, his family, and his friends. *Blood Sugar* is shorter, but the subject is similar. Antonio of *Antonio* is the filmmaker's father. *Nell and Fred* is about the filmmaker's grandmother and her lodger. *The Man Who Can't Stop* is about the filmmaker's uncle. *Coming Home* documents, for ninety minutes, the filmmaker's visit to his parents' home, where generational tensions culminate in an argument about the length of the filmmaker's hair. (These last two films were completed after the Pool System had technically ended.)

Some of the older or more conservative members of the Film Board recoiled from the apparent narcissism of these and several other self-expressive films — many of which were not so explicitly about the filmmaker or his circle — made in the late sixties and early seventies. Some blamed the emergence of such films on the removal of the Film Board from Ottawa to Montreal, where English-Canadians were a disliked minority, confined, although largely out of choice, to English-

Canadian ghetto neighbourhoods. (This was not a compelling explanation, however, because it was the older and more conservative filmmakers who tended to reside in English-language neighbourhoods.) Poor recruiting during the reign of the Pool System was another scapegoat. Others blamed the "do-your-own-thing" spirit of the sixties. But not only had the influential Brittain-Kemeny report promoted self-expression, even the Film Act's command that the Film Board "interpret Canada to Canadians" allowed such films, for the filmmakers were, after all, Canadians (either citizens or resident aliens), and their films were the interpretations of themselves and their own sub-Canadian worlds to the rest of Canada. The Board's happily ambiguous mandate allowed these filmmakers to pursue a course inconceivable in any other government filmmaking organization.

And yet the existence of these films needs no apologetic explanation. Like films of any genre, most of them were mediocre. A few were good, such as *Antonio*, and at least one was outstanding — Richard Todd's *Nell and Fred*, a sympathetic but uncondescending study of how two elderly people cope with the narrowness of the range of options a mobile, rootless society offers retired persons of little means. These two films were about the filmmaker's relatives, not the filmmaker himself, and each did attempt to treat a serious social issue, but even the most apparently self-indulgent films were seriously meant. They shared in a subcultural trend of the times — the inward search. And the fact that most of the lesser ones appear undisciplined and disordered offers a clue to their positive significance. Although self-absorbed, these films do not represent an undue emphasis on the "creative" or ordering aspect of documentary to the exclusion of the "actuality" side. On the contrary, they signify the extension of the permissible domain of actuality to include a formerly taboo subject: the self. In many of these films, the self is not merely the creator (the filmmaker), but also part of the puzzle of reality. However unsuccessful most of the attempts were, they helped raise the potential sophistication of the Film Board documentary toward the level of the modern novel, the "new journalism," contemporary social science, or even contemporary physics, where the act of observation had become as intriguing as — and considered inseparable from — what is observed.

Dramatic features constituted the other aspect of "mainstream cinema" which younger NFB filmmakers wanted to enter, and since Don Owen's *Nobody Waved Good-bye* (1964) many of them began to think it was possible. In 1966, Owen started a film intended as a feature, but for lack of funds was completed as a fifty-four-minute film.

The film is called *Notes for a Film About Donna and Gail*. It is a more mannered film than *Nobody Waved Good-bye*, and it attempts to adapt some of the techniques that Godard had been developing with great success in France (e.g., very long takes and titles introducing scenes). In 1967, Owen made *The Ernie Game* (a co-production of the Film Board and the Canadian Broadcasting Corporation), a film about a social misfit who at first seems maladjusted but then, progressively, is revealed as psychotic. The two main female characters in the story are the Donna and Gail from Owen's *Notes for a Film About Donna and Gail*.

Because of the cost of features, only a few others were produced during the Pool System: *Waiting For Caroline*, *Don't Let the Angels Fall*, and *Prologue*. *Christopher's Movie Matinee* had a fictional aspect. In 1970, two more features, *Cold Journey* and *Running Time*, were started, but they weren't finished until midway into the seventies. A few other English-Canadian features were made at the Film Board in the early seventies.

Since the beginning of the Film Board feature production, not a single feature, English-Canadian or Québécois, has been distinguished. One reason is that the Board's features have been too few and too scattered. Any feature film industry that has achieved distinction has produced hundreds of mediocre features for every really good one — just as the Film Board has produced hundreds of good but undistinguished documentaries for every outstanding one. Another reason is that most of the Board's features, consistent with the broad purposes of the Film Board, attempted to address a serious social problem, but nowhere in the world has the combination of explicit social purpose and dramatic entertainment been solved adequately and consistently. Third, although the budget for the typical Film Board documentary is high by commercial standards, the typical Film Board feature-film budget has been low by commercial standards. Fourth, there does not seem to be an adequate reservoir of writing and acting talent available to the Film Board to support distinguished feature production.

There is a sense, though, in which the Board's own distinguished tradition in documentary contributed to the disappointing quality of the features. Probably all of the Board's filmmakers who attempted features assumed that documentary film could serve as a training ground for fiction, and many of them tried to apply documentary techniques in their dramatic work. By the time the Board entered the feature field, the art of its documentary had advanced to a stage at which it embraced an enormous range of actuality. The best documentaries, increasingly, were being made with high shooting ratios, the merest trace of a script, and a long editing period — as in the *Candid Eye* series, the French-Canadian direct cinema films, and *Memorandum*. The director of a Film Board documentary typically began his project supplied with hundreds of rolls of film and the best equipment, supported by excellent cameramen and sound recordists, aided by outstanding editors, sound mixers, laboratory technicians, post-production facilties, and plenty of time in which to edit. This system by no means guaranteed a great film, but it did guarantee a reasonably good film. Even if the director had totally bungled the shooting, he had masses of technically fine material; and if he himself could not make anything out of it, a host of post-production talent was available to bail him out. As a producer at the Film Board accurately has observed, "An idiot could make a reasonably good documentary here."

If this approach to documentary enhanced the best films and saved the worst ones, it was a dangerous method for fiction. Fiction films seem to require an opposite emphasis. Pre-production is to fiction what post-production is to documentary. In fiction, at least a core of a script has to exist beforehand, either on paper or in the director's head. The director has to know how each scene is likely to fit into the final film. If this structural effort is postponed, then the director, as in *Nobody Waved Good-bye*, runs the risk of filming little more than the ability of his actors to make up lines under pressure. Even asbestos mining or paper-making is more interesting. Or if the direction itself is done with too little preparation or concentration, the technical excellence of the footage will only call attention to mistakes in casting, acting, writing, continuity, or atmosphere. In a remarkably lucid, honest self-appraisal, a director said of his first, disappointing feature, "I thought it would be easy." As a producer recalled of the first feature he had produced, "Watching the rushes, it suddenly hit me, with a shock, that you can't make a feature in the editing room." When there is "practically blood dripping off the Steenbeck" after editing a documentary, the film is likely to be very good; but a bloody Steenbeck is a bad omen for fiction film.

The Film Board feature is caught in a dilemma. If a director (or the people surrounding him) assumes he can make a feature simply on the basis of documentary training, he tends to wind up with a rambling, incoherent film lacking strong characterization or dramatic impact. If he *does* work from a script, then producers and other management people are forced into roles that they're not trained for, either. They become script-doctors without the necessary background. There is a tendency to perform surgery on the script — which it may well need — without sewing up the holes. So if the filmmaker does work from a script, it is either an over-cautious or conventional one, or one that has lost key structural elements that give the film meaning and coherence.

If the immediately observable effects of the Film Board's English-language feature-film adventure were deleterious ones, diverting money, energy, and attention away from the kind of work the Board could do best, possibly the adventure, like the experiments in self-expression, had some positive effect on the Film Board documentary. Story-telling failures themselves, the features may have sharpened the sense of story in Film Board documentary. If so, this was no small contribution. The master himself, Flaherty, had used the story as the structure for his best films.

In order to consider the possible contributions of self-expressive documentary and feature films to the documentary work of the Film Board, it is necessary to note another development that occurred during the Pool System. It was a less obvious development, because it cut across the two other adventures. This was a growing sense of Canadian identity.

When, in 1964, the Department of External Affairs, for fear of "offending the Americans," had hindered the release of *Bethune*, the Film Board management sided with the Department. As Brittain remembers, it was action by the filmmakers themselves that finally secured the distribution of the film:

> We held an informal screening for CBC and some critics. CBC bought it instantly, and we got the support of critics and even editorial writers. Then the film won a prize at the Leipzig Festival in East Germany. The film still wasn't released, so Kemeny and I went to [Grant] McLean [the Director of English-Language Production]. We said we would quit the Film Board and call a press conference. Grant took our case to the Board of Governors, and they rescinded the embargo on the film.
>
> But it *still* couldn't be released in the States. I was invited to the States to talk about the film, and we used this to get Distribution to do something about it.

Two years later, the Department of External Affairs objected to *Memorandum*, as Brittain remembers, because the film might "offend the West Germans." This time, however, the Film Board ignored the objection.

In 1969, Robin Spry's *Prologue*, a feature film chronicling a young man's journey from activism to inwardness, was accepted for screening by the Venice Film Festival. The film included documentary footage of the 1968 Chicago Democratic Convention riots and footage taken from televised news reports of the Vietnam war and other events. Spry remembers that

> the Commissioner [Hugo McPherson] said, "If you want that film to go to Venice, you'll have to take out those shots of Johnson [which ridiculed Johnson] and that shot of a U.S. Army officer kicking a Vietnamese in the face." It *did* ridicule Johnson. So I made the cuts.

After Spry cut out those two brief scenes, which he admits were unnecessary and glib, the film was released without difficulty.

The Film Board was becoming less fearful of exploring a subject that might offend an ally. It was as if the Board recognized, with Alexander Solzhenitsyn, that "there are no internal affairs left on our crowded earth, and mankind's sole salvation lies in everyone making everything his business."

In 1970, Michael Rubbo, an Australian whom the Film Board hired in 1966, completed a documentary which synthesized elements of the three main post-Brittain aesthetic trends of the Pool System era. This film, *Sad Song of Yellow Skin*, began as a modest project. Rubbo got approval to make a film on a Canadian foster-parent programme for Vietnamese orphans. After a few weeks in Saigon, he discovered a group of three young Americans on unofficial missions of atonement for their country's devastation of Vietnam. One ran an orphanage; two others worked for the Liberation News Service. Abandoning his original idea, Rubbo built a film around the work of these three Americans.

The result was an indictment of the brutally destructive American venture into Vietnam, but if that were all it were, the film would not stand out particularly from the dozens of similarly motivated films made about the subject. Several key things, however, distinguish *Sad Song of Yellow Skin* not only from other Vietnam-era documentaries but also from documentaries about other wars. For one thing, the Americans become our guides to the damage being done to the fabric of Vietnamese culture. This irony (rare as a serious *structural* tactic in documentary) helps insure the film against an easy and uninformative anti-Americanism. The film thus penetrates ideology and becomes a film about people. In addition, by using the Americans as guides, Rubbo is showing us, in effect, how he did his research. It is a way of being methodologically above-board.

In addition, the film avoids the obvious. There are only a few gunshots in the entire film, and they are heard simply as a reminder in the distance, over the final credits.

Furthermore, Rubbo adapts several of the "self-expressive" techniques of the sixties and transforms them into something resembling "self-reflexivity." Although he does not appear in the picture, he speaks the commentary himself. His voice sounds almost embarrassingly unprofessional, and at one point he even complains that the kids in the orphanage had swiped his still-camera. This introduces a scene in which Dick Hughes, who runs the orphanage, confronts the street-hardened kids with the incident. An argument develops about Rubbo's camera. Hughes also criticizes the kids for accepting money from Rubbo for an earlier interview. He reminds them of a house rule against accepting money from guests. Although the camera, which had already found its way into the black market, cannot be returned, the kids reluctantly fork over the money taken for the interview. This extended sequence constitutes a more natural and more honest revelation of the filmmaker's manipulations and attitudes than almost all the more explicit, and more pretentious, confessions of the filmmaker's presence and influence uttered in films made before or since.

The film contains a subtle story structure — achieved after a year of struggling with footage. Tom Daly, the film's producer, remembers that Rubbo's first efforts at structuring the material were failing to realize its potential. The first cuts of the film resembled essays. Daly suggested that Rubbo attempt a structure analogous to his experience in filming Saigon — that just as Rubbo discovered his material and his theme while he was filming, he might try to lead the audience through a process of discovery, rather than "summarize his findings" as in a research report. Rubbo tried this, and it worked. The film seduces the audience with a "discovery method," structured analogously to Rubbo's own adventure.

Perhaps the toughest, most critical, uncompromising documentary to emerge from the Pool System, *Sad Song of Yellow Skin* was perhaps as well the era's strongest documentary expression of Canadian identity. And yet, the *theme* of Canadian identity appears nowhere in the film, the film lacks "Canadian content," and it was made by an Australian. Several filmmakers at the Board criticized Rubbo for operating outside the Board's mandate to "interpret Canada to Canadians." But if the film does not *interpret* Canada, the film — in an era when "there are no internal affairs left on our crowded earth" — *expresses* Canada far more impressively than films preoccupied with Canadian identity. As a devastating moral indictment of the most politically sensitive policy of the United States, *Sad Song of Yellow Skin*, which no one tried to censor, was an indication of remarkable diplomatic courage. For the

Film Board documentary, this film marked the achievement of the virile dimension that Flaherty had said the British documentary movement lacked.

Not unfittingly, *Sad Song of Yellow Skin* won the Robert Flaherty Award for the best documentary of 1971. But the film's aesthetic achievement is broader. It comes as close as any film has to fulfilling the criteria of Grierson's early aesthetic, which was built on an appreciation of both Flaherty and the Russians. In *Sad Song of Yellow Skin*, there is the same respect and affection for alien cultures that Flaherty's work embodied. (Unlike Flaherty but like Brittain and Spotton with *Memorandum*, Rubbo achieved his closeness to his subject over a short but intense shooting period. It is said of Rubbo that when he was just starting out at the Board, his pace was so demanding that "replacement crews had to be sent out to relieve the original crews," although this could not occur with *Sad Song of Yellow Skin*, a film shot 12,000 miles from Montreal.) There is a story structure, although the story lies in the filmmaker's, and our, discovery of Saigon rather than in any external event. But whereas Flaherty was drawn to the theme of man-against-nature, Rubbo's theme is something like man-against-him-self. Rubbo's world is contemporary, and the film participates in a raging issue. Even the cutting of the film seems to bear, however indirectly and unselfconsciously, the Russian influence. Although some scenes are long, there is a large amount of cross-cutting, and this montage is a significant component of the discovery method that the film employs. From the dual heritage of Flaherty's humanitarian values and the Russians' social concern, Rubbo forged what may be documentary's first full realization of the early Griersonian aesthetic, a positive vision constructed unflinchingly out of the ugliest realities.

Thus in only six years the Pool System, the experiment in "the dictatorship of the creative artist," yielded two of the finest documentaries ever made anywhere: *Memorandum* and *Sad Song of Yellow Skin*. Like the Unit B classics, these two films were "by-products of a job of work done." Much sweat and persistence, trial and error, were expended before the pieces of actuality that finally composed the films were transformed into documentary art. The films were further indications of the depth of Grierson's early remark that "beauty will come in good time to inhabit the statement which is honest and lucid and deeply felt and which fulfils the best aims of citizenship."

The Unit B classics, however, had been by-products of jobs of work in an additional sense — of the work done in the other units (and in other Unit B films), the Board's documentary mainstream, the sponsored films, the educational films, the instructional films, the ordinary, self-effacing documentaries, all of which contributed to the "whole picture" of Canada so crucial to the Film Board's existence. If under the Pool System the quality of the by-product improved in the extreme cases, the main product seemed to have suffered. In an organizational sense, there was an undue pursuit of the by-product at the expense of the utilitarian documentary tradition by which the Board fulfilled its mandate and satisfied its large and varied constituency. The young filmmakers identified more with the developments of mainstream cinema than with the Board's own documentary tradition, and their values were becoming more like those of the youth culture of the sixties and seventies than those of self-effacive service to a national purpose. The self-expressive and fiction films of the sixties and seventies contributed little to the "whole picture," and there was an increasing aversion to making sponsored films, an area of work that younger filmmakers regarded as the "salt mines."

The widening gaps in the "whole picture" were matched by an atomization of the staff that was almost the polar opposite of the unity that characterized the wartime NFB. Those who promoted the concept of the Pool System had hoped that the filmmakers, freed from the bureaucratic restraints of belonging to hierarchically structured units, would coalesce spontaneously into congenial and productive teams, like the old Unit B Inner Circle. This did not occur. Team filmmaking continued, of course, and still continues, but the production teams during the Pool System tended to be formed on an ad hoc basis, and they weren't lasting.

The failure of enduring production teams to emerge in the Pool System was perhaps central to the Pool System's problems. An enduring production team is an informal organization which informally and perhaps often tacitly exercises sufficient control to allow the pursuit of the team's goals. Because the Pool System almost totally had abolished *formal* structure, the non-emergence of informal production structures meant that the burden of control rested almost entirely on the filmmakers themselves, as individuals. Technically the filmmakers were still responsible to the Director of Production. But with no effective subordinate positions between him and the filmmakers, the Director of Production could not monitor closely the progress of the roughly one hundred members of the Pool.

The lack of small production groups, formal or informal, also meant that younger filmmakers were given little attention. Often they made their first films without undergoing any kind of an apprenticeship. A new employee might get $40,000 — or more — for his first film, but he would get very little training or guidance.

Not only did cooperative, productive teams fail to emerge, the necessary ad hoc pairings or groupings were often antagonistic in character, particularly in the relationships between producer and director. The role of producer, having lost much of its authoritative weight, lost much of its definition. Some filmmakers, lacking direction or interest in ideas of their own, expected producers to act as they always had — to initiate projects, to control and shape their development, and to oversee their progress. Other filmmakers now thought of producers as little more than administrative assistants, whose job it was to facilitate the realization of the filmmaker's unquestioned aims and talent. But even the role of "filmmaker," or director, although now carrying more authority, also lost definition. Nearly everybody wanted to become a filmmaker, and nearly anyone could. An editor could become a filmmaker simply by announcing himself so. Even some people in the Camera or Sound Departments, which remained outside the Pool, followed John Spotton's example (under the Unit System) and took salary cuts in order to transfer into production and become filmmakers.

Relationships between producers and directors were sufficiently strained by 1966, only the third year of the Pool System, that a committee of five filmmakers and producers made a formal study of the problem.[7] In the spirit of the Pool System philosophy — and indeed of the Film Board tradition, which had always included a measure of "role freedom" as one of its organizational traits — the committee prefaced its report with the disclaimer that it "unanimously rejects any attempt to set up detailed rules and definitions of the separate functions of 'the producer' and 'the director,'" noting that:

> The Pool System is, by its nature, a flexible and sophisticated structure which presupposes intelligence and responsibility on the part of both management and the staff.

The committee proceeded to list innumerable principles that should apply in producer-director relationships. The underlying theme in these various principles was that in any production there should be respect for and understanding of the potential contribution of each role to the quality of the film.

But the larger share of the problem seems to have lain with the filmmakers, the directors. The two most successful directors (in terms of "the creative treatment of actuality") of the Pool System were also open and teachable. Brittain — who had the same producer, John

Kemeny, for his two best films, *Bethune* and *Memorandum* — had admitted an admiration for Unit B. Rubbo was not above following a suggestion of his producer, Tom Daly (Unit B's Executive Producer), concerning a possible structural device for *Sad Song of Yellow Skin*. And each of these directors — unlike many other directors — actively sought advice and criticism. The thirteen structures that Brittain, Spotton, and Kemeny attempted for *Memorandum* were evaluated openly, not behind closed doors. The different cuts of the film were shown to anyone interested. Rubbo was similarly solicitous of advice and criticism from others.

Unfortunately, too many filmmakers interpreted criticism and advice as suppression of creativity. Some filmmakers preferred to work secretively so that their films would elude the contaminating influence of producers or peers. It should be noted, however, that in some cases there might have been reasonable cause for filmmakers to be suspicious of the intentions of producers and other old hands. The Film Board had become expert at "saving films" — another tradition reaching deep into the Film Board's past, and beyond it to the British documentary movement, when the EMB Film Unit had "saved" Flaherty's *Industrial Britain*. Sometimes producers tended to assume as a matter of principle that every film needed to be saved. Producers were prone to be insensitive to the particular merits and potential of the director's work. The overall tendency of "saving films," if left unchecked, is toward increasing sameness of product. Filmmakers sometimes had reason to complain that their film had not so much been "saved" as denatured.

The shortage of creative cooperation between directors and producers contributed to aesthetic shortcomings in many of the films. It also contributed to administrative problems. Part of the producer's function was administrative, and additionally there were budget officers and other administrative personnel with whom the filmmaker had to cooperate if the Pool System was to work. Since the war, there had always been a tendency for filmmakers to hold the administrative function in low esteem, but the Unit Structure ensured cooperation, however begrudged. Under the Pool System, cooperation depended mostly upon the filmmaker's disposition. Unfortunately, there developed an undisciplined attitude towards budgets and schedules subtly different from the Unit B example that had inspired it. In Unit B, budgets and schedules were secondary values, but they were still values. Only when a particularly intriguing aesthetic potential appeared within reach would Unit B exceed the budget and the schedule. Under the Pool System, this proclivity of Unit B's was misinterpreted such that some filmmakers tended to think that *only if* one went over budget and exceeded the schedule could one come up with a great film. There may have been some truth in the observation, but it tended to ignore other ingredients in the outstanding film. In other words, filmmakers tended to think that going over budget was the main condition for aesthetic achievement, sometimes even a sufficient condition. Even management was somewhat infected by this view. They didn't exactly believe it, but they weren't so sure it wasn't true. Attitudes toward budgets became unduly cavalier. An accountant remembers that:

> There used to be a $50,000 limit on programming budgets. So filmmakers would budget an expensive film at only $50,000. They knew they'd go far over that. This resulted in many overages. Which made it very hard to . . . plan.

Partly as a result of the increasing unmanageability of the Film Board's English Production Branch, the radical "de-routinizing" implied by the Pool System was countered by an increase in administrative staff and functions. In 1968, a committee of several production staff investigated the problems of the Pool System. Whereas the Brittain-Kemeny report of 1963 had identified the role of executive producer (the head of the unit) as the crux of the Unit System's problems, the *Internal Study Report*[8] identified the role of Director of Production as the key problem. He had — like the executive producer a few years earlier — simply too many things to look after. He was overextended. To assist him in the administration of the Branch and the execution of the Board's overall mandate, the committee recommended the establishment of a Planning Office reporting directly to the Commissioner, a Management Committee, training programmes to be administered by the Personnel Department, additional and larger Programming Committees, a Planning and Programmes and Policy Committee, more thorough accounting procedures, and a new Public Relations Office. Most of these suggestions were adopted. This tendency toward increased administration was reflected in costs: for the last three years of the sixties, the cost of administration grew at nearly three times the rate of the cost of production.[9]

As in the forties, a large part of this administrative growth was the result not of directly bureaucratic tendencies, but of the character of the Pool System which eschewed routine. The administrative additions were means of coping with the uncontrollability of the organization. To a large extent, the purpose of the measures was not to exercise prior control, but to "pick up the pieces," to rationalize, after the fact, the irrational character of the operation so that it would appear to conform to government operational norms. In other words, to a large extent it was the very freedom of the Pool System that contributed to increased administrative functions, devices, and costs.

The experiment in "the dictatorship of the filmmaker" appeared to be a failure. *Memorandum* and *Sad Song of Yellow Skin* represented significant advances in the art of the Film Board documentary, but the "whole picture" was threatened. The growing unmanageability of the organization was, however, the larger factor in the increasingly negative evaluation of the Pool System.

And yet the performance of the Pool System proved little. *Bethune* and *Memorandum* seemed to owe their existence more to the transition from the Unit System to the Pool System than the Pool System alone. Although *Sad Song of Yellow Skin* benefited from tapping Unit B's "attitude toward the craft," the odds are that the film would not have been produced at all had the Unit System continued, because the director, who joined the Film Board in 1966, would probably have been assigned to one of the units other than Unit B. Moreover, the seeds of the movement into dramatic features and self-expressive films, which seemed to have had mostly harmful effects but some good ones, were planted in the Unit System. Additionally, the problems of the Pool System were to some extent the problems of Western culture, which in the sixties experienced a growth in the popularity of anti-authoritarian, individualistic, welfarist, and iconoclastic values.

Another problem in evaluating the Pool System against the Unit System is that the Pool had fewer resources upon which to draw. When the Pool System was established, French-Canadian production had become autonomous. Animation, once part of Unit B, remained outside the pool. In 1967, the innovative Challenge for Change experiment drew off a number of the more socially conscious filmmakers. And in the late sixties, several of the Film Board's most accomplished, well-known, or promising English-Canadian directors left the Film Board. Some left out of frustration with the increasingly "bureaucratic" character of the Board. Some left to test themselves on the commercial market. Some left in the hope of cashing in, financially, on the skills they had acquired at the Film Board. Some left for more than one reason. Among those leaving were Donald Brittain and John Kemeny, the authors of the report which urged the adoption of the Pool System. Brittain became a free-lancer, although much of his free-lance work would be with the Film Board. Kemeny, via Challenge for Change, went into commercial film production.

Furthermore, in comparing the two structures we must remember that the Pool System lasted only seven years — a third as long as the Unit System. The Unit System was ten years old before its first classic documentary films emerged. Had the Unit System lasted only seven years, films such as *Corral*, *Paul Tomkowicz*, *City of Gold*, *Universe*, the *Candid Eye* series, *Jour après jour*, *Golden Gloves*, and *Pour la suite du monde* would not have been associated with it, if they had been made at all. The Pool System yielded not only *Memorandum* and *Sad Song of Yellow Skin* during its reign, it harboured the beginning of at least one major project that was completed much later: the *Corporation* series — which had begun as a single film but grew into a series of six half-hour films, and one longer one, explaining the workings of the Steinberg Corporation, one of Canada's largest supermarket chains. Although fairly traditional in style, the series, directed by Arthur Hammond, incorporated a few of the aesthetic developments of the sixties. It is exhaustive — over four hours of film time in all. Its topic, corporate growth and expansion, has become a hot issue for the seventies and eighties. The director narrates the films himself. The scriptless, direct cinema approach is used to great advantage in the seventh film, *After Mr. Sam*, which documents a process few have been privileged to witness. This film is specifically about the selection of a successor to Sam Steinberg, who had built the organization from a tiny neighbourhood grocery store into a multi-million-dollar operation. Most of the "actuality" comprising the film was taken during meetings of the Corporation's top executives. We witness the deliberations, jockeying, arguments, and strategies employed as the participants try to influence Steinberg's selection of a successor. Some want the job for themselves; others know they themselves don't have a chance, but want so-and-so to get it, and not someone else. The film has, additionally, a larger implicit theme — the transition from business run by individual entrepreneurship to business run by corporate decision-making based largely on statistical analysis, organizational theory, market research, and specialization.

Finally, in its *making*, *Corporation* was an "advance" in the delegation of budgets and schedules to secondary status. The series took five years to make. As had *Universe*, the series benefited from the "on-again-off-again" process. Unlike *Universe*, however, the process in this case had not been intended from the beginning. Only when the material proved to be particularly rich and promising was the project re-programmed from a single, one-hour film into a seven-film series. Also, Hammond was in the early seventies a member of the union executive staff, a job that took him away from the project for extended periods.

George Pearson, who produced the *Corporation* series, remembers an occasion which recalled not only the making of *Universe* but also of most of the Board's classic documentaries:

> There was a period [in the editing] of several months when *nothing* was accomplished. The [structural] problems were *insoluble*.
>
> The "aha" experience literally happened with Arthur. One day, after months of frustration, he came in and said, "I've got an idea. There's a concept we haven't dealt with: 'motivation'. What if we extract all the stuff touching on 'motivation' from the other films and make a separate film out of it?
>
> Not only did "motivation" become a film of its own, it got out of the way of all the other films. It was like a jigsaw puzzle falling into place.
>
> That ability to see patterns results from looking at it [the material, the actuality] and looking at it and looking at it ... struggling with it ... and finally discovering the key. That kind of thing you *cannot* schedule.

But the final and most crucial difficulty in comparing the Unit System with the Pool System is that the latter, as an experiment, was severely contaminated by a development largely outside its control, a development that affected the whole Film Board, but perhaps most deeply the English Production Branch. In early 1967, the Canadian Parliament authorized collective bargaining in the public service.[10] In anticipation of collective bargaining, the Film Board froze normal pay increases, and put a near-freeze on hiring. In 1968, partly in response to the freeze, the production staff (English and French filmmakers, technicians, and some producers) formed a union, *Le Syndicat Général du Cinéma et de la Télévision — Section ONF*. The union drew up a proposed agreement and submitted it to management. In July 1969, after months of negotiation, the two parties signed an agreement, approved by the Treasury Board, that called for over one million dollars in back pay. In August, the Canadian government announced an "austerity programme," whereby all departments and agencies would have to cut back their staffs by ten percent.

The union was convinced that the Treasury Board knowingly had allowed the union to negotiate some of its members out of their jobs. The undeniably capricious behaviour of the government — which first authorized collective bargaining, then approved the Syndicat's pact with management, and then invoked austerity — seemed deeply immoral. Moreover, as months passed, it appeared that the Film Board would be the only organization severely affected by austerity. In all other government departments, most of the required reduction in staff would be accomplished by normal attrition. At one point, it appeared that about fifty percent of the total employees being laid off in the entire government service would be Film Board employees. In addition, it appeared to the union that the Film Board management was cooperating too pliantly with the austerity programme. Worse, although the staffs of the two production branches constituted only about 25 percent of the Film Board's total staff, 52 percent of the cuts were to be from the Production branches — and an inordinate share from the English Production Branch.

The Film Board eventually accomplished the cutbacks in staff largely through attrition. Only a few production staff were laid off, and the union managed to win back the jobs of all those who cared to file a grievance. But the whole affair was quite costly to the Film Board. It left the filmmakers with a deep and still-enduring distrust toward both the government of Canada and the Board's own management. The filmmakers felt that the government was out to destroy or at least severely weaken the Film Board, and that management did not really mind.

By 1970, then, the authority of the individual filmmaker had been severely diminished, and so had his confidence. A growth of committees had sapped a portion of the productive energy of the filmmakers, who increasingly had more hurdles to jump before being able to start a film. And the events surrounding unionization and austerity had polarized the Film Board into something resembling a labour-management dichotomy. In only six years, the vertically structured organization of the Unit-System era had shifted through a brief, fluid, and nearly structureless stage, to a horizontally arranged organization.

In 1970, an internal "Crisis Committee" reported on the problems resulting from both the Pool System and austerity.[11] Whereas the 1963 Brittain-Kemeny report had spoken of the need to enter the "mainstream of modern cinema," the "Crisis Committee" report announced the need of finding ways "of re-establishing contact with the people, particularly the Canadian people, and their elected representatives, and of better-serving their interests." With reference to English Production, the committee resurrected the theme of "wholeness," which it presented as the premise of the report:

> The film process, from concept through production to distribution, is considered a whole process, and cannot be dismembered.

The committee then recommended the adoption of a "Studio System," whereby studios would "be comprised of voluntary associations of filmmakers, maybe 5 to 15 per studio, dealing with areas of common concern." The borders between studios would be flexible;

movement between studios would be fluid. The Studio System, in concept, was the old Unit System without the rigidities that had marred it. In early autumn, 1970, not long after the completion of the "Crisis Committee" report, Sydney Newman was appointed Government Film Commissioner. Newman, who had joined the Film Board during the war and had stayed until 1952, had experienced the Unit System. Like the authors of the "Crisis Committee" report, he thought that the Pool System was unworkable. In Newman's view:

> The Pool System was "democratic," but that meant that the best people were underused. In addition, there have to be structures under which the lesser talents can develop. When I came, there was no middle management, no real producers. The Pool System was a tragic mistake.

In 1971, the Studio System was adopted, but the studios proved to be larger than expected. This was partly to save money, because each studio needed its own budget officer and other administrative staff. Perhaps it was also partly because in the atmosphere of distrust, management could identify few filmmakers or producers to whom it would entrust a studio. At any rate, in the words of one producer, the system "is somewhat pseudo — just a collection of individuals grouped under executive producers." Intended as a Unit System without the flaws of the old Unit System, the Studio System was more like a hybrid of the Unit System and the Pool System. But whether it possessed hybrid vigour or not has remained an open question.

9
MIRROR, MIRROR, ON THE WALL: STOP, YOU HAVE GONE TOO FAR

The English-Canadian complaint against the Unit System was that the structure was too rigid. Québécois filmmakers complained that the system was paternalistic. They felt that they weren't taken seriously and that they weren't understood. On both counts, they were probably right, and yet, on both counts, the Québécois had enjoyed a curious measure of freedom under the Unit System, perhaps more than their English-Canadian counterparts. The language and status barriers, irritating as they were, protected the Québécois from management's full scrutiny, meddling, and control. Under the banner of "direct cinema," a film proposal consisting of a terse paragraph or two might be approved for production. Management perhaps would hear nothing more of the project until presented with a *fait accompli*, which might be a *Normétal*, a *Bûcherons de la Manouane*, or a *Jour après jour*. Management might demand certain alterations or cuts, but nothing more radical, because the filmmaker had a bargaining position: biculturalism. As a Québécois producer later recalled, "It was much easier to deal with an English-Canadian Director of Production than with a French-Canadian one."

While the English-Canadian Director of Production was attempting to cope with the Pool System's experiment in anarchy, his French-Canadian counterpart, Pierre Juneau, installed a hierarchical structure and top-down direction in the new French Production Branch. He placed production under the administration of four executive producers — a structure which resembled the old Unit System. In addition, he himself developed guidelines, policy, and projects for the Branch. Juneau's two-year regime left French Production with a degree of order and efficiency in the process of production that it still enjoys today, and as the years passed, the control of production became increasingly democratic, allowing greater filmmaker representation in the chief decision-making body, the Programme Committee. During Juneau's reign, however, Québécois filmmakers experienced a reduction in the freedom they had had under the predominantly English-Canadian Unit System. Juneau saw little value in the scriptless, direct cinema that the more talented Québécois filmmakers had developed, and there was little sympathy for dramatic features — which obsessed the Québécois even more than their English-Canadian counterparts. Not only did Juneau seem to the French-Canadians to be unresponsive to what they had developed in the late fifties and early sixties and to what they wanted to do in the subsequent years, he unintentionally insulted the filmmakers with some of his co-production and visiting filmmaker suggestions. When, for example, he suggested that the Québécois could learn from working with so-and-so from Europe, whom the younger filmmakers regarded as a hack, they felt doubly unappreciated. (Juneau also brought over Roberto Rossellini — no hack — for a visit, but Rossellini, according to Jacques Bobet, told the filmmakers to keep doing what they were doing. It even is said that he was so taken with their work that he sought — unsuccessfully — employment at the Film Board.)

The filmmakers wanted neither to return to a scripted approach to documentary nor to keep doing what they'd been doing in direct cinema. It was in April 1964, shortly after Juneau's appointment and shortly before the Board's twenty-fifth anniversary, that five of the best young Québécois filmmakers — Jacques Godbout, Gilles Carle, Clément Perron, Denys Arcand, and Gilles Groulx — publicly denounced the Film Board in the radical separatist journal, *partis pris*.[1] They called the Film Board "a gigantic propaganda machine" and proclaimed that the chief tool for the propaganda was the objective documentary, documentary that pretended not to take sides but which by virtue of that stance supported the values of the status quo. The Québécois filmmakers had personalized documentary in the last years of the Unit System, but they felt they had reached the limits of what — at the Film Board, particularly — they could say in documentary. As the Film Board would not permit deeper personal engagement in the Quebec documentary, then fiction was the logical form in which to work. The Film Board, however, did not provide sufficient scope or support for fiction, and — they claimed — it actually hindered the development of outside sources of support. The filmmakers felt caught in a contradiction: they were securely employed in the most luxurious and able government filmmaking organization in the world, free to make any kind of film except what they wanted to make: films expressing their perceptions of Québécois reality.

The Film Board management reprimanded the filmmakers for the *parti pris* venture. (Successive Film Board Commissioners had reinforced the Civil Service tradition that employees should not make public statements disputing policy matters.) What Jacques Bobet later called a "counter-revolution" had begun. By 1966, filmmakers Michel Brault, Arthur Lamothe, Gilles Carle, Gilles Groulx, Bernard Gosselin, Jean Dansereau, and a few others had quit the Film Board. Producers Fernand Dansereau and Jacques Bobet had been demoted. Bobet wrote:

> In fifteen months the counter-revolution destroyed the work of fifteen years: the finest group of filmmakers ever assembled in Canada is decimated, scattered, thrown into the void, with vague promises, never kept, of aid in film production.[2]

But it should be noted that if the filmmakers had felt themselves to be suffering from a contradiction as members of the Film Board, there was probably an element of contradiction in their own motives. Although their complaint against the Film Board was that the Board inhibited the expression of truth, their pursuit of the truth was not without egotism. Some of the filmmakers left the Film Board partly because opportunities were developing outside the Board for feature production. They, like some of the English-Canadians, wanted to enter the "mainstream of modern cinema." An outspoken Québécois filmmaker, Roger Frappier, later characterized their post-NFB careers as "an individual race to get famous."[3]

Some of them did get at least mildly famous, often with the Film Board's help. Several continued to work on and off at the NFB as free-lancers. One who broke ties completely was Gilles Carle, who became one of Quebec's most prolific and successful directors. His career got its start, though, with an enjoyable Film Board feature released in 1966, *La vie heureuse de Léopold Z*. Michel Brault most recently returned to shoot Anne-Claire Poirier's *Mourir à tue-tête*, which employs both documentary and dramatic techniques to examine rape as a political and economic phenomenon. Claude Jutra's *Mon oncle Antoine* was made at the NFB with an advance from a commercial distributor. Jean Beaudin left later, and then returned to direct *J.A. Martin photographe* in 1976, and *Cordélia* in 1979, but most of the features which constitute modern Québécois cinema are not Film Board films. Dramatic features are simply too expensive for the Film Board to support on a large scale; what's striking is that the NFB has been able to keep its hand in at all.

Two of the *"parti pris* five" would owe some of their fame, or notoriety, to Film Board *documentaries* they would make as returning free-lancers. Gilles Groulx (who in the late sixties had made the dramatic features *Où êtes vous donc?* and *Entre tu et vous* as a Film Board free-lancer) and Denys Arcand (who later directed *Réjeanne Padovani* commercially) would in the early seventies probe the limits of political expression possible in government documentary, and others would join them. Their efforts would culminate in great conflict, but the conflict was not a clear case of left against right, freedom against suppression, or truth against propaganda. It was a murky, confused conflict between two dimensions of liberalism.

The "counter-revolution" of the mid-sixties was merely another temporary aberration in the Film Board's traditionally increasing "tolerance of ambiguity." The Board's mandate, of course, by calling for the "interpretation of Canada to Canadians," implied that Quebec, too, should be interpreted to Canadians. The separation of French from English production implied a recognition that the realities of the two cultures were significantly different. The gradual democratization of French Production allowed the pursuit of a wider variation of perspectives. The internal ambiguity reflected in the paucity of unbreakable rules gave the filmmaker with an approved project a large measure of autonomy.

The location of the National Film Board of Canada in the cultural centre of separatist-inclined Quebec was a further ambiguity. When the new French Production Branch was established, Quebec had even less of a film industry than English Canada. There was English production in Toronto and Vancouver. What there was of French-Canadian production was in Montreal. And the mid-sixties was a time of intense interest in cinema, particularly in Montreal. For the English-Canadian filmmaker, the Film Board had become simply one of several career options available to him, north or south of the border. For the Québécois filmmaker, who generally was more intellectually inclined and politically conscious than his English-Canadian counterpart, the Film Board's French Production Branch was the centre, and to a large extent the creator, of a burgeoning Quebec cinema. As one Québécois filmmaker has put it:

> We never thought of ourselves as working for a federal agency. We were the French-Canadian film industry.

It was a situation that allowed the Québécois filmmaker to enjoy the benefits of filmmaking in the Civil Service without incurring the full force of its obligations. He could, as a character in *Le chat dans le sac* had recommended, "play the game and cheat at the same time." As a Québécois producer has observed:

> When a film is going well, the French-Canadians call themselves Quebec
> filmmakers. When it is going badly, they're federal filmmakers.

The Québécois filmmaker could hardly avoid the frustrations and advantages of such a dual identity — not if he wanted to make films. As one of them has remarked:

> It's like a seat on the plane. If you want to fly on the plane, you have to take a seat. Each Quebecker pays $3000 a year in taxes. This money belongs to me. I have a right to grab it.

Some of the Québécois, however, demanded more than just a seat on the plane. They wanted to share the cockpit — as the separation of the two production branches had seemed to encourage — and dispute the destination.

This many-faceted organizational tolerance of ambiguity was matched by a growing political tolerance in Quebec. By the spring of 1970, the Liberal Party was firmly ensconced both federally and in Quebec. The values of the Liberal Party in Quebec were in some respects like those traditionally associated with the Left. For example, medicine in Quebec had been all but socialized. But the Liberal Party also enjoyed the support of big business, especially in Quebec, where the only alternative seemed to be the separatist Parti Québécois. The Liberals thus enjoyed a broad basis of support. Freedom of expression was equally broad in Quebec, broader than it had ever been.

And yet it was the confluence of these two circles of ambiguity that, in the early seventies, led to a clash between the filmmakers' freedom of expression and the Film Board's limits to that freedom.

To understand how this is so, it is necessary to reach back into the history of government-sponsored documentary in England and Canada and note two paradoxical facts: that although government documentary filmmakers traditionally have been "leftist" or "progressive" in outlook, almost invariably it had been the conservative political mind, not the radical or progressive one, that supported the idea of government documentary.[4] Grierson was speaking to his fellow leftists when, in 1945, he defined the limits of expression in terms of "the degree of general sanction":

> ... nothing can be expected from governments beyond what I shall call the degree of general sanction. [This] is not the degree of sanction by the party in power; it is the degree of sanction allowed by all the parties of Parliament or Congress.... I say, as an old public servant, that if the degree of general sanction is accurately gauged maximum support is forthcoming for creative work. Where, however, advantage is taken and the degree of general sanction is estimated on partisan lines, ineffectiveness and frustration result.[5]

It has been remembered of Grierson during the war years that

> one time he was very busy lobbying . . . with Coldwell, minority leader of
> the then only socialist party, and Coldwell said very frankly . . . "Just how
> left are you?" And Grierson said, "I am an inch to the left of any party in
> power." And Coldwell said, "And when the socialists are in power?"
> And Grierson said, "I would then be one inch to the left of you."[6]

Grierson never had to undergo such a test. His governments were conservative, and so he and his British filmmakers in the thirties and his Canadian filmmakers in the early forties could make mildly leftist or progressive films and thereby feel both "radical" and secure. (Mackenzie King's wartime government was Liberal, but in those days, the Liberal Party was small-c conservative.) But in the seventies, in Quebec, the conditions existed for such a test. All the room was on the right. In 1974, a Québécois producer explained:

> For years, there was lots of room for freedom of expression in Quebec. But
> now, with [Robert] Bourassa [Quebec Premier] . . . if you're *just a little
> left* of Bourassa, you're in the Parti Québécois. There is no room between
> status quo and sedition . . . no space. . . . There is no political party or
> organization on the left of Bourassa except the Parti Québécois.

The Parti Québécois stood for the separation of Quebec from Canada and the subsequent nationalization of all major industries. This was what lay "one inch" to the left of the party in power.

The clash that occurred was not, however, between the filmmakers and the Liberals directly. It was between the filmmakers and Sydney Newman, who became Commissioner of the Film Board in the autumn of 1970.

Newman had been one of the brash young filmmakers of the wartime Film Board, and one of the most successful. He had quickly become the producer of the *Canada Carries On* series. In 1952, he left the Film Board to work in television. In the late fifties and the sixties, he became the head of the British Broadcasting Corporation's drama department, and is generally credited with bringing "kitchen sink" drama to British television screens. In terms of filmmaking and the administration of filmmaking, he was by far the most experienced Commissioner the Film Board had had since Grierson.

Unfortunately, Newman did not speak French. And he had been away from Canada for a long time. It is said that shortly after he assumed the Commissionership, he asked the new Assistant Commissioner, André Lamy (who would become the Commissioner in 1975), "Is it true that there are separatists in French Production?" Lamy reportedly replied, "Yes — one hundred percent. But don't worry. They're talented."

Additionally, Newman began his job as Commissioner at a time when morale was low. The austerity crisis had shaken the Film Board's confidence in the security of its role, and the division between filmmakers and management had never been deeper.

Newman didn't help heal this divisiveness when, after viewing about 250 films within the first three months of his reign, he called the staff together and gave his frank (and probably accurate) evaluation of the films. As Newman remembers:

> I told the staff that ten of the films were brilliant, about forty were pretty good, and as for the rest — blah. They stank with probity. I was grateful for the probity, but not the stink.
>
> Production hated me after this. They agreed with me, but I had had the ill-grace to say it to them in front of the distribution people.

In addition, Newman, who correctly perceived that the Film Board was losing its hold on the mass audience, promoted increased television series production and suggested that filmmakers might have to accept commercial breaks in their films. This did not go over well with filmmakers.

And only a few weeks after Newman's arrival, a small group of separatists in Montreal kidnapped a British consul and a Quebec minister. Thus began the October Crisis of 1970. The separatists threatened to kill both hostages unless certain conditions were met. Prime Minister Trudeau invoked the War Measures Act and sent federal troops into Montreal. The separatists killed the Quebec minister, Pierre Laporte, before they were located and captured. It was a tense few weeks. "My bosses in Ottawa," Newman recalls, "were in absolute hysteria."

One of Newman's first decisions regarding censorship was to uphold the decision of his predecessor, Hugo McPherson, to refuse the release of Jacques Leduc's *Cap d'espoir* (1970), a one-hour fictional film in the form of a confessional, a film influenced by the trend toward self-expression that had infected the English Production Branch. The one main character, an alienated Québécois youth, lashes out at society, venting his anger at its corruption and repression. For Leduc, it was a film about despair. A supporter of the film says that *Cap d'espoir* "interrogates by its subjectivity objective things and events." A non-supporter points out that the film opens with "a rather gross shot of a man defecating in a toilet." At one point in the film, the youth shouts at the audience, "Mange de la merde!" This vulgarity was the official grounds for refusing the film's release, but Leduc and others believed that the film's gloomy, negative picture of Quebec was the real reason.[7]

Pierre Perrault, who in 1963 had made *Pour la suite du monde*, in 1970 made a long documentary called *Un pays sans bon sens! ou Wake up, Mes bons amis!!!*. The title was a *double entendre*. For the older generation, the phrase meant "an unbelievably enormous country"; for the younger generation, it meant something like "an irrational, illogical, crazy country." The film, consisting mainly of interviews with alienated Québécois, lacks the beauty of Perrault's earlier films but it is more direct. The message is that the Québécois are spiritually lost, and will remain so until they have a country of their own, a free Quebec. Although the interviews convey the burden of the message, there are some symbolic scenes, such as a shot of an airplane chasing a herd of caribou into a hunter's net. In violation of the Film Board's tradition of non-partisanship, an explicit, favourable reference to the Parti Québécois appears in the film. Newman allowed this film to be released to groups who specifically requested it, but the film could not be shown on television or in theatres. (Newman later lifted this restriction.)

Also in 1970, Denys Arcand, on a free-lance contract with the Film Board, made a three-hour documentary called *On est au coton*. An openly Marxist film, it shows the Quebec textile industry from the workers' point of view. The industry is seen as greedy, exploitative, repressive, callous, and controlled by United States capital.

It was reported in the press that Newman liked the film initially, but changed his mind after showing the film privately to representatives of the textile companies, who, it was reported, expressed the view that "every possible legal means should be taken to prevent the release of the film."[8] Newman admits that he liked parts of the film, but he denies holding a private screening for the textile industry. At any rate, he refused to release the film on the grounds that naïve audiences might not be able to detect that the film was biased. In one scene, for example, a worker says that if he were working at the same job in the United States, he'd be paid more than he is in Canada, even though the company was owned by Americans. Newman says that, in fact, the worker was getting one cent more than his American counterpart. Newman says that there were other errors of this kind. Newman says that "it had so many untruths in it that I thought the Film Board would be accused of *lying*." In Newman's view, the integrity of the Film Board was therefore at stake. "If that film had been without errors of that kind," Newman says, "I would not have been able to stop it."

The carrying-out of a censorship decision, however, was becoming a game of cat-and-mouse. The Québécois had developed a simple strategy for dealing with the banning of a film. Before any film is finally complete, several test prints have to be run until details such as colour-balance and sound-track quality are perfected. All prints preceding the final print are called "n.g." prints ("no-good" prints). The Film Board, a profligate operation when it comes to technical quality, didn't care what happened to the "n.g." prints. The filmmakers usually would get them. When the Québécois had a film for which they anticipated censorship problems, they would run several extra n.g. prints. After they had all the prints they needed, they would show the film to management. If the final test print were censored, or if alterations were demanded, the filmmakers had a supply of n.g. prints for clandestine distribution.

Newman had put a stop to this practice. N.g. prints were no longer allowed out of the laboratory. No such prints of *On est au coton* escaped. But the filmmakers made a videotape of the film, and soon there were dozens of copies floating around Quebec — mostly in colleges and left-wing *salons*. In Newman's own rueful words, the film became "the greatest underground film in Quebec." Arcand himself laughs that the film itself was an "arid, three-hour black-and-white" documentary which would not have attracted much of an audience, but that the banning of the film established "at one blow my reputation."[9]

When Gilles Groulx, who by the early 1970s was probably regarded as Quebec's top filmmaker, was making *24 heures ou plus* on a free-lance contract, Newman was prepared. He made sure that he saw the film before the editing was completed. He recalls:

> It was an endless vomit of at least two hours. I took action within twenty-four hours after seeing it. Now it's dispersed all over the place, a piece here, a piece there. It would be a mammoth job to find all the pieces and spirit a copy out. In this particular case, I was able to outsmart them.

The outcry was immediate and loud. There were condemnatory editorials, fervent speeches, irate letters — as well as expressions of support for Newman's action. One problem for the critics of Newman's decision was that almost no one outside the Film Board, and only a very few inside the Board, had seen the film. When it was learned that there was to be one more internal screening at the Film Board (before the dispersal) for select members of staff, several reporters raced to the Board and attempted to see the film. They were denied entrance to the screening room. But one enterprising reporter — Gerald Godin of the leftwing *Québec-Presse* — sneaked into the projection booth and managed to see most of the film before being discovered.

According to Godin's account,[10] Groulx's film was a chronicle of events that had occurred in Quebec over a two-month period in early

1971. The title refers to one of the scenes, wherein a group of workers votes to support a general strike lasting "twenty-four hours or more." There is a scene of violent demonstration that took place during a strike. In another scene, the president of the Quebec Federation of Labour urges Quebec workers to destroy the system. There are scenes of ghastly high-rise apartment buildings situated in areas of heavy air pollution. The sequence that was most often mentioned in subsequent press reports included a scene of Premier Bourassa swimming in a pool under the watchful eye of his bodyguard. This scene is followed by a televised interview in which he says that he often makes decisions while swimming. In addition, Groulx had added a comment of his own. Groulx himself speaks the film's commentary, and he appears on camera himself, calling for the overthrow of the capitalist system and the establishment of a new, socialist society. In Godin's summary description, *24 heures ou plus* was

> a film-mosaic which shows, on the one hand, the degree of alienation or political unconsciousness of certain Quebeckers and, on the other hand, the passion of those who want to make others conscious. A documentary film about the obstacles which those who want to truly change the situation will have to overcome. A dangerous film. . . .

And it was, it might be added, an extreme combination of the Québécois filmmakers' penchant for personal expression and for political content.

A few days before Godin's story appeared, Newman had issued the following statement explaining his position:

> No matter how much I personally believe in the freedom of the artist or filmmaker to express his own views when he makes a film for us, he must understand that the National Film Board was created by the Parliament of Canada and is paid for by the taxpayer. For these reasons, the filmmaker — like a citizen in any professional discipline — is limited in his freedom by the terms of the place he works for.
>
> I expect filmmakers to push their freedom to the utmost. Because of this, it sometimes becomes necessary for me to say "stop, now you have gone too far." This is my burden and the burden of my Board. It is not the burden of the filmmaker or anyone else. I maintain that if *24 heures ou plus*, as it is, was released, the NFB would never be forgiven by the majority of Canadians who uphold the Canadian democratic system.
>
> It is indefensible for the NFB to put out a film which advocates the over-throw of the entire political system as it operates in Canada. I take it for granted that we do and must continue to make films which criticize elements in our society, such as employment, social democracy and so forth just as we also make films showing positive and healthy elements. Can we in all honesty think that the Film Board, financed by the taxpayers who have representatives in Parliament, [can] make a film in which the

ultimate conclusion is that our society is entirely corrupt and needs total change?

Now that this internal matter has become publicly distorted, I fear it may prevent a free and objective evaluation of this film. It amazes me how some staff members are so naive as to not see that such leaks to the public become just a political football in the hands of people who take malicious pleasure in knocking the Film Board.

When they knock the Film Board, they are not merely defending the freedom of the highly politicized filmmaker — but they are also inadvertently knocking the dozens of others whose work has no overt political flavour and which gives pleasure and indeed hope to our audiences of millions in Canada and abroad. It's the totality of the Film Board I am duty bound to uphold and protect.[11]

Newman denied that his action constituted censorship: "I'm not a censor, I'm the boss."[12] Even by this interpretation, however, Newman was guessing what the government of Canada, as representatives of the Canadian people, would tolerate. He was thereby committing the Film Board to organizational self-censorship. Newman's stand was, of course, consistent with the NFB's past, but by assuming full responsibility for it, he was pitting himself against the whole of Quebec film culture, for which the Film Board's French Production Branch was regarded as the centre. To the Québécois, he was meddling in the Quebec film industry. And it was not easy to isolate Groulx from the French Production Branch, because Groulx's film had not deviated in substance from the proposal he had submitted to the Branch's Programme Committee, and which the Committee had approved.[13]

In an often-quoted remark, Pierre Perrault called Newman a "celestial imbecile." Groulx likened Newman to a "little Latin-American dictator." Newman, in turn, characterized the more outspoken Québécois filmmakers as "a bunch of blind idiots."[14] This name-calling set the tone for the debate, which could descend to that level for the intriguing reason that the ambiguity-rich tradition of the Film Board allowed both sides to be right and both sides to be wrong. The issue had its roots in the very origin of the Film Board, and the present affair was another manifestation of one of the Board's peculiar strengths: that imaginatively consummated unholy union between the needs of the state and the needs of the artist or truth-teller, a union reflected in the structural and philosophical contradictions instilled into the Board from the very beginning. Even Grierson's attempt to characterize the freedom of the government documentary filmmaker had reflected the contradiction. He had warned filmmakers against narrow partisan stands, but he had said that he would always be "one inch" to the left of the party in power, even if that be the socialists.

Newman had shown acute awareness of this essential characteristic of the Film Board when he said that he expected filmmakers to "push their freedom to the utmost," which in turn required him to say, "Stop, now you have gone too far." That is, he understood the tension between what made the organization creative and what kept the organization funded by the government. But in his defence of his definition of what constituted excess, he had invoked "the terms of the place he works for." Unfortunately for his position, but not for the art of the Film Board documentary, the "terms" of the Film Board had evolved considerably since his post-war departure. The ambiguities implied in the mandate had been explored. There was nothing in the Act that qualified the mandate to "interpret Canada to Canadians," and there was no reference to pleasing the majority of taxpayers. The Film Board's role had always included a "cultural expression" component as well as a propagandistic one, but the cultural one had become larger over the years, and the interpretation of what was "cultural" had evolved considerably since the days when "cultural" meant folklore and sing-along films.

Canada and Quebec had changed, too, since Newman's post-war departure. Gilles Groulx's interpretation of Canada could hardly be called bizarre or eccentric or irrelevant. As many of his supporters pointed out, the issues and ideas presented in his film were discussed openly, every day, in the newspapers and colleges of Quebec:

> There is nothing in Gilles Groulx's film that is not in print in Quebec. Even professors are teaching more than you can find in his movie. Yet his film was censored by the NFB. You can find all kinds of newspapers on revolution — but it's in print. Even from a purely liberal point of view that film is representative of what people think. And if you want to be a liberal — that's a film that should be done.[15]

Moreover, there was nothing especially *undemocratic* in calling for the overthrow of capitalism and the construction of a socialist regime. Nor was there anything particularly un-Canadian about it. Two of Canada's democratically elected provincial governments were socialist at the time. Another porous argument against the censored films was that they presented an imbalanced view. Groulx could argue that a wealth of documentary material had been produced supporting the system he had attacked. Arcand could argue, as he did, that his *On est au coton* gave voice to 110,000 textile workers at a time when Radio-Canada was broadcasting a series of television programmes showing the industry from the owners' point of view.[16] And no one could have said of the Film Board's two finest documentaries,

Memorandum and *Sad Song of Yellow Skin*, that they were *balanced* in the sense of giving both pro and con views of their subjects. Further, whatever the merits of Groulx's claim that Canadian society was totally corrupt, what was the difference, Pierre Perrault asked, between the Soviet censorship of Alexander Solzhenitsyn, who argued that the socialist system was entirely corrupt, and the Film Board's censorship of Groulx, who had argued that the capitalist system was entirely corrupt?[17] And finally, as Gilles Groulx correctly pointed out, "They [the critics of his film] have never said that the film is not true."[18]

And so, increasingly it was Newman, rather than the filmmakers, who appeared to be acting outside the democratic spirit. He had censored a film that the French Production Branch's own Programme Committee, itself consisting partly of filmmakers elected by their colleagues, had approved. He had stopped a film that attacked an economic system, not a political one, save for the latter's alleged corruption by capitalist economics. He had refused to distribute a film that reflected a large minority opinion in Canada, and of millions upon millions of people abroad. His action thus seemed to violate what was becoming perhaps the most important interpretation of the Film Board's role in a democratic society. As NFB filmmaker Clément Perron wrote:

> For it is profoundly true that *the essence of the democratic society ... lies in the preservation of the very mechanisms which allow for a permanent interrogation of the quality of the lives of the citizens*. And in relation to our own professional lives, it is also true that *one of the grandest roles of the Film Board*, through its cinematographic function, *is to be a forum for such permanent interrogation*, both for the representatives of the people and the people themselves. If in any way these two truths are restricted, then the country is a dictatorship and the Film Board its Goebbels.... Breaking mirrors to avoid seeing the wrinkles on a face ... can cause irreparable damage to the entire society.[19]

To counter the undue attention that these largely unseen films were getting, Newman stepped up the promotion of two major bilingual or bicultural projects, one a series of forty films to help French-Canadians learn English and English-Canadians learn French, and the other a series of half-hour television documentaries, half of them about English Canada but directed by Québécois filmmakers, and half of them about Quebec, but directed by English-Canadian filmmakers. For both projects, experienced television producers were brought in from outside the Board. Newman announced:

> We've got some marvellous things going, and I believe that, in two years, this country will have a totally different view of its own Film Board.[20]

The Film Board, Newman urged, was being "transformed into an effective instrument to promote national unity."

But two years later, the language series had been transformed by the filmmakers into opportunities for making short- and feature-length fiction movies, which for the most part proved to be of dubious aesthetic merit and suspect didactic power. And the television series was only half-way realized. The Québécois filmmakers refused to do films on English Canada, and many of the English-Canadian filmmakers dissented very strongly from the idea of making films on Quebec. Eventually, only the series on Quebec, *Adieu Alouette*, was completed, mostly by English-Canadians. Three episodes were made by Québécois. The films by English-Canadians were mostly harmless reportages, disappointing aesthetically even to the Board's more conservative members, one of whom described the films as "teeny, weeny, mousey things." A Québécois filmmaker had stronger words for

> this fucking series of *Adieu Alouette*! This series was done by the English on French Quebec to show the rest of Canada, "Look how the guinea pigs have grown up and can walk by themselves!" They had problems with only three films in the series — the three done by French filmmakers. One was Jean Pierre Lefebvre's on theatre; the one on *Le Devoir* had a sentence of [Parti Québécois leader] René Lévesque's cut out when he said, "We have to change the system now — we have to have independence now!"; and the third by Fernand Dansereau on union workers is still censored.
>
> It proves that our way of seeing our problems is different — but they don't consider us competent. [We have to go through the English culture to have a reflection of our situation.] Sydney Newman said something very funny, "You can liken our work to a clear mirror, an eye for all to see the turning points in the progress of Canadians — their joy and pain. . . ." Yes, but what kind of mirror? Only *his* mirror! One that shows *his* reality! If our mirror shows something different, they break our mirror![21]

But just as Newman's position lacked convincing force, the filmmakers' position lacked a certain compelling quality. André Lamy had been right when he assured the Commissioner that the separatists in French Production were talented; what Lamy didn't foresee was that the filmmakers would largely forsake that talent. The films were either confessionals (expressions of opinion rather that revelations of reality) or they were arid (as Arcand admitted of *On est au coton*) or they were diatribes, giant complaints, tracts. Pierre Perrault had invoked the films' lack of aesthetic quality as a defence, arguing that it was "Griersonian" to use films primarily as a means for social change.[22] But Grierson had never rejected craftsmanship — only artiness — and certainly not for the expression of narrowly partisan political views. It seems more likely that the filmmakers were once again influenced by

Jean-Luc Godard, the inimitable French genius, who in 1969 had publicly rejected his previous work (which included such radical masterpieces as *Masculin-Feminin*, *La chinoise*, and *Weekend*) as "bourgeois," and proceeded to make a series of film-diatribes (which he later admitted were failures). We can never know, but Newman's censorship of *24 heures ou plus* may have worked to Groulx's advantage, not for the notoriety that the banning gave him but for the embarrassment that it may have spared him. At the time that this debate was raging in Quebec, the English author and critic, George Steiner, made the following remark in a totally different context:

> Borges has said that "the tremendous advantage of censorship is that it makes me find metaphors." That's very simple and very deep. Any damned fool can shout it out.[23]

The censored films "shouted it out." Interestingly, Groulx's two NFB dramatic features, *Entre tu et vous* and *Où êtes vous donc*, were not censored, even though, according to Denys Arcand, they "say exactly the same thing." But, Arcand added, in those earlier films the message "was conveyed by fables, illusions, and symbols, while in the last the denunciation is unveiled."[24] And Arcand himself, after the censored *On est au coton*, made a film called *Québec: Duplessis et après* . . . , in which he suggests that the governing Liberal Party is totally corrupt. Except for the original opening scene, which showed a current politico handing out dollars to constituents (not an illegal practice), the film was approved. Arcand asserts that the film says the same thing as *On est au coton*, but that it says it "in a complex way, harder to understand." Newman says that he released *Québec: Duplessis et après* . . . because the film did not favour one party over another:

> Arcand thinks he knocked the Liberal Party. He didn't. He knocked *all* democratic institutions in Canada. He also knocked Lévesque [the Parti Québécois leader]. He showed how *all* parties use tricks. That was the film's merit. It revealed the tricks of politicians.

There is a sense in which by "shouting it out" the censored films were not really saying much, at least not as films. That is, whether or not there was an objective truth to the messages of the films, the truth was not expressed with the full communicative powers of *film*. The films avoided a true "creative" struggle with "actuality." Like the wartime documentaries, they began with a received premise and then collected material to tack on to an unoriginal and rather hackneyed message. The issues in the films were discussed openly in Quebec. What would the films have added if they did not use the aesthetics of film to illuminate the issues?

The censored films, to varying degrees, also violated — although perhaps unavoidably, because of the "one-inch" squeeze — the Film Board's tradition of avoiding direct political partisanship. When Grierson told Coldwell that he'd be one inch to the left of the socialists if they were in power, Grierson was speaking of his general orientation. Grierson tried to avoid partisan films, believing that "truth transcended politics" and that it was "in the hands of artists, and artists alone, that truth becomes a principle of action." The wartime attempt by Mackenzie King to use the Film Board for his own narrowly political ends (to help him get elected) had informed the entire history of the Film Board. On this point, Film Board tradition was solidly behind Newman. Guy Glover recalls that in 1969 he sent a press officer of Prime Minister Trudeau's secretariat away "with his ears ringing" when the officer proposed that the Film Board make a series of films on the Prime Minister and his cabinet colleagues. But it should be noted that by the seventies, there were signs that the tradition might be weakening. The Film Board had made an interesting documentary about Newfoundland leader Joey Smallwood, *The Little Fellow From Gambo* (directed by Julian Biggs), in 1970. The Board considered this an exception, justified because Smallwood had brought Newfoundland into the Confederation. At the same time, Donald Brittain, who had returned to the Film Board as a frequent free-lancer, was making a documentary about a minor Canadian-Indian activist, Noel Starblanket. The film, *Starblanket*, was an acerbic undercutting of the young activist. Even if, as Brittain says, Starblanket was even worse than the film showed him to be (which is a debatable point, especially among Indians), the film could be a dangerous precedent for preserving the status quo by turning documentary's critical eye on fringe leaders but not on established ones.

Finally, there is a sense in which the censored films, although intended by the filmmakers to complete the essential "whole picture" of Canada, may have threatened the rest of the picture. Just as Newman had spoken of the need to protect "the totality" of the Film Board, some of the Québécois support given to the makers of the censored films was somewhat begrudged by a similar concern, although from a different point of view. Newman says that when he screened Groulx's film internally, Groulx lost a lot of support among the Board's Québécois filmmakers, who didn't think the film was very good. A Québécois producer, who in his career has supported and encouraged the more radical filmmakers, complains that

> almost any film can be destroyed if it is taken out of context. It's wrong to get into the position of defending films one by one. We should say, "You don't like this? Then let's try *this*."

Another producer has noted that many Québécois filmmakers, although sympathetic to Groulx and his political view, felt afterwards that

> that's not our job, to try to attack any particular party or policy. Let's work on deeper levels.

It is, in sum, hard not to conclude, with Paul Larose, who was the producer of *24 heures ou plus*, that "the history of censorship of the Film Board is far from tragic." Compared to any other so thoroughly governmental an organization, the censorship has been amazingly mild. The freedom, in fact, is astounding by comparison to any other known government communication agency.

And the films are no longer censored. In 1975, André Lamy succeeded Sydney Newman as Government Film Commissioner. One of his first acts was to lift the ban on the completed censored films, and to offer Gilles Groulx another opportunity to finish his. The films now are publicly available.

But it would be wrong to conclude that the issue of censorship was sound and fury over nothing, because it is misleading and unadventurous to compare the Film Board only to other organizations and not to its own capabilities. The stubbornness, aggressiveness, and courage of the Québécois filmmakers — especially Gilles Groulx and Denys Arcand, who were free-lancers, without job security — made an important contribution to the development of the Film Board. If there was little space for their own films within "the degree of general sanction," their work, by attracting most of the Film Board's censoring energy, probably created more space for others. That is, their efforts probably stretched that one-inch gap between the acceptable and the seditious. In the seventies, the "whole picture" of Canada was probably, on the average, a little tougher than it had ever been. Many films of a critical nature were being made. The censored films brought the tough documentary "home," or at least potentially so. If *Memorandum* had criticized the Germans, they were the Germans of twenty-five years earlier. *Sad Song of Yellow Skin* criticized Canada's neighbour for something occurring across the Pacific. The Québécois films tried to turn the same ruthlessly critical attitude onto Canada itself, to make government documentary film an uncompromising instrument of national self-criticism.

Arcand's *Québec: Duplessis et après* ... is perhaps one example of a radical, critical film that slipped through the space that the censored films created. Perrault's *L'Acadie l'Acadie* (1971) is another. *L'Acadie l'Acadie* is a long documentary about Francophone students in New

Brunswick who protest the lack of recognition given their language and culture. Newman says that

> L'Acadie l'Acadie was a fine film, a tough film. I thought that it was so honest and good and worthwhile that the English-Canadians should see it. I urged Perrault to make an English version. But he was very suspicious. It took him four months to agree.

Perrault made an English version, Newman got the film on CBC, and Perrault remained suspicious.[25]

Two more films which found their way to the public were Robin Spry's *Action* and *Reaction*, a pair of honest if detached documentaries about the October Crisis. Tom Daly, the producer, remembers that at the rough-cut stage, Newman

> had plenty of suggestions. About a third were really good, and improved the films. Another third were debatable, but we made the changes. The last third we rejected, and he didn't press the matter. On the whole, his involvement improved the films.

Once again, though, the Film Board shrank from fully admitting that independence for Quebec was a legitimate issue. One of the debatable but accepted changes concerned the last line of Spry's commentary. After noting that the October Crisis and its aftermath marked Canada's loss of innocence, the narrator concluded that the central question remained the issue of Quebec's potential separation. Spry had to relinquish this last point before the film could be released.

If the history of censorship at the Film Board is "far from tragic," especially when compared to the performance of government filmmaking organizations of other countries, it *is* mildly tragic that in 1976, when the Parti Québécois won the provincial election — which was decided mainly on the issue of economic and political corruption, the subject of Groulx's film — the National Film Board of Canada had produced and disseminated very little to prepare Canadians for the shock that many of them felt. The results of the election make the Film Board, in hindsight, look bad. A great opportunity had been lost, and there was a large smudge on the mirror.

10
CHALLENGE FOR CHANGE: THE ARTIST NEARLY ABDICATES

The organizational changes of 1964, which established a separate French Production Branch and an experiment in anarchy for the English Production Branch, were in part the results of internal stress and external pressures. Within the Board, the Unit System had alienated English-Canadians by its rigidity and Québécois by its paternalism. Outside the Board, Canada was increasingly committing itself to biculturalism; the traditional emphasis on duty and responsibility in the public service was yielding ground to an emphasis on rights and opportunities; and cinema was rivalling the status of the more traditional arts.

At the same time, however, the changes were bold adventures, courageous experiments. They involved organizational and aesthetic challenges to the Film Board's overriding principle of "wholeness," of "central powers and central purposes." The challenges were met, and the result was a widening in the scope of that "wholeness" so that it embraced a wider variety of purposes and powers. The destination had been reached, however, along with a train of heavy baggage: infatuation with "mainstream" modern cinema and a degree of glorification of the filmmaker as cultural hero or political revolutionary.

In 1967, only three years after these organizational changes, the Film Board initiated two large-scale programmes which likewise reflected outside events and internal attitudes. One of the programmes, Challenge for Change, achieved almost instant fame. By 1970, it had its imitators around the world. The other programme, Regionalization, developed by fits and starts — more fits than starts until the mid-seventies, when it began to become a reality. Both programmes were, in part, interpretations of federal policy. The government had announced a commitment to the principles of cultural democratization and cultural regionalization. Equally, however, the programmes were internal reactions against the main trends at work in the two branches of production.

Colin Low, the one-time member of Unit B's Inner Circle and one of the Board's most talented filmmakers — *Corral*, *City of Gold*, *Universe*, and *Circle of the Sun* were among the Unit B films to which he contributed prominently — was a key figure in both programmes. He was involved first, however, in Challenge for Change. He directed its prototypal project and served a stint as the programme's executive producer. Low went to Challenge for Change partly as a reaction against the glorification of the individual filmmaker:

> the illusion that *I* can communicate through film — that *my* films can communicate, that *I* am effecting social change.[1]

He was also disturbed by the increasingly shrill tone of some of the films with political or social themes. While the Québécois, especially, were recalling Grierson's wartime characterization of film as "a hammer," Low thought that "eventually all weapons will have to be beaten into ploughshares and that includes media weaponry." But the motivation was not simply discomfort with the dominant trends of the sixties. A colleague has remarked of Low that he was one of the very first people at the Film Board to sense the enormity of the problems of the environment and of the disparity between the haves and the have-nots. The latter concern permeated Challenge for Change from the beginning; the problem of the environment eventually would be addressed mainly by a specialized programme of films made outside Challenge for Change.

The developments in self-expression and politicization of the sixties had been associated with an increasing detachment from government purposes or priorities. And although the two developments may have raised the quality of sponsored work, by making the filmmaker more demanding when dealing with a sponsor, the two developments monopolized the creative and critical energies of the Board. Challenge for Change, in some ways more radical in intention than the dominant trends, sought to re-establish close government contact in order to realize its own aims. This was directly within the Griersonian tradition. Grierson had written:

> The nature of cinema demands collaboration and collusion with others and with many variant purposes; and its significance derives from those who can operate and command purposively within these conditions.[2]

But Low and the others associated with Challenge for Change added a new twist to this collaborative relationship. In Low's view:

Early documentary was dominated by the educated elite middle class — Grierson's boys. Very pompous. Early Canadian documentary was dominated by the whiz college kids with all the answers — mildly left wing camp stuff — very serious and scholarly but without great understanding of the country.

To counter that elitist danger, Challenge for Change would attempt to reverse the collusory relationship. The traditional sponsored film conveyed government's message to the people; the Challenge for Change films would convey messages from "the people" (particularly disadvantaged groups) to the government, directly or through the Canadian public. Films would be like government briefs — expressions of citizens' opinions elicited by, and submitted to, the government, with the aim of directly influencing specific government policy, by criticizing it. This is what made the programme unique.

Seven government departments participated in the establishment of Challenge for Change: Indian Affairs and Northern Development, Agriculture, Health and Welfare, Labour, Regional Economic Expansion, Secretary of State, and Central Mortgage and Housing. The participating departments put up half the money for the programme; the Film Board put up the other half. Both the filmmakers working in the programme and the participating departments could submit proposals for projects. An Interdepartmental Committee exercised authority over the approval or rejection of proposals. The committee was directly responsible to the Secretary of State via the Privy Council.

The overall purpose of the programme was to encourage experimental approaches to the use of film and television in the fostering of social change. Three kinds of film were proposed: films for the departments and the general public explaining a problem; films for social workers and change-agents; and "film activities among the poor." Above all, the emphasis would be on making films with disadvantaged people rather than merely about them.

As Challenge for Change evolved and became known and respected, Grierson (who at first was sceptical about the programme — he called it "eight-millimeter films for eight-millimeter minds"), and others associated with the origins of the British documentary film movement, tried to claim *Housing Problems* (1936) as a forerunner of Challenge for Change. In *Housing Problems*, slum-dwellers speak to the camera, describing the conditions in which they live. Grierson called *Housing Problems* a film made "not *about* people but *with* them,"[3] and Edgar Anstey remembers that the idea was to let "slum-dwellers simply talk for themselves, make their own film."[4] But a critic had noted at the time that *Housing Problems* "posit[ed] a social enquiry and resolve[d] it superficially by concluding that slum clearance has been ended by the Gas Company [who sponsored the film]."[5] This kind of suspicion was later voiced of Challenge for Change. Community activists wondered if it were not a contradiction in terms for government agencies to be promoting social change; a Canadian-Indian spokesman noted that "the major unifying factor among Indians all across Canada is their common dislike for Indian Affairs."[6] How could Indians and Indian Affairs work together?

Alert to these dangers, the writers of the original Challenge for Change proposal urged:

> Above all we must aim for honesty. There should be no smell of public relations in the pejorative sense. No amount of skill, imagination and cleverness will substitute for honesty; the objective must be social change, not a rationalization of things as they are. To be honest will not be easy; with the best of intentions there will be a natural tendency to be optimistic about projects, to shade reality, to confuse hopes with results. We must constantly be aware of this tendency and resist it.[7]

But exactly what honesty was, and how to achieve it, would be subject to various interpretations as the programme evolved. George Stoney, an American documentary filmmaker (perhaps best known for his film, *All My Babies*, a quasi-documentary about rural southern midwives) who in 1969 began a two-year stint as the programme's coordinator, found that "each person working in the programme had his own idea of what Challenge for Change should be doing." (That same year, the French-language counterpart of Challenge for Change, Société nouvelle, was generating an even wider diversity of viewpoints.)

Of the three kinds of films that had been proposed, all three were made within the first years of the programme. *The Things I Cannot Change*, filmed in 1966 as a pilot project for Challenge for Change, was primarily a film that attempted to explain a problem to the general public. The film is an hour-long documentary about a poor Montreal family of ten children. The father is unemployed and perhaps unemployable. The welfare allowance does not go far enough. What seems to give the parents occasional moments of joy or the will to endure are the children — so they keep having children. There appears to be no hope for this family, and the film acts as a witness to their pathos.

A popular film at the time, *The Things I Cannot Change* influenced the development of Challenge for Change more by its failures than its strengths. After the film appeared on television, the family suffered the ridicule of their neighbours. They were hurt by the film, not helped.

And the film seemed to lack any significant positive value. It was structurally weak. It expressed hopelessness rather than some course of remedial action. It was actuality without the positive component of creativity.

In 1968 the programme produced, for social workers or change-agents, a series of films about Saul Alinsky, the late American community organizer. Titles in the series include *Power and People*, *Deciding to Organize*, *Building an Organization*, *Through Conflict to Negotiation*, and *A Continuing Responsibility*. One of the Alinsky films, *Encounter with Saul Alinsky: Part II*, is especially memorable. A very simple recording of Alinsky trying to communicate with some young Indian leaders, the film presents a remarkable example of cross-cultural non-communication, and it has a philosophical dimension as well — in the tradition of Arthur Koestler's *The Yogi and the Commissar*. The hard-nosed Alinsky, who had been brought to Canada to teach community organization, keeps stressing to the Indians that he can't help them until they can specify their goals. He demands that the Indians tell him what they *want*. If they can tell him what they want, then he can tell them how to get it. The Indians have trouble thinking in terms of goals and strategy. They prefer to emphasize integrity of culture, non-competitiveness, and values of character. Although he is sympathetic to the Indians, Alinsky finally becomes impatient and angry. By the end of the film, however, it is not at all clear that the Indians have understood Alinsky any less than he has understood them.

But it was under the third category of work — "film activities among the poor" — that the key differences in interpretation of the purposes and policies of Challenge for Change arose. This was partly because the category could include the other two kinds of film, and partly because of the words "activities" and "among." Yet it was under this category that the central innovation of the programme — government sponsorship of specific, critical feedback — was most directly pursued. The famous prototype was a series of films made by Colin Low in the Fogo Islands, a tiny group of sparsely populated islands off the northern coast of Newfoundland.

The five thousand inhabitants of the islands had lived almost entirely from commercial fishing, but the catch had declined. Their fishing methods and equipment were antiquated. They knew nothing of marketing techniques or development strategy. There was almost no communication or cooperation among the islands, because of distance, religious differences, and hopelessness. Despite their condition, the islanders were resisting an attempt by the federal government, in conjunction with the Newfoundland government, to relocate them. Colin Low remembers the origin of the project as follows:

> I began my work on Fogo *after* I had examined a couple of federal-provincial resettlement projects in another part of Newfoundland. They were criminal in their indifference to people and were an example of political porkbarrelling I could not believe. I could have shot an indictment of the programme easily but I realized that it would be politically suicidal — it would have ruined any chances of the Challenge for Change programme in that province in the early stages of the programme.... [And] I thought it was a lot better to examine a situation, the outcome of which was not yet determined, rather than look at another melancholy social mistake.

Low began the project with the intention of making two or three films about Fogo, but he encountered apathy about the project, an apathy rooted in deep hostility and bitterness toward the government. But the islanders were open to the idea of Low making several individual films, each one a record of a single interview with an islander or about a single event or issue. Low also found that this approach seemed to treat the people more fairly. The traditional documentary structure was, in Low's word, "horizontal," moving from one scene to another, cross-cutting between different points of view. Invariably, no matter how conscientiously the filmmaker tried to present a balanced, objective picture, the editing would introduce an element of bias. Any scene invariably would seem to be a comment on the one that preceded it. The "vertical" approach of expressing each point of view in a film of its own alleviated this problem. Additionally, giving each person or point of view or issue its own film helped combat the tendency for documentary films to exploit their subjects by using bits and pieces for some overall theme or structure that did not necessarily serve the ends of the people who had been filmed.

After five weeks of filming, Low and his small crew returned to the Film Board with twenty hours of film. They edited the material into twenty-three films, totalling about five hours. (The shooting ratio of 4:1 was quite low for documentary.) The topics included the need for cooperative fisheries, the relationship between the merchants and the fishermen, boat-building, the education of Fogo children, and many others. Before making final prints of the films, Low took the rough-cuts to Fogo and showed them to the islanders concerned. Each person was asked if the film said what he meant to say, and if there were anything he wanted to add or delete. Only one change was requested: a three-minute deletion of a question and answer about the standard of education on one of the islands. The islanders resented the tone of voice of the person asking the question.

The finished films were shown to government administrators and politicians. As one filmmaker said, "We finally had fishermen talking to cabinet ministers."[8] The government scrapped the relocation plan, and in its stead provided assistance and encouragement to the islanders to start a fishing cooperative and a marketing board.

In addition to their direct influence on government, the films are said to have affected the islands directly, by breaking down the isolation among the communities. The films allowed an exchange of viewpoints that was not likely to have happened otherwise. This encouraged inter-island cooperation.

The Fogo experiment has served as a model for projects around the world. The films have been used extensively in Newfoundland and by specialized audiences across Canada and abroad. The project informed the future development of Challenge for Change, but also raised some difficult questions for the programme.

Challenge for Change could point to the Fogo experiment as an example of using film as a social tool with immediate observable effects: the scrapping of the relocation plan and the renewal of initiative and hope among the islanders. No longer was film merely something to be shown to a mass audience in the hope of changing their attitudes or opinions a little. But the immediate, observable, favourable effects of the Fogo films may have been matched by indirect, obscure, undesirable ones. Four years later, according to the programme's own follow-up film, *A Memo from Fogo* (1972), neither the co-op nor the marketing board was doing well. The community leaders had been "put on a pedestal through the films." The films had not exploited their subjects; they had glorified them. The new leaders, however, lacked leadership qualities. A fisheries expert and community organizer had to be sent in to help sort out the resulting difficulties. But, the film suggests, the problems in the islands were now problems of growth, not decline. A fisherman says, "It's like Fogo come up out of the grave." And Colin Low, in 1976, commented that:

> Fogo Island, I understand, had one of its best years last year in the fishery. Its battle helped bring the 200-mile-limit issue into focus for the Federal Government. Its Co-op is now functioning very well. The people movement is in reverse. [i.e., more people are returning to the islands than leaving.]

It is always difficult, and usually impossible, to ascertain the effects of a film. This difficulty posed a special problem for Challenge for Change, because the programme stressed so heavily the importance of direct social effects of film. Traditionally, films had been evaluated largely against a commonly held general frame of reference. The aesthetic criteria were no longer applicable, and so the observable social effects became all the more important. To this day, however, Challenge for Change has not devised a means of adequately evaluating the effects of its "film activities among the poor." (Various methods have been attempted. For example, when the *En tant que femmes* series was shown on television in 1974, Société nouvelle set up a bank of phones, manned by filmmakers and social animators, and invited viewers to call in with comments and questions. The data provided some indication of the series' impact, but only in terms of immediate, verbalized responses. As in most of the attempts to evaluate Challenge for Change projects, it yielded no clue to the project's enduring effects, if any.) As Low himself has noted:

> Time is the best measurement of anything. Evaluation has never been practical because there has never been an *adequate commitment* to a time base that would mean something in relation to social change.

Even assuming that the effects of the Fogo project were, on balance, favourable — and the evidence, slight as it is, does suggest that they might have been — the project was not a cost-effective model. Traditionally, films have seemed to make economic sense when used as mass communication. Twenty-three films useful mainly to a small community of five thousand people constituted very expensive social change. It is true that the films were used widely, but they were interesting to national and international audiences mainly for their prototypal value, as examples. And although the twenty-three films were produced at a cost comparable to what the Film Board spends on a typical one-hour television documentary, the amount of money represented was no trifle and the audience differential was quite large. The Fogo project was too costly to be emulated in the programme's future film work. Challenge for Change began to require that its film projects have potential value all across Canada. For projects of interest mainly or exclusively to small communities, the programme preferred videotape, which was cheaper and faster. But it was only the size, scope, and cost of the project that could not be emulated. The approach itself influenced Challenge for Change deeply.

Another problem for Challenge for Change lay in the apparent contribution that the *process* of making the films gave to their apparent success: "Far more important than the films themselves," an evaluator wrote, "was the process of making them."[9] And the Fogo *process* became more widely known than the films themselves. This, of course, was no contradiction of the stated aims of the programme; problems arose because of two interpretations that could be given to the importance of process. One was that the process of involving the people in making the films insured fairness and non-exploitiveness. This made for better, more honest, and less superficial films. The other interpretation was that the process itself — forget about the films — was what really counted. The important thing was to be "a sparkplug for process rather than a creator of product."[10] By this interpretation, filmmaking or videotaping could become simply a pretext for "getting people together," for stimulating interaction, communication, and cooperation among the participants. The filmmaker was like a recreation director in a summer camp, who arranges games and other activities in order to stimulate interaction. But the effect of a process is as hard to determine as the effect of a product, and there developed a tendency in Challenge for Change to judge that if participants in a project seemed to enjoy themselves, to interact and to cooperate, to act confidently or appear happy, then the project "worked." Compounding the doubtful validity of such criteria, the "evaluator" tended to be the project leader, who was deeply involved in the project and especially desirous that it be judged successful.

But the first interpretation of "process" contained some deeper implications. The islanders themselves had helped make the films. They helped choose the topics, and they passed judgment on the editing of the films. This, and the "vertical" structuring of the films, minimized the possibility of distortion or exploitation. This "democratic" approach to filmmaking appealed strongly to people working in Challenge for Change, and its pursuit seems to have taken two divergent forms. In both, though, the preferred medium was video rather than film. Video was cheaper, the equipment less cumbersome, and technically simpler. A Challenge for Change worker announced:

> There is no doubt about it. It's here. Half-inch video is everywhere, and so are cable companies, and the number of people behind cameras and in front of cameras is multiplying unbelievably. Television will no longer be the medium of a small elite, programming for the masses. It will be the forum through which the many segments of the community will be able to talk to each other, a medium for everybody.[11]

Because videotape allowed wider access than film:

> We may now hope to see the expression of experiences by individuals to whom such expression was previously denied.[12]

One direction that this democratization took was toward extending access so that the people themselves could use Film Board equipment and make their own films or, especially, tapes. The classic example is

166

Vidéographe, a project developed by Robert Forget in Société nouvelle. In Forget's view:

> One realizes that there are many more people all around who are already awakened, who have things to say, who want to get involved in certain [media] work, but who don't have access to the means.[13]

Opening in 1971, *Vidéographe* operated out of a small centre in downtown Montreal. Videotape equipment and professional consultation were made available to citizens who submitted proposals to *Vidéographe*. By the end of the first year, four hundred proposals had been submitted, a hundred and twenty were accepted, and sixty projects were completed. Nearly six hundred people had been involved in producing the tapes, and about twenty thousand people had visited *Vidéographe* in order to view them. [14] In 1973, the Quebec Ministry of Communication took over the sponsorship of *Vidéographe*.

The other form of democratizing the media was less extreme, and more like the original Fogo project. Instead of turning equipment and facilities entirely over to the people, the filmmaker or videotaper would still maintain technical control over the project, but would function only minimally as a director. In a brief submitted in 1971 by Challenge for Change to the Canadian Radio-Television Commission, the programme stressed

> involving citizens in the production process — choosing their own subject areas, controlling the editorial process, and determining who would see the film.[15]

This movement to democratize the media led to some unforeseen entanglements and puzzling dilemmas for Challenge for Change.

Once a project like *Vidéographe* was legitimized, every single Canadian able to hold and point a video camera became a potential Film Board director. Forget and many others desired this. But if economics prevented the realization of this ideal, economics did not prevent the increased involvement or participation in individual Challenge for Change productions. But the more the public's involvement in production increased, the smaller the contribution of the filmmaker. Ultimately, the filmmaker became no longer a filmmaker, but a technician, a facilitator of filmic expressions by "the people." The movement to democratize the media thus led to a further devolution of authority at the Film Board. Only a few years earlier, filmmakers had assumed the authoritative centre of gravity for Film Board production decisions. Now, filmmakers were abdicating the authority, turning over the role of filmmaker to "the people." Filmmakers — it could be argued — were "copping out."

As mediators for the people, the filmmakers working in the programme found it difficult to cooperate creatively with the Interdepartmental Committee. The Committee expressed frustration that its role seemed to have been reduced merely to reacting to proposals rather than helping initiate and develop them. The Committee's distance from the work being done on a project like *Vidéographe* led its members to feel that they had no meaningful role at all.[16]

The Committee's frustration was matched within the ranks of Challenge for Change. In the words of one Challenge for Change worker, "It's like, 'Here's a quarter, Sonny, go out and change the world.'" Additionally, the fear of acting autocratically or in any other way outside the democratic spirit led to a proliferation of committees, a development that frustrated the programme's first executive producer, John Kemeny, as well as his successor, George Stoney. And a major examination of the programme's structural difficulties recommended even more committees.[17]

Moreover, there was a sense in which being a mediator was a more constraining *role* than being a filmmaker had been. The programme thus tended to resemble a bureaucracy in some ways. Challenge for Change seemed to spend more energy on keeping projects alive than on examining them critically. A Challenge for Change worker mused:

> Sometimes I think Challenge for Change is a devious plot to make poets think like bureaucrats.

A disgruntled filmmaker complained of the people in the programme that

> they become what they set out to change. If you challenge *them* to change, they get incensed. I criticized Challenge for Change once. They got very angry. They said it would harm the programme's image.

And the programme's image apparently was very important to Challenge for Change. In the early seventies, Challenge for Change published a widely distributed newsletter called *Access*. A few years later, when a revival of the newsletter was being considered, a Challenge for Change worker reviewed past issues and

> found them notable for many of the characteristics against which the programme always tried to work. Though the programme adopted a critical stance in relation to society, the magazine was remarkable for its lack of self-criticism; though the programme from the first was to be based on honesty, the magazine ... unjustifiably clothed the work of the programme in the glowing verbiage of success.[18]

The programme was emitting the "smell of public relations" which the original Challenge for Change proposal had warned against.

The shift in authority from filmmakers to "the people" had aesthetic implications as well, not just for the programme but for the whole Film Board. Filmmakers, acting not as artists but as mediators, facilitators, technicians, consultants, or whatever, wanted to minimize their manipulation of the film material, i.e., the actuality. But to do this, it was hard not to throw the baby out with the bath water. The craft of filmmaking, developed laboriously over three decades at the Board, began to lose currency. To edit carefully or imaginatively was an imposition. To choose an interesting angle or to compose an intriguing shot was distortion. Music or effects were intrusions. To comment was an abuse of power. And perhaps most important, a working-out of a structure for the material was to steal the right of self-expression from the subject. In terms of "the creative treatment of actuality," the creative half of the formula fell into deep disrepute. This was the implication of the "vertical" structuring of films.

As a result, the "talking head" achieved a predominance in Challenge for Change films, as if, in the words of Guy Glover, "simple quotation were the only guarantee of veracity." Ironically, the self-expression that Grierson had abhorred, and which he noticed in some of the Board's work when he visited Montreal in 1964, and which Challenge for Change had meant to counteract, was re-emerging. Only it wasn't the filmmakers who were expressing themselves, it was "the people." Challenge for Change, which sprang up in part as a recoil from the aesthetics of self-expression, got rid of the aesthetics, but not the self-expression. "Often," as Low himself noted, "all a group gets is its own boredom played back."

It should be noted in passing that the same overall tendencies were evident in Société nouvelle, even though the French-language programme started later, was smaller, and, because of the deeper prior politicization of most Québécois filmmakers, was less of an adventure than the English programme. And, in a sense, Société nouvelle worked through them earlier. In 1969, Fernand Dansereau completed *St-Jérôme*, a two-hour documentary about the effects of technological change on a small town. A few years earlier, Dansereau had been involved in making *A Saint-Henri le cinq septembre*, a film which backfired against its subjects in much the same way as did *The Things I Cannot Change*. In the Winter 1968/69 issue of *Challenge for Change Newsletter*, Dansereau recounted how in *St-Jérôme*, a film regarded widely as marking the beginning of Société nouvelle, he attempted to avoid the undesired results of *St-Henri*:

> To avoid a repetition of Saint-Henri, I adopted a special principle: I pledged to all the people (except the politicians) . . . that they would have the right to censor the material that I would shoot with them. . . .
>
> Because of this initial pledge . . . the major part of the shooting was taking the form of interviews. . . . I simply listened to people. . . .
>
> When, a little later, I . . . attempted to intervene as a director, I always had the same feeling of disrespect, of unjustified manipulation on my part. The final footage was composed entirely of interviews and events that had authentically happened quite outside my control. . . .
>
> At different stages of the filming, we invited our principle participants to screen rushes with us. We continued to do so at different stages of editing. . . . [The] screenings could, in certain cases, exercise an effect of collective therapy. . . .
>
> The film . . . is long. Most of the time all you see is people talking. . . .

The forces of craftsmanship in both English and French production were strong enough to prevent wholesale adoption of the "talking head" interpretation of authenticity, but the fear of manipulating the material had some effect throughout the Film Board. Again in the words of Guy Glover, there developed a tendency

> to use terribly simple means, no matter how much it costs you . . . *underplaying* everything to the point where it becomes kind of mousey . . . sanctimonious. . . . Quiet, whispering, mumbling films . . . as if to raise yourself, to move fast, to dance, would in some way *violate* the notion of sanctity about the subject.

Nothing, however, is ever simple or one-dimensional at the Film Board. A description of the tendency of a programme or a structure does not describe the totality. When the emphasis on respecting the integrity and the rights of the subject did not cow the filmmaker into complete submission, when he or she did not abandon the creative function entirely, the resulting film could be better and truer than it might have been otherwise. In addition, the emphasis on process might have added a new dimension to Grierson's early hope that documentary film could play a truly important role in the life of the *polis*. By involving the subjects in the filmmaking, the filmmaker encounters challenges to his or her preconceived notions and natural elitism. Colin Low describes and dismisses elitist filmmaking as follows:

> There is an assumption in all elitist filmmaking that the filmmaker "knows" what the changes in institutions should be for the betterment of people and society. History demonstrates this to be crap.

But sometimes it is not elitism but simply the habits of careerism which active involvement with the community can penetrate. Low comments:

> A sustained career of filmmaking alone is a very artificial activity over several decades if it is not a *real* part of the community we belong to. You

> have to think of the mental health of the filmmakers also. They cannot spend their lives as observers and skilful interpreters — they must act and interact also.... It ... means that filmmakers should either have experience in several fields before they [become] filmmakers or they [should] be encouraged to distribute and utilize their own films in situations that the films were intended to influence.

Much valuable work has emerged from Challenge for Change. Several of the programme's films since the Fogo project seem to have met the original intention of using critical feedback directly and constructively. *Wilf* (1968) is said to have influenced the government to recommend legislation, which Parliament approved, for subsidizing small farms. Another film is said to have helped establish a plastics factory in a small town. *Up Against the System* (1969), a film about what it's like to be on welfare, was shown at several Department of Health and Welfare conferences across Canada, and at three major political party conventions.

Additionally, some films have been made which may not have affected legislation but which are nevertheless beautiful documentary briefs. *Nell and Fred* was a Challenge for Change film. *Encounter with Saul Alinsky: Part II* is a rare, technically simple, but philosophically rich, anthropological document. Michel Régnier's ten-part *Urba 2000* series, and fifteen-part *Urbanose* series (both Société nouvelle), constitute an exhaustive cinematic inquiry into a mammoth contemporary, and future, problem.

An early example of Challenge for Change at its best is the film, *You Are On Indian Land* (1969). The film was made on the initiative and with the participation of a Canadian-Indian film crew, which Challenge for Change had trained. A tribe of Indians living on an island in the Saint Lawrence was planning to block a bridge connecting the island and the Canadian side of the river to the United States. The Indians were protesting the sudden enforcement of a previously ignored law that required Indians to pay duty on groceries brought back from the United States. A day before the blockade was to occur, Mike Mitchell, a young Indian leader and a member of the Indian film crew, proposed over the phone that Challenge for Change make a film about it. Overcoming some bureaucratic obstacles and by-passing others, Challenge for Change managed overnight to organize a production.

The film was almost everything that the programme stood for. It was a "film activity among the poor." It was experimental. It involved Indians themselves in the making of the film. The main subjects of the film were invited to rough-cut screenings of the edited material. The film led to an agreement that the Indians could establish their own police force for the island. The film revealed an amazing degree of gentleness on the part of both the police and the Indians. And finally, *You Are On Indian Land* was a brilliantly shot and edited example of direct cinema. It was widely shown. It was a good film.

Whatever the successes of Challenge for Change in channelling criticism to constructive use, a limitation with the programme became visible after a few years. The more remote from the Canadian mainstream the people criticizing the government were, the more critical they or the films were allowed to be. Films about, or by, or with, Eskimos or Indians, not regarded as a threat to the fabric of Canadian society, could be highly critical. Films with threatening groups could sometimes not even be made. The Interdepartmental Committee rejected a series of proposed films on militant trade unions in Quebec (perhaps justifiably, because union members are not as disadvantaged as so many other groups, and they have a voice). At any rate, generally the kind of change that the programme promoted was mild and non-threatening. A film could criticize practices, policies, or situations that tended to bar certain groups from equitable participation in the mainstream of Canadian life. The thrust of the programme was to raze whatever barriers hindered such participation. But films which criticized something fundamental about society were not encouraged and rarely permitted. As Sydney Newman, the Board's Commissioner during the early seventies, remarked:

> The [Interdepartmental] Committee has a general wisdom ... well, let's just say that I'm not aware of any film that has shaken any fundamental institutions.[19]

The Interdepartmental Committee's "general wisdom" was not necessarily censorship. It was consistent with the programme's aim, and it was practical. The participating Departments themselves lacked the power to change fundamental Canadian institutions, should they have had the inclination. And yet, there were those at the Film Board, and those in Challenge for Change, who were beginning to think that the shaking of fundamental institutions was ultimately necessary. If you really wanted to "do something" for the Indians or the Eskimos or the poor, you should not advise or help them to enter the "mainstream of Canadian life." You should help them resist it.

In 1974, Tony Ianzelo, Boyce Richardson, and Virginia Stikeman completed a pair of films which, although about Cree Indians in remote northern Quebec, struck at the heart of a fundamental institution. These films demonstrated not only that Challenge for Change principles could be incorporated into the full original Griersonian aesthetic, but also that the administrative entanglements of Challenge for Change did not preclude the making of deeply political films. The films, and the way they came to be made, illustrate Challenge for Change and the Film Board at their best.

The idea that led to the films came not from the filmmakers but from a member of the Interdepartmental Committee. The issue of aboriginal land rights had interested him for a long time, and he suggested that Challenge for Change do a film on the issue. Challenge for Change engaged Boyce Richardson, a journalist who had written a series of articles for the *Montreal Star* examining the effect of economic ventures such as the James Bay Hydroelectric Project on the ecology of the North and the people who lived there. Apparently, some very powerful interests did not enjoy seeing these issues raised, for the *Star* dropped Richardson.

While Richardson was helping Challenge for Change prepare its proposal for the film on aboriginal land rights, the Film Board itself became a little nervous. A decision was made to go to Ottawa to feel out the government. "The next thing we knew," a filmmaker associated with the project recalls, "the Interdepartmental Committee had cooled to the idea. They said that the timing didn't seem right for the film, that they had got this from the 'highest authority.'"

No one associated with the project wishes to say, for publication, who he thinks the "highest authority" was, but there is reason to suspect that the "highest authority" was indeed the highest authority. Prime Minister Trudeau was adamantly against even acknowledging aboriginal rights as an issue. In a press conference held in Vancouver in 1970, Trudeau had said:

> It is inconceivable that one group of people should have a treaty with another group of people within the same society. The Canadian people cannot be put in the position of guaranteeing the aboriginal rights of the Indian. It is imperative that Indians enter the mainstream of Canadian life. It is important that they become Canadian like any other Canadian.

Challenge for Change went ahead and submitted its proposal to the Interdepartmental Committee. In apparent collusion with Challenge for Change, the Committee neither approved the proposal nor disapproved it. They could have referred it to the Department of Justice, but they were sure the Department would kill the project. Consequently, the Committee, in its "general wisdom," simply did nothing.

Challenge for Change then submitted a substitute proposal. Instead of a film on aboriginal rights, the new proposal suggested four half-hour films on "Indians and Canadian Society." The Committee approved this vaguer concept, and Challenge for Change proceeded to make not only their film an aboriginal rights, *Our Land is Our Life*, but also a spin-off film, *Cree Hunters of Mistassini*, each an hour long.

Cree Hunters of Mistassini is a quiet, compelling record of a Cree winter. The film shows us a culture that has evolved relaxed social relationships, deep ecological awareness, and subtle religious beliefs suitable for the land they have lived in for centuries. The film tells us briefly at the beginning, and reminds us at the end, that this way of life is doomed by the huge James Bay Hydroelectric Project, on which construction already has begun. But as we learn in *Our Land is Our Life*, the land which the Project will submerge belongs to the Crees, by treaty. The Crees don't want to give this land up. They refuse offers of compensation that rise to hundreds of millions of dollars. They prefer their own modest but proud economy to all the glitter of mainstream Canada. The film does not suggest the Crees will win this particular battle. They won't stop the James Bay Project. They'll probably accept the money, eventually, because the land will be taken anyway. But the film does serve as a witness against the values and imperatives of a society based on an insatiable demand for energy, and in this sense is not only an honest film but also a deeply political, prophetic document.

Taken together, as they should be, the films challenge a fundamental institution — "progress" as we know it — and at a rather deeper level suggest that saying no to promiscuous change might constitute a much larger, far more significant kind of change than that required to enter and succeed in mainstream Canada.

Of the two films, *Cree Hunters of Mistassini* (the spin-off film) achieved the more immediate success. CBC bought it and aired it. It won the Robert Flaherty Award in 1974. The Department of Indian Affairs, which on its own probably would never have sponsored such a film, paid the Film Board $30,000 to have its name listed as a co-sponsor. And among the Crees of northern Quebec, the film's reception was almost overwhelmingly enthusiastic. A Challenge for Change worker describes the response of a key northern community as follows:

> Fort George is the focal point of the James Bay project. Already, work on the project is affecting the traditional way of life and a malaise was setting in. The film had an unexpected and almost unbelievable impact. Following the first few days of screenings, Fort George was virtually abandoned as people returned to fishing. . . . Many of the trappers announced they were making plans to return to the bush in the winter. . . . The reasons given were the film, which revived memories of what life was like.[20]

Our Land is Our Life never got on CBC, and the NFB doesn't promote the film as enthusiastically as it does *Cree Hunters*. But the film has served both the Film Board and Canada marvellously. At a Third World conference on government information, the film stunned most of the participants, who hadn't conceived of government information as the honest examination of issues. The film has been just as successful in Cree communities as *Cree Hunters*. And if not widely promoted, the film exists and is available.

In the spirit of Challenge for Change, the Cree films were briefs from a group of people to the government and the public. They also represent the way the Film Board works best. Rather than trying to confront the government (or the Interdepartmental Committee or the Film Board management) with shrill political diatribes of dubious aesthetic merit, the filmmakers worked quietly, unaggressively, but persistently, not just to get the films made but to get them made properly. The skills of the filmmakers were applied exhaustively and with deep commitment; the films were by-products of work, work in which the Crees participated. The films stand as evidence for Grierson's claim that serious film work demanded "collaboration and collusion with others and with many variant purposes," and they are very impressive examples of the uses of ambiguity. The "highest authority" had tried to stop the films, and he couldn't.

Partly in response to the success of the Cree films, the values of craftsmanship, which in certain Challenge for Change circles had fallen into disrepute, were reaffirmed. In a statement of Challenge for Change guidelines, Dorothy Todd Hénaut urged the activist filmmaker to

> make a beautiful film, with the highest quality of shooting and editing you can reach. Honest and sincere mediocrity is not enough, if you want to make a film that can help people change their world. In fact, people expect you to bring your professionalism to your work....To involve people in the editing doesn't mean having them decide every shot. It means helping you judge whether you have put the right emphasis and balance on what they have to say, or whether you have left anything out. They want you to be an artist as well as a filmmaker.[21]

Thus Challenge for Change was able to retrieve and incorporate the aesthetic values it had all but rejected. The synthesis, when reflected in work like the Cree films, represented a remarkable achievement. And yet there is a sense in which the maturation of Challenge for Change marked the beginning of the programme's decline and perhaps its ultimate demise. For just as Challenge for Change eventually incorporated the Film Board's traditional craftsmanship, the Film Board as a whole eventually incorporated most of what was valuable in Challenge for Change, such as its involvement of subjects of the film in the making of the film. In 1979, a producer outside the programme observed that

> Challenge for Change seems to have outlived its former usefulness. It was supposed to be — and was — an innovative thing, to blaze new trails. Now it's part of the heritage. The thinking unique to Challenge for Change has now permeated the whole place. Government departments also realize this.

Government departments also recognize a deeper problem in Challenge for Change: its original guiding ideology. In the late sixties, participation in "the mainstream of Canadian life" seemed within reach of all Canadians, but by the end of the seventies the survival of the mainstream itself was in doubt. In a few short years, Challenge for Change had fallen behind the times. By 1978, the number of participating government departments, once nine, had dwindled to two. In December 1979, the number remained at two and the programme stood in abeyance.

To rekindle government interest, Challenge for Change administrators are attempting to redefine the programme's goals. A draft document[22] outlining a new orientation for Challenge for Change makes no reference to "film activities among the poor"; instead, it emphasizes, at great length, the need to help Canadians understand and adjust to a new age of scarcity. The document also suggests that Challenge for Change be renamed "Horizons."

11
FILM BOARD
REGIONALIZATION:
WILL THE CENTRE HOLD?

In times of soaring costs and diminishing resources, non-profit organizations, especially cultural ones, tend to retract and consolidate. They halt, draw the wagons in a circle, and prepare for the siege. But the National Film Board is an unusual organization, and as the nineteen-eighties begin the Film Board is engaged in what may be its most radical organizational venture yet: regionalization of production. The programme's radicalism lies in its deep ambiguity of purpose and potential. Its impetus seems to derive from motivations bold and craven, idealistic and self-serving. From one angle, Regionalization looks like audacity; from another, appeasement. It appears to be both ahead of its time and behind the times. Regionalization of production appears to pose a severe threat to the continued development of the Film Board's documentary tradition — but thereby falls directly within the context of that tradition, the periodic organizational brinkmanship inextricable from earlier major developments in Film Board documentary. That Regionalization could result in either the Film Board's revitalization or its final dissipation simply highlights its organizational appropriateness.

Regionalization, which involves the decentralization of Film Board production and the sharing of authority for this production with local film communities, is frequently described as a natural outgrowth of Challenge for Change. Several Challenge for Change projects, such as the prototypal Fogo Island series, entailed relocating much of the work of filmmaking to remote parts of the country. Most Challenge for Change projects involved at least some sharing of authority with people unconnected with the Film Board. Like Challenge for Change, Regionalization challenges Grierson's insistence on "central powers and central purposes" while finding hints of support elsewhere in his thinking. It was while discussing Challenge for Change that Grierson, shortly before he died, expressed this apparent support for regionalizing production, noting that

> not yet is there a real decentralizing of production. The *cinéastes* may make their films *with* the people and *in* the villages, but they are soon off and away . . . to their normal metropolitan milieu. The old unsatisfactory note of faraway liberal concern for humanity-in-general creeps in, in spite of these real excursions into the local realities.[1]

And finally, as in Challenge for Change, there is a tendency for those involved in Regionalization to boost it uncritically.

But despite such parallels, it is misleading to describe Regionalization simply as an outgrowth of Challenge for Change. Challenge for Change contained its own fruitful ambiguities, but compared to Regionalization it was much more sharply focused, more deliberately thought out, more coherent, self-contained, and limited. Filmmakers in Challenge for Change shared authority with their subjects — noncompetitors, nonfilmmakers at the bottom of the "vertical" filmmaking process introduced by Challenge for Change. Regionalization involves sharing authority at a higher level: with directors and producers from the competing private industry, traditionally at odds with Film Board methods and goals. In this respect, Challenge for Change resembled a capitalist nation extending limited benefits to its poor, while Regionalization resembles a nation entering an uneasy partnership with its traditional ideological enemy. And when the larger political context for Film Board Regionalization is taken into account, Regionalization seems less akin to Challenge for Change than to the establishment of a separate French Production Branch in the early sixties. Film Board Regionalization is a similar acknowledgement of new political realities, in this case the growing disaffection of anglophone provincial groupings from centralized Canada. (Ironically, the comparatively token Regionalization of *French* production *does* resemble Challenge for Change, in that by establishing small production offices in Winnipeg, Toronto, and Moncton, French Production has extended opportunities to politically weak minorities, to groups outside the mainstream who want to get in. Regionalization as a significant organizational venture is essentially an English-Canadian phenomenon.)

One simple fact, however, sufficiently belies the claim for Regionalization's origins in Challenge for Change. Grant McLean conceived the regionalization of production in the early sixties. He established regional offices in Halifax, Toronto, Winnipeg, and Vancouver in 1965, when Challenge for Change was at most a vague idea. The primary mission of these offices was to serve as listening posts, to send ideas to headquarters. Beyond this, however, Regionalization was not thought out very deeply. Peter Jones, whom McLean assigned to Vancouver, was directed to refer to himself simply as a Film Board "representative." He remembers that there

> wasn't much real thinking about regional production when it was made policy in 1965. In fact, I was told I would have to work out my own "job description" *after* assessing the situation. A real Canadian approach.[2]

Partly because it lacked a clearly articulated, compelling set of purposes, Regionalization enjoyed little support from either the Film Board or the Canadian government. When the austerity crisis of 1968 hit the Film Board, Challenge for Change, then only a year old, survived while all the regional offices save Vancouver were closed.

Peter Jones's determined and successful effort to keep the Vancouver office open established a foothold for Regionalization during the subsequent few years of official indifference to it. Jones wanted the office to be more than just a listening post; on a very small budget he managed to engage the office in some training and involve it in at least some production. According to Ron Dick, now retired, Jones was "the first guy to sense that there was more to the regional possibility than just the untapped talent, that there was an angle on the national dream that could be seen only from the regions." The current executive producer for the Pacific Studio, John Taylor, whom Jones recruited and trained, recalls that Jones was able to keep the office going partly because "he was strongly supported by the local film community, who took him and his ambitions for Vancouver to heart, and lobbied for him."

Challenge for Change began contributing to the development of Regionalization only in the early seventies. Recalling his response to the conditions on Fogo Island, Colin Low remembers, "It was just like Alberta in the thirties. I got angry as a Canadian regionalist." As an adjunct to the Fogo project, Low helped set up the Memorial University Film Unit, which now works on projects in conjunction with the Atlantic Studio. He later served as coordinator for regional production. The current executive producer for the Atlantic Studio, Rex Tasker, became interested in Regionalization largely from his experience on a Challenge for Change project which sent him to Thunder Bay to train young people how to do community programming for the local cable channel. But this new spurt of interest in Regionalization did not arise solely from Challenge for Change. Even the austerity crisis helped recruit supporters for Regionalization. Tasker recalls:

A bunch of filmmakers got together. Most were concerned with how the
Film Board could survive. I was more concerned with how to make a better
Film Board. I thought the Film Board needed to get in closer touch with the
people of Canada. Challenge for Change had done some of that, and
Regionalization seemed a way of extending it.

Other filmmakers, equally interested in making "a better Film Board,"
turned to Regionalization without significant reference to Challenge for
Change. Mike Scott, executive producer for the Prairie Studio, remembers:

The last few years I worked here [at headquarters, in Montreal], I felt there
were all these great minds that had cut themselves off from the rest of the
country. They had lost their commitment. When Regionalization started
getting talked about, it was the *first time* that I sensed a new future for this
place. It was like a door opening. For many of us, it has been a kind of
salvation, like having a blood transfusion.

And there is little doubt that some of the filmmakers who transferred to
the regions were primarily interested in escaping headquarters and
Montreal. For them, the ideology came later.

At least as important as the revived interest in Regionalization
among some filmmakers, however, was the changing political climate
in Canada. In the seventies, Regionalization suddenly appeared conso-
nant with a growing political point of view. At least two persons with
Regionalist views had been appointed to the Board of Governors. The
growing network of independent film communities found increasing
support in regionalism for their demand for greater access to the Film
Board's resources. Commenting in 1976, after the Film Board had
re-opened the regional offices, renamed them "Studios," and provided
them with reasonable operating budgets, Colin Low observed:

Regionalization is happening whether it is led by the NFB or not. The Film
Board started it, then got nervous, but now is getting on the bandwagon
again, perhaps for its own survival.

Referring to this renewed official interest and investment in Regionalization, the Film Board's Assistant Commissioner noted:

at this point no great think-piece had been produced. It was only *after* it all
started to work that the paper started. There is a moral in that somewhere.[3]

As a consequence of the varied purposes and sporadic enthusiasm
behind its development, Regionalization lacks the comparative unity of
vision that characterized Challenge for Change, the development of
Québécois filmmaking at the Board, Unit B, or even the Pool System.
The clearest official statement of the aim of Regionalization reflects the
programme's mixed motivations:

> The objective ... is to provide each region the opportunity to interpret a
> regional subject to a national audience or a national subject from a regional
> point of view.... [Its two goals are] to provide more diversified pro-
> gramming, reflecting regional concerns [and] to encourage the develop-
> ment and employment of filmmakers locally.[4]

The statement also contains a fair measure of the Film Board's
traditional ambiguity. This has allowed each regional studio to interpret
its mandate according to the characteristics of its region and the
orientation of its executive producer. Perhaps the ambiguity is doubly
appropriate; a Canadian writer, referring to regionalization as a broad
federal policy, has observed:

> The term "regionalization" is very vague and subject to different
> interpretations.... In fact, there may be as many definitions of "region"
> as there are persons defining it.[5]

John Taylor, executive producer for the Pacific Studio, describes his
region as

> a transient culture, settled by miners, loggers, fishermen, who'd come,
> take, move on. They were not root-setting people. We reflect this. Our
> interests are eclectic, cosmopolitan.

This was not always the case, especially in the years of threadbare
budgets:

> In the early years, we limited our subjects to our own backyard. And there
> are those who think that regions should be concerned solely with the
> regions. But that way of thinking is a trap. Naturally, there should be
> regional content, a regional slant, but really there's only one mandate: to
> interpret Canada to Canadians.

An example of this broader orientation is a recently initiated film on the
lottery industry in Canada. But the geography of the Pacific region,
traditionally somewhat separated from the rest of Canada by the
Rockies, encourages it to look westward, across the ocean. Consequently, the Pacific Studio's programming is beginning to take on an
international aspect. "Our future role," predicts Taylor,

> will be the interpretation of Canada's role in the Pacific Community, and
> we've started what we hope will be an ongoing series of films on this. The
> first two films are on business in Japan. One film will examine the
> structure of Japanese business, which is so different in many respects from
> the North American way. The second film will be about a Canadian doing
> business in Japan.

A film community existed in Vancouver before the opening of the
Film Board office there, and this community included a few ex-NFB
filmmakers. Thus the Film Board's presence on the west coast is not

entirely the result of Regionalization. In this respect, Taylor views Regionalization as coming full circle from something begun in 1939:

> Originally — forty years ago — the filmmakers came *from* the regions to the *centre*. This had to be. They had to learn from each other. But they carried with them their regional interests and points of view. And there are people out here who long ago went to Ottawa, learned filmmaking, then returned. In this sense, Regionalization is entirely within the Film Board's tradition.

But despite the existence of a community of filmmakers in Vancouver, the Pacific Studio has maintained a training programme for several years. "We found a need," Taylor explains,

> to teach filmmakers — not all, but a lot of them — how to work in the NFB style. Most of them learned filmmaking through industrials, commercials. They aren't used to high shooting-ratios, extensive sync-shooting, the Film Board candid documentary approach. So, since 1972, we've set aside ten percent of our "outside" money for training and experimental purposes. The idea is to take a guy who already has the basic skills, put him to work with a filmmaker experienced in the NFB way, and bring him to a professional, NFB level. This is often a stepping stone to getting his own contract with us, or with someone else, like the CBC.

The film industry in Toronto is the oldest in Canada, the most commercially oriented, and historically the most antagonistic to the NFB. This resentment still surfaces occasionally, but the industry has grown so large that it seems only vaguely aware that the Film Board has established an Ontario Studio. And Don Hopkins, the Studio's executive producer (until August 1980), deliberately maintained a low profile, especially in the early years:

> We wanted to get the office opened with a minimum of political flak. There was a lot of resistance. "Why does the NFB have to come here?" people asked. So we've done a lot of quiet listening, and we've contracted out all our work to independent producers and freelancers.

Consistent with this studied inconspicuousness, Hopkins defines Regionalization more abstractly than do other regional executive producers:

> The basic assumption of regional philosophy is that a people made consciously aware of their individual origins and characteristics will be more secure, more flexible, and more successful in framing and achieving not only individual fulfilment but also collective fulfilment as a people within their national society.[6]

What this means for Canadians, Hopkins explains, is that with Regionalization "we have a better chance of telling the truth of the country to ourselves." Hopkins shares Taylor's interpretation of Regionalization as a natural, timely renewal of the Film Board's original regional input. "People are no longer prepared to move to Montreal," Hopkins adds, "and the Film Board hasn't had the turnover of staff necessary to continue representing the regions from Montreal."

The Prairie Region, embracing Manitoba, Saskatchewan, and Alberta, presents altogether a different situation. In executive producer Mike Scott's words:

> A big problem here is that our region is so enormous. It's half of Canada. It's very difficult for us to address all the different communities.

It is also difficult to tap all the talent available in the Prairies. Scott has found that the strength of Winnipeg's small film community lay principally in animation, while out in Edmonton — a thousand miles away — there existed a small core of documentary talent. In response, Scott set up a regional "desk" in Edmonton. In April 1980, the Edmonton "desk" became a regional studio of its own (the North West Studio).

In Scott's view, Regionalization does not entail a new mandate for the Film Board, but rather a new way of fulfilling it:

> Regionalization is an attempt to do what Grierson started forty years ago. The idea is to open up the doors of the institution to Grierson's idea of giving access by the country as a whole to the Film Board. Regionalization could be a way of creating a national sensibility rather than a parochial one. Part of this involves giving people some self-respect, a sense of their own cultural identity.

Despite the geographic dimensions of the prairies, Scott perceives common cultural characteristics underlying the work being done out of his studio:

> Prairie films are different from, say, the Maritimes or B.C. There's more humour in our films. Our films are more people-centred. And our films are more concerned with culture, that is, with artists, than, say, with fishing.

Wood Mountain Poems is a film which seems to exemplify Scott's definition of Prairie sensibility and his interpretation of his mandate. A quiet, half-hour portrait of a minor poet who lives in a small prairie town, the film is distinctly different in its particular combination of scope, subject, and tone, from films emerging from the other regions.

Although not the largest region in either land area or population, Atlantic Canada (Newfoundland and the Maritime Provinces) is in one sense the most dispersed and complex, a region of fishermen, small farmers, small towns, a weak economy, and very little inter-provincial communication. It also possesses the fewest existing film resources. This situation has had its advantages; Rex Tasker has been freer than the other regional executive producers to define and shape his studio:

> The mandate we gave ourselves — because no one else did — was to make films about the region, to use *regional* filmmakers, and to develop local film communities. This meant, of course, that we had first to engage in training, since virtually no film communities existed.

To avoid creating a monolithic Film Board operation confined to Halifax, Tasker has helped develop NFB "sub-regional" offices in Newfoundland, Prince Edward Island, and New Brunswick. The offices serve mainly as focal points for local film communities, which Tasker also helped establish. "We *have* to create these film communities," Tasker explained to a questioning Montreal programming committee shortly after initiating the effort, "because we can't keep absorbing these [newly trained] filmmakers ourselves."[7]

Largely due to his Challenge for Change background, Tasker's self-defined mandate has implied that the films made in Atlantic Canada reflect the practical concerns of the region, Canada's poorest. And just as the Pacific Studio has begun to extend the scope of its programme to include the Far East, the Atlantic Studio has begun to look to coastal Northern Europe. Because there appear to be immense deposits of oil off the shore of Newfoundland, the Atlantic Studio, in conjunction with Memorial University, sent a crew to Norway and Scotland to examine the social impact of off-shore drilling. Out of this material, the Film Board and Memorial University made a group of videotapes which circulate locally as stimuli for discussion. The tapes are revised as new material becomes available. Another project involving Norway is a film on fish-farming, which is almost non-existent in Canada, although many parts of the country are ideally suited for it and could benefit economically from its widespread adoption. Besides promoting fish-farming for its particular benefits, the film presents it as an example of what Tasker regards as "a more imaginative approach to regional development."

Although the emphasis in the Atlantic Studio's programme is clearly utilitarian, Tasker resists making it exclusively so:

> I believe in Grierson's basic ideas and have used them as guidelines in my work. But one thing I particularly like is his definition of the Film Board's mandate being as ambiguous as possible. The vagueness is useful. I don't want to lock ourselves into any particular area. The more variety, the better. There are no no-no's. And we don't want to make purely local films; they have to have appeal on a national level, even an international one.

This national concern emerges in a recent Atlantic Studio documentary, *Empty Harbours, Empty Dreams*. The film is one of a projected series of films, each produced by a regional studio, on Canadian confederation from a regional point of view. The first of the series to be completed, *Empty Harbours, Empty Dreams* on at least one criterion sets a high standard for the other studios to meet in at least one area. The film is a quiet but unrelenting historical analysis of how each Maritime Province was drawn into confederation. One by one, each is shown to have entered confederation as a response to fear, economic or political coercion, or promises which were never kept. Although stylistically rough-edged and rather pedestrian, the film is notable for the honest criticism it addresses to the issue of confederation. The film is soft-spoken but fearless.

Empty Harbours, Empty Dreams stands on its own as a film, but it also serves as an excellent example of the way Tasker believes Canada's diverse peoples, cultures, and regions should interact:

> What we're talking about is a redefinition of the word "confederation." Up until now, it has meant a central authority. But *we're* defining it as a coming together of more or less equal parts. It means groups of people working together rather than dispersed people working for a central authority.

Thus the regional studios attempt to define themselves. Each reflects the character and concerns of its region and the values of its executive producer. Each appears distinctly different in orientation from the others.

But despite the clear differences among the regional studios, each executive producer either does or could invoke Grierson in support of the direction his studio seems to be taking. Rex Tasker's Atlantic Studio seems guided primarily by Grierson's belief in using documentary as an instrument for social and economic improvement, but Tasker also has applied Grierson's strategy of encouraging a variety of production. Mike Scott has adopted Grierson's cultural interests and his insistence on a close relationship between filmmakers and their communities. Both Tasker and John Taylor have rediscovered Grierson's internationalism. In its attempt to establish a foothold in Toronto's industry, the Ontario Studio echoes Grierson's early insistence that a significant portion of the Film Board's work meet North American commercial standards. And all the executive producers find in Grierson's cross-country recruiting and promotional forays a sensitivity to the positive potential of Canada's regional nature, and thus can interpret Regionalization as the final lap in the fulfilment of one of Grierson's most cogent formulations of the Film Board's mandate: to "see Canada and see it whole."

This remarkable feature of Regionalization's development to date — four distinct orientations, each consistent with Grierson's early documentary conception — would seem to augur well for Region- alization's potential contribution to the Film Board's overall pro- gramme. It suggests the continuity of a rich tradition enriched by new creative impulses. It promises unity in diversity. For example, the overseas orientation of both the Atlantic and the Pacific Studios revives and adapts the Film Board's early internationalism. Largely suppressed after the war, this internationalism lay dormant for two decades. It re-emerged in the sixties, in films like *Bethune* and *Memorandum*. Even then, a film shot overseas was required to have "Canadian content." This persisting inhibition is doubly ironic, because some of the Film Board's very best documentaries have been international in scope, and nowhere else in our increasingly troubled world is the phrase "global village" (invented by a Canadian) heard more frequently than in Canada. Even if the overseas films of the Atlantic and Pacific Studios should remain limited in aim, they might legitimize once and for all the Film Board's right to demonstrate an interest in the world outside Canada.

Another example of Regionalization's creative potential is in pro- gramming for national audiences. One criticism of the Film Board in recent years has been its alleged insularity from the nation as a whole. Just as the French-Canadians in the fifties argued that the job of interpreting Quebec should not be left to English-Canadians, filmma- kers and other people in the anglophone regions have maintained that career civil servants based in Montreal cannot authentically interpret the Maritimes, the Prairies, Ontario, or the West Coast. The establishment of a French-language production unit in the fifties, then a second one, and finally a separate French production branch, was acompanied by a spate of films which presented a far richer, truer interpretation of Quebec than the films made earlier. By the same token, the champions of Regionalization insist that regional films will be more vital and truthful than films made at headquarters about substantially regional subjects. Those who make this claim will find corroboration from the confederation series if the rest of the films match *Empty Harbours, Empty Dreams*, a film whose evident authenticity would be inconceiva- ble had the film been made by Montreal-based filmmakers.

In addition to its thematically Griersonian features, Regionalization seems to retrieve a principle of organizational strategy central to Grierson's thinking: staff impermanence. In his analysis of the Motion Picture Bureau's ossification, Grierson identified "the permanence of its staff'' as central to this process. He believed that permanent employment ran counter to creativity and commitment. Those NFB filmmakers who were especially needed during Grierson's wartime reign were kept on by a succession of three-month contracts. Within the past ten years or so, the Film Board has increasingly been chided for its permanent payroll, which eats away an increasing percentage of the Film Board's budget. Even within the Board, staff permanence has come to be viewed by many as detrimental to the Board's creative vigour. The regional studios' reliance on local independent filmmakers reintroduces the principle of job impermanence, although only partially (the executive producers are permanent employees; some studios have other permanent filmmakers on their staff, and two studios hope to lure more staff filmmakers out to their regions), and in a somewhat different form (generally the contracts between studios and independent filmmakers represent agreements between equals, which the wartime contracts certainly did not).

But the promises of Regionalization are matched by perils, for there is a sense in which the positive thrusts of Regionalization necessarily threaten the life-blood of the organization which spawned it. This paradoxical feature is what makes Film Board Regionalization, like the political regionalization of Canada which it so closely parallels, an adventure both daring and reluctant, the outcome of which could be either a new array of creative centres or a disastrous Balkanization of a rich, unique tradition.

What was particularly strong about Grierson's concept of Canadian documentary, especially around the time of the Film Board's birth and early development, was his sense of wholeness. There are at least two connotations to ''wholeness'': comprehensiveness and integrity. It is unremarkable for something to be ''whole'' if the range of its elements is severely restricted. And something is not necessarily ''whole'' if it is merely complete, if it is a collection lacking any underlying significant structure. Grierson's concept had both. His definition of documentary as ''the creative treatment of actuality'' equally emphasized structure and comprehensiveness, and his idea of the Film Board programme embraced a stunning variety of forms and purposes, yet sought to relate each and every film to a broader, overall purpose. When Grierson defined the Film Board's purpose as being to ''see Canada and see it whole,'' he did not mean that the vision be merely complete, i.e., representative of Canada's diversity, but that also it forge a unity. What that ''unity'' was may never have been seriously examined, and perhaps never fully achieved, but it remained as an ideal; and it certainly seems to have manifested itself, however elusively, in the development, over time, of the Film Board documentary tradition, in a continual process of increasing the range of "actuality" and the reach of "creativity," or structure.

While Regionalization promises to expand the range of the Film Board's ideal of "wholeness," it threatens the unity of the ideal. This is not a flaw in the concept of Regionalization, but a necessity. If Regionalization did not pose such a threat, it would not be genuine. All important advances in the Film Board documentary have involved similar threats to the integrity of the whole; Regionalization threatens it by definition.

Tension between these two poles of "wholeness" pervades the interaction among Film Board headquarters in Montreal, the regional studios, and the independent filmmakers, groups, and companies who now make almost all the NFB regional films. It is present at all levels of interaction, in questions of budgets, questions of administration, and questions of aesthetics.

Official Film Board policy is that fifty percent of all NFB production occurs in the regions.[8] In times of austerity, when the overall Film Board budget fails to keep pace with inflation, the development of regional production obviously affects production at headquarters. In 1978, when the government cut the Film Board's overall budget, the Board of Governors voted to keep the budget for regional production intact. This raised the ire, and paranoia, of headquarters' filmmakers. The regional studios, acknowledging that the strength of headquarters was threatened by this, jointly offered to transfer a substantial portion of their allocation back to Montreal. NFB management rejected the figures, but did approve a smaller rollback in the regional budget, making the headquarters deficit less severe.

Despite the regional studios' attempt at compromise, headquarters' filmmakers still bristle at the very economics of regional production. At headquarters, only about twenty percent of a film's costs are for outside goods and services — travel, film stock, per diems, etc. "Inside" costs — personnel, facilities, overhead — constitute the rest of the budget. In the regions, however, about seventy percent of a film's costs are outside costs. But the regional studios can convert the same basic facts into an argument that the true inefficiency lies in maintaining such a large and underused capability in Montreal. Regional executive producers can point out that although their outside costs are proportionally higher their overall budgets are lower. They can argue that their higher outside costs are more than offset by their savings in inside costs. As for the underused capability in Montreal — the labs, the equipment, the facilities — the solution is, according to one regional executive producer, to sell it off.

But a number of independent filmmakers, in turn, have developed ambivalent attitudes toward the Film Board's regional presence. Many of them had thought of Regionalization as just another funding opportunity, but Regionalization has turned out to be a little more complex than that. A Winnipeg filmmaker says:

> One thing about Regionalization that pisses off independents is that with the NFB in hard times cash-wise, they are essentially *competing* with us for money from provincial governments and foundations. Independents resent this deeply.

Independents also resent the paper entanglements that regional NFB production entails. The independents are used to working under commercial contracts or on grants. The NFB paperwork may irritate the regional studio staffs, but at least they continue to receive their pay-cheques. For the independents, however, delays in the processing of productions affect their ability to pay the rent, and sometimes to eat. Regional filmmakers have had to take out bank loans to continue functioning while payments on NFB contracts slowly worked their way through the administrative maze.

Regional executive producers are caught between the needs of the independent filmmakers and the demands of headquarters. An executive producer notes:

> Any proposal that originates here has to be sent to the programme committee in Montreal. It won't be sent back until the programme committee acts. Often I have to fly to Montreal in order to get something approved or accomplished. All in all, we need at least a month's lead time for anything, and the *waste* — the money, the travel, the time — is considerable.

Another executive producer remarks that although every project his studio has submitted has been approved, "In each case it took months and months to *get* it approved."

Even headquarters suffers. John Spotton, the current coordinator for regional production, explains:

> The work's being done out there, but approval of projects and financial matters is all done out of Montreal. So there's a *lot* of paper.

In a memorandum favourably reviewing the progress of Regionalization, Colin Low has eleborated on this bureaucratic burden:

> The National Film Board at the centre is a very complex organization. . . .
> The stresses at the centre get transmitted, if not amplified, at the regional

level. The stresses at the regional level are almost impossible to transmit to the centre with any degree of effect and absolutely *no* modification of procedure. It is impossible to achieve a delegation of fiscal responsibility because of the pyramidal levels of responsibility at the centre and their relationship to the treasury board. It is impossible to achieve greater autonomy of programming because of the jealousy of the Programme Committee in relation to its function. (This programme committee evolved in order to secure the rights of creative individuals in relation to the limitations of management and is not adjusted easily.)

... The heavy use of contracts in the regions and the necessity of contract approval at headquarters is one problem. The amount of paperwork at all levels of activity ... is another. There are many others. This is standard regional/headquarters bureaucracy, but agonizing when you, as a regional executive producer, are faced with the mythology of the efficiency and "superiority" of the "private sector" ... .[9]

Of these problems, the key one, according to John Taylor, is the programme committee, which

is at the centre but has no representatives from the regions. They try to assess filmmakers, subjects, projects without knowing much about the particulars. They don't know the *context* of the subject for the studio. Their decisions, as a result, are sometimes quite arbitrary. For example, we wanted to make a film called *Danny and Eleanor*, a film about two key characters in the 1979 Yukon federal election. This was scuttled by headquarters. Someone on the programme committee had "heard from a friend" that these two characters were not very interesting or important.

In an attempt to alleviate the problem, George Pearson, the director of the programme committee, issued a memorandum recommending significant changes in programming procedure. For some years programme committee guidelines had stipulated that no project could be approved without a detailed proposal, a final budget, a shooting and editing schedule, and several other documents or certifications. This was despite the fact that each project had to be approved by the filmmaker's executive producer (whether regional or headquarters) before it could be submitted to the programme committee. In Pearson's view:

This approach has ... two serious weaknesses: ... executive producers must make a separate appearance before the committee for each item — a particularly difficult situation for the regions — and the committee is constantly forced to consider individual items, ad-hoc, without the benefit of a larger context of overall programme plans and objectives within which they can deliberate.[10]

Pearson goes on to propose that each studio present an *annual* programme of well thought-out *ideas* rather than a detailed proposal for each film.

Pearson's proposal manages to relate the mainly administrative frustrations of the regional executive producer to the primarily aesthetic issue of programme coherence. It would also provide him the time and space first to think out his regional programme for the next year or so and then compare it with those of the other executive producers and test it against the critical scrutiny of the programme committee. Such a procedure would seem to be closer in spirit than the current one to the philosophical attitude behind Regionalization, an attitude which calls for a collaboration among equals rather than an orchestration directed by some (resented) central authority. *Empty Harbours, Empty Dreams* suggests that meaningful programme coherence is within the reach of such an approach. Moreover, if the rest of the confederation series matches this film, then Regionalization will have demonstrated that it can achieve meaningful coherence in a format which historically has been difficult for the Film Board: the series. A flaw in the Film Board's approach to series has been that typically a series idea is thought up by somebody for the wrong reasons, who defines it too rigidly, then assigns or recruits filmmakers to make individual films. The confederation series seems to have escaped the pitfalls. It has a common subject which filmmakers should feel deeply about. Each individual project has enjoyed the protection of an executive producer sympathetic to its point of view. No single authority controls the series. Confederation was an obvious theme, but already regional studios are planning a second series, this one built around the North American Energy Plan, a theme rich in implications and issues for every region, for Canada, and for the United States and Mexico.

But as promising as *Empty Harbours, Empty Dreams* is, there is also something disturbing about it. Its craftsmanship is well below the level achieved by the Film Board's best work. The Atlantic Studio, of course, wants to train its own filmmakers, for reasons which are defensible; perhaps the craftsmanship will come in time. Nevertheless, the question is raised: is the new relevance which Regionalization may bring to the Film Board's documentary necessarily tied to a regression in craftsmanship? Or, in Grierson's terms, will this new aspect of "actuality" opened up by Regionalization involve a forfeiture of "creativity"? Is such a trade-off inevitable?

It is Regionalization's almost total reliance on talent from the local free-lance markets that raises doubts about its ability to extend and revitalize the Film Board's documentary tradition, to keep it on the leading edge. Not only does Regionalization rely on these markets; it also intends to serve them. One of Regionalization's avowed purposes is to create employment opportunities. Although the establishment and growth of the National Film Board generated thousands of employment opportunities, this was never its goal. Its purpose was to create opportunities to serve an ideal. This sense of purpose, however difficult to pinpoint, was, as Grierson later remarked, "at the heart of the matter."[11] The later development of Unit B, the Québécois filmmakers, the best of the Pool System, and Challenge for Change all involved at least some measure of commitment to something "outside oneself." The comparative lack of bold reference in the official rhetoric of Regionalization to an exterior ideal worries some of the Film Board's old hands. John Taylor, who speaks enthusiastically about the programme's potential, also warns:

> There is a real danger that "regionalization" could become synonymous with "privatization." It could lead to commercialization. Yes, it could become just a job-creation project. It is a serious danger.

Although the programme's reliance on free-lancers seems to echo Grierson's antipathy towards permanent payrolls, the comparison is misleading in at least two ways. Most of Grierson's recruits had little or no film experience before reporting to the NFB. They were bright and broadly educated. They were idealistic. But of film they knew nothing. Grierson and his cohorts immersed them into the craft of filmmaking almost immediately. The education was total. The wartime NFB was a boot camp for filmmakers, all trained to serve a national and aesthetic ideal. By contrast, most of the free-lancers participating in the regional programme already have achieved competence in filmmaking. They've been trained in either the private or the grant-getting sector. They are beyond their impressionable years as craftsmen. When they enter contracts with the NFB, they do so with far more cockiness than did the raw recruits of the Grierson era. Conversely, the charismatic authority exercised by the Grierson-led NFB is almost non-existent in the regional studios, which some perceive as little more than outposts of a tired institution. It is therefore easy for the regional filmmaker to regard the NFB regional studio as "just another funding source."

But despite the free-lancer's comparative strength vis-à-vis the regional studio, he does not enjoy the security of the permanent employee at headquarters. Grierson feared this security, but it seems to have been a necessary condition for the Film Board's most innovative documentary work. The Film Board began making prototypal documentaries only after job security had been won. And although the Film Board has always made use of free-lance talent, almost every truly innovative Film Board documentary has been made by permanent employees or by teams of filmmakers led by permanent employees, filmmakers secure enough to take the extra time needed to turn an ordinary film into a great one, or the political risk necessary for turning a safe film into a daring one.

Regional filmmakers escape not just the vices of a large centralized filmmaking operation, but also the virtues. It is possible to take any truly major Film Board achievement, for any period, and trace its genesis to a variety of contributing sources almost all existing within the huge complex now in Montreal. Filmmakers working at headquarters inevitably, even if in spite of their own inclinations, absorb a tradition of film craftsmanship which may range in its expression from a variety of perspectives on a single cut to a broad philosophical frame of cinematic reference. Even if they do it reluctantly or unconsciously, young filmmakers in Montreal can sift through this plethora of ideas and approaches and discover what works for them. They can do this only because there are hundreds of skilled people at headquarters and because it is very difficult to make very many films without confronting a number of them. Like it or not, the filmmaker employed at headquarters is forced to learn. But the filmmaker working on a regional contract can strike a "take-it-or-leave-it" attitude toward the Film Board tradition, and thus miss out on the creative tension associated with most of the Film Board's best documentary work.

The success of Regionalization may depend on its ability to reproduce and maintain the sometimes stressful dynamic that has always operated between the Film Board's cumulative tradition and the energy and freshness which new filmmakers bring to it. One Film Board veteran who seems to perceive the issue in this way is Colin Low:

> There is an essential symbiotic relationship between the regions and headquarters. Much of the activity, transference of learning, co-production, training and information exchange will not take place with a partisan approach to regional activity. The reason the regional experiment has worked is that it has had a professional umbrella, a sounding board, some practical help when a film gets in trouble, and standards to aim at. The situation is paradoxical. There must be more regional freedom and the accountability pushed outwards to gain simple administrative efficiency. If we are to make substantial improvements in quality, standards must continue to be set by headquarters and the interaction between regions and headquarters increased, if anything. . . . Regional executive producers urge me to help establish a firmer delegation of responsibility . . . to the regions, yet they are also loath to cut themselves off from the full range of goods, services, talent and advice and cooperation at the NFB headquarters.[12]

In Low's view, the burden of extending the tradition falls heavily on the regional executive producer. There's a widespread feeling at headquarters that the regional studios should be reinforced with additional staff filmmakers from Montreal. The Ontario Studio's Arthur Hammond, who directed the *Corporation* series and then the programme committee before moving to Toronto, shares this view:

> My own feeling is that Regionalization could perpetuate the tradition, especially if there were more staff people down here, so we could exercise some influence.

In other regional studios, however, the importance of headquarters is not assumed so readily. John Taylor complains that

> headquarters regards itself as the brain trust, but the fact remains that you can't get an honest interpretation of a nation from an English-speaking ghetto in a French-speaking province. There are creative, energetic filmmakers in Vancouver with a strong feeling for the role of the Film Board.

Rex Tasker takes an even stronger position:

> Our philosophy is to train the regional people, not to import filmmakers from Montreal. We're developing our *own* competent filmmakers from scratch, and we'll develop our *own* critical mass.

Mike Scott would like to lure more staff filmmakers to the Prairie Studio, but he sees some value in his inability to get them to relocate:

> Maybe it's a benefit. We have had to do it ourselves. We've learned to be self-reliant, innovative, to work within resources.
>
> Out here, the Film Board becomes a community, not an institution. It's much healthier. We're not insulated. We're not protected, either. So you really get a stronger sense of what the Film Board is all about.
>
> There is really a much closer relationship with the film community as a whole here.

All the regional executive producers share Scott's desire to integrate their studios with the local film communities, but their ability to establish close relationships seems inversely proportional to the size and strength of the local film industry that existed before the Film Board arrived on the scene. In Atlantic Canada, where very little film work was being done before Regionalization, the relationship seems closest. Tasker has had the opportunity to re-apply, forty years later, Grierson's approach to training. By contrast, in Toronto the relationship is weakest, and the job of building it is hardest.

The movement toward identification by the regional studios with their local film communities may be the most promising trend in Regionalization. If the regional studios become identified with the local film communities, then they can reproduce, if in a different guise, those apparently essential organizational characteristics that Regionalization so far has threatened to undermine. For one thing, such an identification would allow the studio to expand, if not officially. An NFB-oriented "critical mass" might develop. This critical mass could serve as a matrix for the formation of filmmaking teams committed to strengthening their ability to do serious documentary work, and perhaps more able to do it. For another, a true community, confident of its roots and determined to survive and develop, should help compensate for the lack of federally ensured job-security. And finally, such a film community seems more likely to generate an ideal of service, however the community defines it, than a film "community" that is really just a film industry. In this way, Regionalization could become more than "just another job-creation project." It could constitute a genuine extension of the Film Board's reach.

Such a move, however, is likely to encounter resistance from some of the local film communities, especially in the matter of aesthetics. Colin Low has observed:

> There is a specific quality in the best work of the National Film Board that is not easy to transmit to younger people or to people experienced in commercial films. It is this quality of maturity which can criticize or celebrate the circumstances in the films so that the result is ... the discipline of a superior cinematic journalism, theatre and art. Only this kind of expression has any hope of forming an answer to the high density, predominately commercial, expensive — often cynical — international media. I don't see us responding with more and more "production values" and glossy expensive product, but with an expression of faith in our own roots and experience, honestly and passionately and inventively portrayed. That requires a lot of energy, faith and commitment....[13]

With reference to this "specific quality," a regional filmmaker complained to an NFB representative in 1979 that

> you have a "house style," but we're not interested in that. You also tell us the subject. We're not interested in that. We want to make the films *we* want to make.

A Prairie filmmaker says:

> The NFB is very pratriarchial. Do it their way or not at all. They put a great deal of direct and indirect pressure on the local community. Even their way of spending so much time on a film can exercise its own kind of tyranny, because you're *not* working to a deadline, and you've got all that footage. This looks great to the outsider, but it becomes a real trap. One of our people has been editing a twenty-minute film for thirteen months. They will endlessly argue over an interlock.

A Toronto filmmaker predicts that the Ontario Studio

> will be having more involvement in the projects. I don't particularly welcome that. It's good perhaps for the younger, inexperienced filmmakers, but I don't need it. To me, the NFB is just another funding source.

A Vancouver filmmaker says that there is some value in the NFB tradition, but adds murkily that "you have to realize where it's coming from." Mike Jones, a filmmaker from St. John's, Newfoundland probably puts the case against the NFB tradition most articulately:

> Our feeling for the last few years is that the NFB deteriorated to the point where the films coming out are basically products of the *institution*. The institutional "touch" shows up in all the films. By the time an idea emerges from the NFB as a film, the film feels like every *other* film coming out of there.

Although the "institutional touch" which Jones resents is what has made the Film Board unique in the world, it is not necessary that filmmakers stand in awe of it. It is only necessary that they deal with it, and take from it what they can. There are favourable signs in every region that lasting and genuinely creative collaboration between the NFB and the film communities may develop. Jack Long worked at the post-war NFB in Ottawa before returning to his native west coast. In his assessment:

> Regionalization is working very well here. It's not a closed shop. Anyone with ideas is listened to. Almost all the films made out of this office are from ideas brought in by outsiders. They all like to work with the Film Board. They like the freedom from the commercial constraints, artistically speaking, and also with regards to content.

In Winnipeg, Tom Fletcher, a frequent critic of the NFB, says:

> Without the Film Board here ... well, its presence has meant that the support industries have grown up much more than they could have otherwise. We now have a full-service sixteen-millimetre lab, for example. We wouldn't have that without the NFB.

Don McBrearty is an established Toronto free-lancer who is working on his second project with the Ontario Studio:

> I just got an investigate from them to research a subject I'm extremely interested in. It's a big social issue. It will take a year or more to make. As critical as I often may be of the Film Board, I'm probably one of the few filmmakers in Canada who can look forward to spending a year or more on a film idea I really care about.
>
> The Film Board, despite its bureaucracy, definitely has a place. The private industry is just dreadful.

Ramona MacDonald is a member of the Atlantic Filmmakers' Cooperative. Of the NFB Atlantic Studio, she says:

> It's a very open place.... When we need help, they always help us, on our *own* projects, not just Film Board projects. They give us advice and provide technical resources.
>
> When the Film Board finished criticizing my film [*Sarah Jackson*], it sort of came back the same film I had, but much better.

196

> The Film Board couldn't be replaced. We often criticize it, but we need
> it. We'd die without it.

It is often much easier to perceive the problems and the potential of a
new idea than it is to see how the problems might be overcome and the
potential realized. It may very well be that new constellations of
creative commitment will emerge from one or more of the regions. One
historical fact favouring Regionalization is that the Film Board has
usually managed to keep itself more or less "on level with the problems
of the time," as Grierson urged documentary filmmakers to do in the
thirties. Canada's biggest political "problem of the time" is, of course,
regionalism. The matter of its solution may be one area in which
regional studios and regional filmmakers will find some common
ground. NFB critic Mike Jones seems to be echoing Rex Tasker when
he observes:

> Canada as we knew it in 1976 — since the Parti Québécois came to power
> in Quebec — is gone. The old glue doesn't work any more. We have to
> find again what binds us together. To be viable, the Film Board has to
> pursue this.

There is therefore a sense in which, regardless of the problems and
risks involved in regionalizing production, the Film Board has to pursue
it to the end. The Film Board can't avoid this challenge without going
against its own tradition of keeping "level with the problems of the
time."

Perhaps Regionalization is beginning to succeed. *Empty Harbours,
Empty Dreams* shows that regional studios can employ the toughness
introduced to the NFB aesthetic by the Québécois filmmakers. *Nails*,
from the Pacific Studio, was an Academy Award nominee for 1980,
which demonstrates that the professionalism present since 1939 can be
transmitted to the regions. Perhaps genuine innovation will come in
time. Ron Dick, who spent a career at the Film Board, sees perhaps a
more basic cause for optimism:

> You know, the proof that Regionalization has *something* is this: I know
> almost all the headquarters people. I know the regional producers.
> Recently I saw a screening of regional films, but when the credits streamed
> by, there was hardly a name I recognized. The films were all of high
> quality. So there's talent out there.

12
WEEDPATCH IN A HUNGRY WORLD: THE FILM BOARD IN THE EIGHTIES

In 1964 the Film Board reminded Grierson of "a musk-ox, maddened by its own perfume." The challenges that filmmakers were posing to the organization's structure, purpose, and tradition were confident, even arrogant, ones. Although these challenges led to excesses and failures, they also widened the aesthetic scope of the Film Board documentary by bringing both the filmmaker, and broad political concerns within the range of permissible actuality. On balance, they were creative. The Challenge for Change programme, although created in part as a reaction against the excesses of the sixties, added a new dimension to the Film Board documentary: no longer were the social concerns in a film interpreted solely by the government or the filmmaker, but now, in a large part, by citizens themselves. Whereas the self-expressive trend turned the filmmaker into part of the actuality, Challenge for Change made the subjects into creators. With Regionalization, the Film Board appears to be extending its reach in yet another direction — *laterally*, so as to bring the work of a growing, dispersed independent film community at least partially within the Film Board's tradition.

By the end of the seventies, just about anything, aesthetically, seemed possible at the Film Board. Its unequalled heritage of technical and professional craftsmanship was at the disposal of a similarly unmatched variety of approaches and attitudes toward the documentary art — not to mention other film arts, such as animation. The nineteen-seventies saw the emergence not only of such films as *Cree Hunters of the Mistassini*, *Action* and *Reaction*, the *Corporation* series, *L'Acadie l'Acadie*, and *Nell and Fred*, but also a number of other distinguished films drawing upon the experimentation of the sixties — Mike Rubbo's *Persistent and Finagling* and *Waiting for Fidel*, Martin Defalco and

Willie Dunn's *The Other Side of the Ledger*, Bruce Moir's *Mr. Symbol Man*, Tony Ianzelo and Boyce Richardson's *North China Commune* and *North China Factory*, Torben Schioler and Ianzelo's *High Grass Circus*, Don Brittain's *Henry Ford's America* and *The Dionne Quintuplets*, John Kramer and Brittain's *Volcano*, Mike McKennirey's *Atonement*, Martin Duckworth's *Accident*, and Albert Kish's *Los Canadienses* and *Paper Wheat*.

The aesthetically spartan films of Kathleen Shannon's *Working Mothers* series generated a wide interest across Canada, and helped launch a Film Board studio emphasizing the needs of female audiences and filmmakers. Bonnie Sherr Klein's portrait of a woman struggling through a mid-life crisis, *Patricia's Moving Picture*, came out of the women's studio, as did Beverly Shaffer's marvellously tough-minded but good-natured films on Canadian children, such as *My Friends Call Me Tony* and the Oscar-winning *I'll Find a Way*.

These films, and many others, would seem to suggest that the art of the Film Board documentary emerged from the seventies in an extremely healthy state. The output of the seventies includes several films which should find their niche in the history of documentary and innumerable others of the first rank which help complete that "whole picture" of Canada of which Grierson once spoke. Perhaps in no other decade has the Film Board produced such a variety of excellent documentaries addressing so wide a range of social, political, economic, and personal problems.

And yet, as the Film Board enters the eighties it is plagued by organizational and individual self-doubt. The quiet craftsmanship of Unit B, the reckless confidence of the early Québécois filmmakers, the assertiveness of the younger members of the Pool, the stridency of the early-seventies Québécois dissenters, the certitude of social purpose behind Challenge for Change all seem to have dissolved into a general (if by no means universal) dispiritedness. There are dire predictions of the Film Board's imminent demise. The government wants to get rid of it, some say. Private producers are another threat. Many filmmakers at headquarters perceive Regionalization as a ruse to dispossess the Film Board. Others view it as a hapless floundering for political survival. Some believe the Film Board will eventually become little more than a distribution agency or a film school, and the filmmakers seem to have little will to resist the real and imagined threats to the Film Board's future. A filmmaker who has made some outstanding documentaries sighs that the NFB is "a hotbed of mediocrity — me, too, I'm mediocre." Another remarks, "We're essentially a boring bunch of people, and that's why our films are so boring." Another offers that "if

The Film Board keeps making films, it's because nobody knows how to stop it.''

Perhaps the *Internal Study Report* of 1968, initiated in response to austerity and increasing unmanageability, signalled the coming crisis of confidence with a quote from the Book of Job:

> He putteth forth his hands upon the rock; he overturneth the mountains by the roots. He cutteth out rivers among the rocks; and his eye seeth every precious thing. He bindeth the flood from overflowing; and the thing that is hid bringeth he forth to light. But where shall wisdom be found? And where is the place of understanding?[1]

Some factions at the Film Board seem to think the place of understanding lies in documents, which proliferated in the seventies, prompting one filmmaker to muse, "I guess when you've lost your sense of mission you need an evaluation." At an English Production Branch meeting called for the purpose of self-criticism, someone suggests a need for more research. A filmmaker retorts:

> I don't think the Film Board lacks research. I think the Film Board lacks visionaries. We're quite well equipped to take a rational, moderate, responsible approach to important problems. I'm not denigrating that. It's important. But I get fed up with all this soberness, sick of all this responsibility.

The respect some filmmakers have for documents is only slightly less than their respect for documentaries. "If we were any good," says one, "we'd be in Hollywood." A filmmaker whose Film Board career has been particularly distinguished says:

> Documentary itself will never counterbalance the terrible opiate of media in society. People have not begun to realize the soporific powers of media as a life-destroying force — hypnotic, blinding, time-consuming, and death-engendering. . . . I would like to see a revolt against media itself. I would like to see a smashing of the television sets. That sounds fascist in implication — it is meant to be the opposite. I hate to see people "hooked" on such an artificial system of impressions.

Another filmmaker suggests, in seriousness:

> I don't know if we should make so many films. We work too hard. The old protestant work-ethic trip. Maybe the solution is just to sit around, doing nothing. Absolutely nothing.

There are those who consider the Film Board finished as a creative organization. They would attribute its exhaustion to the most recent wave of austerity, to the organization's bureaucratic overload, to its leadership, or to its age. But as Nietzche warned those quick to assess well-being, "Health and disease — be careful." That the Film Board is troubled there is no doubt; the causes and significance are not

200

necessarily so obvious. The Film Board has endured periods of official austerity at least twice before. The troublesome bureaucratic half of its structure surfaced during the Second World War. And the Film Board was "old," as creative filmmaking organizations go, by 1950. The Film Board's present crisis is not so easily explained.

A factor in the Film Board's vitality over the years has been its responsiveness to the issues of the wider culture. But this wider culture shows symptoms of doubt and dispiritedness, a disintegrating frame of reference, a dissolving consensus of values, of confusion and withdrawal. These symptoms find expression in a wide range of commentators. Norman Podhoretz, editor of *Commentary*, says this of western culture:

> There is no longer a consensus as to what is good, what is bad, what is important, what is minor, what is significant, what is trivial, and how one tells the difference.[2]

Susan Sontag puts it more baldly:

> This civilization is at an end, and nothing we do will put it back together again.[3]

The most relevant interaction between the Film Board's malaise and that of the wider culture occurs in documentary, the Film Board's chief activity. Curiously, the symptoms of a culture coming apart at the seams find expression at the leading edges of what little contemporary thinking there is about documentary. In recent years, a growing dissatisfaction with documentary and its assumptions — or what are perceived to be its assumptions — has been articulated in a variety of places.[4] The assumptions questioned include the value and even the possibility of objective truth, the notion that there is such a thing as social progress, the confidence in an informed citizenry's ability to make wise civic choices, the assumption that there is a difference between fact and fiction, and the assumption that the documentary filmmaker is capable of knowing anything worth communicating.

Thus the troubled Film Board seems to bear a close relationship with a troubled culture through the equally troubled medium of documentary. This unhappy triangle suggests that, although the Film Board's present difficulties could be analyzed conventionally, from a political, economic, or managerial perspective, they can be approached as well from an aesthetic perspective. An aesthetic ideal preceded the Film Board and the organizational strategies and experiments informing its original design and its subsequent development.

Goethe remarked that "Genius is formed in quiet, character in the stream of human life." The two terms of Goethe's aphorism are analogous to the two key terms of art, or perhaps of any creative endeavour: the fashioning of order out of chaos. But Goethe's oberva- tion also helps us see that of all the major arts, documentary, or "the creative treatment of actuality" as Grierson defined it, may be, in at least one sense, the most difficult. The novelist, painter, poet, dramatist, composer, sculptor, or director of dramatic features gathers content for his art in "the stream of human life," but he can do so unobtrusively (even indirectly, through works others have produced: books, scripts, "properties," etc.), and he doesn't have to begin to give it shape until he's in the quiet of his den, or the security of his studio or roped-off location. The documentary filmmaker has to intrude into "the stream of human life," not only to get material, but even to begin to shape it. He has to enter the "blooming, buzzing confusion" of the social world both as an open-minded researcher — an explorer, a discoverer — and as an artist, a chooser of angles and compositions, of what to film and not to film. And because he interacts with, and depends on, citizens as citizens, his face-to-face encounter with the world carries strong moral obligations, both to his subjects, whose lives he may change, and to his audience, whose knowledge of the world he will affect. The debate over the confessional scene in *Blood and Fire* reflected in part the conflict between these two moral obligations, and most cases of censorship at the Film Board involve a measure of conflict between them, however they are interpreted.

Documentary's extreme dependence on "actuality" is the main source of its social relevance, but its relevance comes to nothing if the element of "genius" is absent, i.e., if there is no meaningful ordering of the thousands of pieces of "actuality" the filmmaker has gathered. And because so much of the ordering in documentary occurs on the spot and after the fact, the job of structuring documentary material can be an extremely difficult one. A film like *Memorandum*, or *Sad Song of Yellow Skin*, may take only a few weeks to shoot, but a year or more to edit.

Documentary's requirement that the filmmaker be both artist and citizen may be one reason why, out of the thousands upon thousands of documentaries that have been made since the invention of cinema, only a very few have been memorable, worth seeing more than once, if at all. More often than not, documentaries suffer from false order, the order supplied by a preconceived view of the world, by dogma, government policy, script, an overbearing commentary, a hesitance to encounter the subject, a narrowness in scope or timidity of purpose. Since the invention of lightweight equipment, however, the opposite kind of flaw has emerged: the failure to give order or meaning to the material, an uninspired stringing together of "relevant" direct cinema or *vérité* footage. These are the two common failures of most modern documentaries — order without full encounter, or encounter without order. Documentary, in which it is so easy to achieve a passable competence but so difficult to achieve genuine excellence, is a tough craft. Grierson probably was referring to the economics and politics of documentary, but he could have had in mind the aesthetics as well, when in the sixties, he described documentary as

> a hard game that breaks the hearts of all but the very tough man. . . . [Most of my American contemporaries had died.] I'm alive because I quit.[5]

What seems to differentiate the Film Board from all other documentary organizations is the degree to which the Film Board has managed to provide for both aspects of the craft. To an extent unequalled anywhere else, the Film Board has allowed for both the encounter and the ordering, for character and genius, for social commitment and formal pattern. At the Film Board, the filmmaker can choose his subject — not always, but often enough — and then take the time to become intimate with it, to explore it in depth. Free from serious personal financial worry, the filmmaker can take the year or two which may be required for fashioning a meaningful structure for the material he has gathered, and he can draw upon the vast resources of the Film Board — most importantly, its tradition — for aid.

Yet, to leave it at that would suggest that whatever success the Film Board has had in documentary is a result of giving the filmmaker time, money, footage, and advice, but otherwise leaving him alone. To the extent that this is true, it is only lately and sporadically — and accidentally — true. Where it is wrong, it is wildly wrong. The role of the filmmaker at the Film Board is far more complicated than that of a grant-recipient, and the function of the organization in the development of its documentary filmmakers is infinitely more complex than that of a funding agency.

Two intriguing facts point to the relative importance of the Film Board as a whole against that of the individual filmmaker employed there. In its forty-year history, never has a distinguished visiting filmmaker made a memorable documentary at the Film Board. Equally, never has a documentary filmmaker who developed within the Film Board, and achieved distinction there, done so well in documentary on the outside.

Thus the Film Board seems to function as a unique *system*, which talents developed under different conditions find inhospitable, and which talents developed within find indispensable. It's a hard system to penetrate, but a hard one to escape. Like Hawthorne's Pearl, the Film Board seems to be composed of elements "with an order peculiar to themselves." The Film Board has an organizational *identity*.

But this identity, like Pearl's, is elusive. The Film Board is a complex system that resists conventional systematic analysis. It is not easy to describe. Generalizations that may form as easily as soap bubbles are about as solid. The ancient Taoist principle that "the Way that can be described is not the Way" seems to apply to attempts to identify precisely what it is about the Film Board that accounts for its successes and perhaps its limitations. It seems necessary to explain the Film Board's development by reference to a number of partial truths which do not quite add up to the whole truth. A momentarily promising generalization soon generates its own contradiction.

Perhaps it would seem that the Film Board could be described in precisely those terms: as a series of creative contradictions. The polarity between "genius" and "character" has analogues in the "art" and "social responsibility" of Grierson's original aesthetic. During the war Grierson balanced his utilitarian, propagandistic emphasis by hiring abstract artists like Norman McLaren, whom Grierson called "the most important man on the staff." Similar oppositions can be identified throughout the Film Board's development. The polarity itself, however, becomes paradoxical, especially in essentials. For example, it is in part the Film Board's governmental basis, its public accountability, and its resulting bureaucratic core that require that its documentary work have social relevance, that it be socially responsible. But that same core fears and resents the depth of social encounter that filmmakers want to pursue, which may involve sensitive social or political issues, and which almost invariably requires a high shooting ratio, an unreliable budget, a long editing period, and, more often than not, utterly uncertain results.

There is a similar difficulty with the concept of a tension between "routine" and "charisma." The polarity helps illuminate many things, but not everything. For example, the establishment of permanent positions was *prima facie* a device that abetted routine. The idea of permanent positions ran counter to Grierson's thinking, which held that permanence breeds mediocrity. Although the eventual provision for permanent positions bred no small measure of mediocrity, it also provided space for the somewhat "charismatic" set of attitudes associated with most of the Film Board's most innovative documentary work.

It seems almost impossible to describe the Film Board — or rather that aspect of it which has made the organization great — without mixing the metaphors, and the suspicion arises that perhaps this resistance to systematization, to generalization, is somehow related to the Film Board's development and achievement. Indeed, *ambiguity* is the phenomenon that seems to occur over and over in the Film Board's history, especially at its key points. This ambiguity — and "ambiguity" implies not the lack of meaning but the observer's uncertainty, at the time, about what the meaning is — does not arise in a vacuum, but always in some sort of context — or, to put it another way, from a position of strength. It is this strength, in various manifestations, that *tolerates* the ambiguity. The sources of this strength seem to be several: the close governmental ties established at the outset and never completely relinquished; the strong mandate that gave the Film Board a monopoly on government film production and the power to interpret that mandate largely as it wished; the original charismatic energy inspired by Grierson and the war; the ample budget that allowed the Board to generate projects on its own initiative; the security from the personal economic worries so acute in the commercial film industry; relative freedom from market constraints; the sense of self-effacing discipline that Grierson inculcated in his young recruits; and, perhaps most of all, an aesthetic ideal deeply rooted in a sense of purpose. As Grierson wrote in 1965:

> A sense of purpose was certainly at the heart of the matter . . . and . . . still must be if the documentary film is to command wide and various public support and do justice to its aesthetic potential.[6]

The notion of "tolerance of ambiguity" may itself be too general (or too ambiguous) to unmix the metaphors, but it does appear capable of softening the differences, especially when applied to the crucial dynamic dimension of the Film Board, its development over time. What seems to have happened over the years is that the "ambiguity" that was in any particular era or area "tolerated" became, if productive, absorbed into the "tolerance." During the war, the operational principle of "banging them out and no misses" was tied to a propaganda strategy of seeing Canada "as a whole," which permitted the wide variety of films ranging from *Blitzkrieg* to *Four New Apple Dishes*. By the end of the war, this variety had been absorbed into the general notion of what the Film Board was. The variety of excellent production was probably the main reason for the Film Board's survival. It was now part of the "tolerance." In the nineteen-fifties, this context allowed the ambiguous (at the time) adventures of Unit B and of French production.

Eventually, as the value of Unit B's work became widely recognized, Unit B's "attitude toward the craft," its perfectionism-at-whatever-cost, was absorbed into the Board's mainstream. It became tradition. Similarly, the Québécois desire for cultural engagement and authenticity became absorbed into the general character of the Film Board's documentary work. By the end of the sixties, it was almost "routine" for a Film Board documentary to have a critical aspect. In the late seventies, Challenge for Change seemed to lose its momentum largely because its innovations, particularly its sensitivity to the effect of a film on its subjects' lives and to the added dimension that subject participation could bring to a film, spread through the work of the Film Board as a whole.

This process was not planned, but there was a guiding intelligence behind it, at the beginning. Defending the Film Board's censorship of *On est au coton* and *24 heures ou plus*, a producer who had been at the Board since the early war years repeated an old and unfortunately coarse joke — which, according to Sydney Newman, was Grierson's — as a metaphor for the Film Board's development overall:

> An old bull and a young bull were at the top of a hill. Down below were a bunch of cows. The young bull says to the old bull, "Hey, let's run down and screw one of those cows." The old bull replies, "No, let's *walk* down and screw them all."

Unpleasant as the parable may be to today's sensibility, it does describe the patient, shrewd development of the Film Board's documentary art, and it describes as well the Board's chief accomplishment — the variety of its achievement, the wholeness of its programme — which in turn creates the space for additional experiments and daring adventures.

But equally there is truth in another filmmaker's apparently contradictory observation that "the thing about the Film Board is that the individual filmmaker can separate himself psychologically from the organization." He can think of himself as a dissident from whatever he perceives to be the prevailing values at the Film Board. He doesn't have to identify with the Film Board. He can use the Film Board (apparently) for his own aesthetic ends, or other ends. And it is patently true that almost every notable advance in the art of documentary at the Film Board has been associated with the apparently "irresponsible" impatience of the young bull. Films such as *Paul Tomkowicz, Corral, Universe, City of Gold, Bûcherons de la Manouane, Normétal, Les raquetteurs, Very Nice, Very Nice*, the *Candid Eye* series, *Memorandum, Sad Song of Yellow Skin*, the *Corporation* series, and *Cree Hunters of Mistassini* broke some kind of rule or taboo. Some less successful but more outrageously "irresponsible" films blazed trails for others. As Blake observed, "The road to wisdom is paved with excess."

Thus the continual expansion of the tolerance of ambiguity, of the absorption of ambiguity into tolerance, of aesthetic innovation into tradition, could be seen as a creative conflict between the old bull, who represents prudence and custom, but also wisdom and tradition, and the young bull, who represents innovation and experimentation, courage and adventure, but also recklessness, selfishness and naïveté. When the situation is such that they keep talking to each other, and perhaps even more importantly keep listening to each other, the result is often an outstanding film. One particularly talented filmmaker has described his work in an analogous way. He says, "So far, I feel like I've been driving a car with one foot on the accelerator and the other on the brake." Being a young bull, he adds, "One of these days, I'd like to take my foot off the brake."

From the perspective of the Film Board as a developing organization, the dynamic of this creative interaction is described by Edward Markham's poem, "Outwitted":

> He drew a circle that shut me out —
> Heretic, rebel, a thing to flout.
> But Love and I had the wit to win:
> We drew a circle that took him in.[7]

From the perspective of the filmmaker successfully innovating within this tradition, T.S. Eliot's summation describes the dynamic as follows:

> What happens [to a developing artist] is a continual surrender of himself as
> he is at the moment to something which is more valuable. The progress of
> an artist is a continual self-sacrifice, a continual extinction of personality.[8]

But, of course, it is not "love" on the part of the Film Board, nor intentional self-effacement on the part of the individual filmmaker, that is the agent of this continual expansion of the scope of the Film Board's work. On the contrary, the Film Board, as an institution, does not often appreciate even its devoted employees. If anything, it abuses them. The Film Board's very origin, as Grierson himself admitted, owed much to an act of cruelty. Individual filmmakers, in turn, often regard the institution with contempt. They try to take advantage of it for their own ends, whether those ends involve fame, security, or an easy life. Dissension, abuse, and self-interest have marked the Film Board from the beginning. The Film Board's first experience with a "protest meeting" occurred in 1941, when the permanent employees from the Motion Picture Bureau demonstrated in support of Captain Badgley. It has periodically recurred ever since.

But protest meetings are only sporadic. Conflicts among small groups and individuals occur daily. Intense hatreds exist at the Film Board. Suspicions pervade, paranoia exudes. The Film Board, in recent years at least, resembles a large collection of individual monads, each with its own window on the world. A producer living in the upper middle-class, predominately anglophone district of Westmount condemns another producer for living in the suburbs, out of touch with the "people". The suburban producer, in turn, expresses disgust with filmmakers who have chosen to live in the country, an hour away, far outside "the mainstream of Canadian life." The rural filmmaker regards himself as being in the vanguard of the cultural revolution. A filmmaker complains that NFB filmmakers, who "once they walk into that door are set for life — for *life*," are all on "a security trip, sucking on the teat of Mother Film Board." But another filmmaker shudders that "something must be wrong when I go home every night and can't sleep because I worry about being fired." Another promising filmmaker quits because he is "afraid of the security."

Confusion, yes, but "health and disease — be careful." The observer of the Film Board is like Gulliver among the Brobdingnagians. From afar, the Brobdingnagian woman seems to Gulliver the most beautiful creature imaginable. Up close, climbing over the breasts of the gigantic creature, Gulliver is repelled by the leathery pores, the pungent odours, the beads of oily sweat. The observer's problem, like Gulliver's, is a matter of perspective. As he becomes familiar with the Film Board, he may forget what attracted him in the first place: those marvellous films. The character of the Film Board compounds the problem. The Film Board is so informal an organization that it wears its heart on its sleeve. It bares its pathologies to all but the most formal or myopic of observers. The Film Board is a very easy place to note idleness and unhappiness, but its productivity remains largely hidden. A filmmaker at work is either out on location or locked in his editing room. Creative collaboration occurs most often in the course of filming, planning, or editing, rarely in public arenas. And the filmmakers themselves can be inconsistent in their complaints. In almost the same breath, Donald Brittain says of the Film Board that "they bureaucratize you to death" and that "there's nowhere else in the world I could make the films I do."[9]

Creative organizations are not always harmonious. The Princeton Institute for Advanced Studies, for example, has been plagued by enormously petty, egocentric, backstabbing internal disputes couched in language of principle.[10] A similar phenomenon has been observed in the editorial offices of the *New York Times*.[11] Jealousies, selfishness, and other human foibles attended the discovery of the double helix.[12]

The Film Board is a nearly role-free, rule-free, structureless organization. This characteristic seems related to the Film Board's success. But the other side of the coin is that, in the words of one producer, "there is no protection, at any level in the so-called hierarchy, from stupidity, arrogance, or malice." It is an environment which "drives many to drink, and some to suicide." "There are," a filmmaker observes, "a lot of dead souls around this place." A filmmaker remarks that the stress in the organization is such that "We don't have a lot of angry old men — we have a lot of old drunkards." But then, what is immoral, when there are no longer any operable norms? What is arrogant, when there is no protocol? What is unfair, when there are no rules? And what is achievement, in a field such as art? And yet, whereas the documentary filmmaker working on the outside enjoys the comfort of knowing that only the extremely rare person can make outstanding documentaries commercially, the NFB filmmaker knows, deep down, that no matter how difficult working at the Film Board may at times be, the shortcomings in his work are ultimately his own. That fact can make documentary filmmaking at the Film Board tougher, psychologically, than it is on the outside, where much less is expected.

Thus the Film Board creates its own kind of jungle, in which the prudent easily can survive as job-holders but only the extremely fit can endure and develop as artists. It does not appear to be difficult, at the Film Board, to make a reasonably interesting, informative, entertaining, or useful documentary. But to take full creative advantage of the institution's vast resources — to innovate within its tradition — is terribly difficult. Eliot's observation that "tradition cannot be inherited, and if you want it you must obtain it by great labour" applies in a two-edged way at the Film Board. The filmmaker has to be extremely tough, both on himself and for himself. Otherwise, the tradition will either swallow him or reject him. His film will be either another competent but innocuous "goosing of the nostalgic gap" or something that lies in a can on a shelf, gathering dust. Grierson's remark, in 1964, that the Film Board was "not a playground" was prophetic in a sense he may not have intended.

The Film Board's creative but strenuous structural characteristics — role-freedom, rule-relaxation, informality, fluidity, dispersal of authority, goal-orientation — are not in themselves unique to the Film Board. Organizational theorists have noted them in other organizations. Recent theorists tend to favourably call such organizations "organic," as opposed to bureaucratic, formal, rigorously hierarchical, "mechanistic" organizations.[13] The implication is that such organizations resemble the individual organism.

In no way, however, does the Film Board resemble an organism. If any creature behaved like the Film Board, he would disintegrate into madness. An organism does not experience the conflicts among its elements that the Film Board experiences. An organism does not tolerate ambiguity in itself, at least not in significant amounts. In terms of the harmony of its elements, and the predictability of their performance, an organism is Prussian.

If the organizational structure of the Film Board is "organic," it resembles not an individual organism but an evolving ecosystem. There is a mathematical principle in systems analysis called "the law of requisite variety," which states that given any two systems "in competition," the more complex system, the one containing the greater variety, will, in the long run, win out.[14] The strength of the more varied system lies in its greater unpredictability — its ambiguity.

The law of requisite variety says that a weedpatch, if left alone, will overcome a cornfield.[15] Now the Film Board is to the traditional bureaucracy what the weedpatch is to the cornfield. The cornfield is orderly, everything is in rows, it can be measured and counted, it pulls no surprises, its purpose is determined by the farmer, it is monotonous, it requires tremendous attention, it is efficient — and it is eaten. The weedpatch, by contrast, is inefficient, disorderly, unpredictable, hard to control, and apparently useless. There is nothing neat about the weedpatch, but it is a place where flowers bloom and butterflies abound. You can't market it, but it enriches. Each visit turns up something new. A farmer might intentionally keep his weedpatch unploughed, for it is not a bad place to think over what to do with the other fields. The farmer might also sense that if all the world were a cornfield, we would all starve, that the weedpatch makes the cornfield possible, that it is nature's laboratory.

Thus the notion of tolerance of ambiguity can serve as a conceptual bridge between the "creative treatment of actuality," which is documentary as Grierson conceived it, and the "organization of creativity," which is the Film Board as Grierson originally structured it. Just as the development of the Film Board documentary has involved an ever-widening range of actuality (ugly, horrific, or alien as it may be) that can be brought into some meaningful order, the development of the Film Board has involved increasing decentralization, devolution of authority, role-freedom, and messiness of intraorganizational relationships. The two developments have been closely related to one another; they meet, metaphorically, in the creative tension between the old bull and the young bull. And what seems to constitute the strength that can tolerate and absorb this apparently endless ambiguity is central power informed by a deep sense of purpose.

If this sort of analysis has validity, then we can see that the Film Board's future creativity depends in part on the Film Board's ability to protect its weedpatch character. This may be difficult to do in a time of economic gloom. Government bureaucrats since 1939 have resented the Film Board's unruly nature, but they couldn't deny its productive, goal-oriented performance. Despite periodic attempts to rationalize the Film Board, the weedpatch was never fully subdued. As late as 1976, George Stoney, who after a distinguished career as an independent American documentary film director and producer appreciated the Film Board's uniqueness, could say, "I'm just glad the efficiency experts have never gotten hold of the Film Board."

But Stoney had completed his Film Board stint a few years earlier, and was unaware of the extent to which efficiency expertise was penetrating the Film Board. In the seventies, the Treasury Board, in an attempt to make government departments and agencies more efficient, introduced strategies that go by various names, such as OPMS (Operational Performance Measurement Systems), PPBS (Programme Planning and Budgeting Systems), and MBO (Management by Objectives).[16] The specific aims of such strategies are to clarify objectives, measure results, and accountability. Each government department is required to submit with its budget request a description of the results to be achieved. The anticipated results have to relate to national well-being. The department or agency is required to demonstrate that a need exists for the programme it proposes.

Despite all the anti-bureaucratic, "tough-minded" rhetoric associated with OPMS, PPBS, and MBO, they are classically bureaucratic phenomena. "Bureaucratic administration," Weber wrote, "means fundamentally the exercise of control on the basis of knowledge."[17] There is nothing wrong with that, except that OPMS, PPBS, and MBO demand knowledge that the Film Board *cannot possibly have* as long as it remains a creative, prophetic organization. It takes two or three years to design a programme, submit a budget, and get it approved. But the Film Board has to be able to respond quickly to vague ideas and intuitions the importance of which may be barely discernible at the time. *You Are On Indian Land* was organized overnight. *Waiting for Fidel* was arranged within weeks. At the beginning of a film project, and even during the editing, the filmmaker may still be unsure what his film is about. A novelist has said that he writes "in order to find out what I'm thinking"; an NFB filmmaker has said of one of his films:

> I did it all unconsciously. That was wrong. You need consciousness. But I don't know how to get that without *doing* it first. I can't work from rules that someone has taught me.

Films like *Memorandum*, *Jour après jour*, *Cree Hunters of Mistassini*, and *Sad Song of Yellow Skin* exist because the filmmaker could get money for the production without proving its ultimate contribution to the "well-being" of Canada. A filmmaker laments:

> You used to be able to get money to make a film ... and then justify it with a *good* film. Now you have to justify it first, before you can get the money.

There is no way that the Film Board can function as an "early warning device," as one filmmaker put it, under such a system if fully implemented. If the Film Board has to submit to the requirement of quantifying the future contribution of its films to the "well-being" of Canada, a great folly will have been committed. A shrewd organizational theorist, Charles Lindblom, has argued that in a dynamic system, you can't set quantifiable goals, policy-making is decentralized and disjointed, policy-makers respond incrementally to environmental events, and formal goals and formal analyses are not very important or helpful.[18] E.F. Schumacher has observed that

> to undertake to measure the immeasurable is absurd and constitutes but an elaborate method of moving from preconceived notions to foregone conclusions.[19]

And one of the century's greatest and most creative social activists, Gandhi, remarked that "he who is ever brooding over results often loses his nerve in the performance of duty."[20]

Although a Film Board accountant complains accurately that "the filmmakers don't even want to measure the *basics*," there is a danger even in measuring the basics. The Film Board has introduced a requirement that every "expenditure" be charged to a production number. Watching a film, for example, is considered an expenditure. This means (theoretically, at least) that filmmakers cannot screen a film unless it is directly related to an existing production. If they are between productions, or looking around for an idea, they can't screen a film. And even if they can charge a film screening to a production number, the procedure is elaborate and exhausting. People who measure things naturally want to make their job easy. It is a lot easier to measure

212

something if the process is so defined and distorted that it *generates* data. This requires data-generating structures, preferably so designed that the data arrive routinely at the measurer's in-basket. And so, as a harried producer notes:

> To see a film you first have to find out if a theatre is available. Whoever answers the phone never knows, so you walk up there and find out if a theatre is available. Then you have to go to the budget officer, who must have *two* numbers — a production number and then a work order, which the budget officer has to make out in quadruplicate. That is mailed to the theatre booking office. All this has to be done three days ahead!

The pressures to rationalize the Film Board take on many forms, but mostly they arise from economics and from the outside. The Film Board is not expensive. Its annual budget represents only about a dollar per Canadian, which in turn represents a pack of cigarettes, a gallon of gasoline, a third or less of the cost of one ticket to *Dressed to Kill*, *Apocalypse Now*, *Animal House*, or *Herbie Goes Bananas*. But large and established cultural institutions always have depended on the largesse of political power, and democracies can be among the stingiest, most resentful, and most short-sighted of political systems when the individuals with whom that power ultimately resides are worried about the cost of food, housing, transportation, education, cosmetics, clothes, and creature comfort. Such a polity, harried and harrassed, and morally confused, is unlikely to tolerate the weedpatches among it unless they can produce something unequivocably worth the loss in immediate gratification.

Thus, perhaps unfairly, the burden of protecting and sustaining the National Film Board of Canada as a creative institution falls primarily on the NFB itself. Filmmakers, technicians, and administrators need to regain that sense of purpose which originally was "at the heart of the matter." They have to recognize and meet the challenge filmmaker Michel Régnier posed to his union:

> Our film industry is reputed for a certain kind of documentary . . . and not for its respect for the well-being of its workers. The day I will have to make films with crews that act like American ones, I, unfortunately, will not make any more and a lot of filmmakers will be in my position.
>
> I am not saying this out of meanness or pettiness but in order to protect a certain way of thinking that makes Canadian cinema differ from the others.[21]

They need to prove, by example not rhetoric, the truth of Wolf Koenig's remark that

> "culture" is one of the most *practical* things we can have. It is style. It is purpose. It is something not for itself, but for something else.

Filmmakers need to take the sickness of the age as a challenge to their craft, to create from actuality. They need to recognize, with filmmaker Derek May, that "the human condition is up for grabs," and turn the malaise of the times into fodder for their work. They need to embrace the future with the boldness of a Colin Low, who notes that

> the era of fossil-fuel economy is coming to an end. The end might be apocalyptic. And yet, the sooner we get to the other side, the better. And it will be better, don't you think?

The Film Board should not shirk the responsibility implied by one of Grierson's mentors, Walter Lippmann, when he remarked, "Every complicated society has sought the assistance of special men, of augurs, priests, and elders," and not fear to try to tell the world where it's heading. Filmmakers need to return to that original conceptual lode, the idea of documentary as "the creative treatment of actuality," and mine it for what it's worth. They need to follow Auden's edict, and probe "the bottom of the night" in order to "teach the free man how to praise." And administrators have to let them do it.

This is a tall order, but if no effort is made to fulfil it, Canada will be the loser. As Grierson remarked in 1969, the Film Board was created

> to bring Canada alive to itself and to the rest of the world, it was there to evoke the strengths of Canada, the imagination of Canadians in respect of creating their present and their future ... and it is still there. The duty is still there.[22]

If this duty is not at least pursued, the irony will be great. In a country which for decades has been obsessed with national identity, there seems to be very little appreciation for the one institution that has developed a national art of international fame and import. You could write a solid history of any other art without a single reference to Canada, but you could not write a solid history of documentary without devoting whole chapters to Canada, perhaps more to Canada than to any other country. If this incredible history should come to a close, not only Canada, but the rest of the world, will be the poorer for it.

FOOTNOTES

CHAPTER ONE: A WILL AND A WAY

1. James Beveridge, *John Grierson Film Master* (New York: Macmillan, 1978), p. 238.
2. *Cinema Quarterly*, vol.2, no.1, Autumn 1933, p. 8.
3. Raymond Spottiswoode, *A Grammar of the Film: An Analysis of Film Technique* (London: Faber and Faber, 1935), pp. 284-9.
4. A. William Bluem, *Documentary in American Televison* (New York: Hastings House, 1965), pp. 14 and 46.
5. Jack C. Ellis, "The Young Grierson in America: 1924-1927," *Cinema Journal*, Fall 1968, p. 14.
6. Unless otherwise noted, the quotations used in this explication of Grierson's concept of documentary are from articles he wrote between 1931 and 1935, primarily his contributions to *Cinema Quarterly*, which began publication in Autumn 1932, and ceased publication (it was replaced by *World Film News*) in Summer 1935. Almost all of this material has been reprinted in John Grierson, *Grierson on Documentary*, ed. Forsyth Hardy (London, Faber and Faber, 1966).
7. "In Memory of W.B. Yeats," in *Collected Shorter Poems* (New York: Random House, 1975), pp. 141-3. The poem is dated 1939.
8. *Daedalus*, Spring 1960.
9. Posthumous note to *Will to Power*, quoted in Thomas Mann, *The Short Novels of Dostoevski* (New York: Dial Press, 1945), Preface.
10. Basil Wright, *The Long View* (London: Secker and Warburg, 1974), flyleaf.
11. Eva Orbanz, *Journey to a Legend and Back: The British Realistic Film* (Berlin: Volker Spiess, 1977), p. 32.
12. Elizabeth Sussex, *The Rise and Fall of British Documentary* (University of California Press, 1975), p. 96.
13. *Journal of the Society of Film and Television Arts* vol. 2, no. 4-5, (1972), pp. 5-6. Special issue on Grierson.
14. This version is from a speech Grierson gave at Poona, India, April 22, 1971. Sir Stephen Tallents, head of the Empire Marketing Board, was fond of the quotation also. Tallents' version is, "It is the artist alone in whose hands truth becomes a principle of action." See Stephen Tallents, "The Documentary Film," in *Nonfiction Film Theory and Criticism*, ed. by Richard Meran Barsam (New York: E.P. Dutton, 1976), p. 58.

15. Karl Mannheim, *Essays on the Sociology of Culture* (London: Routledge and Kegan Paul, 1967), p. 233.
16. Forsyth Hardy, *John Grierson: A Documentary Biography* (London: Faber and Faber, 1979), p. 51.
17. *Grierson on Documentary*, postscript.
18. Paul Rotha, *Documentary Diary: An Informal History of the British Documentary Film, 1928-1939* (London: Secker and Warburg, 1973), p. 283.
19. Sussex, *Rise and Fall*, p. 81.
20. Rotha, *Documentary Diary*, p. 269.
21. Evelyn Gerstein, "English Documentary Films," in *The Documentary Tradition*, ed. by Lewis Jacobs (New York: Hopkins and Blake, 1971), p. 113.
22. Harry Watt, q. in Sussex, *Rise and Fall*, p. 41.
23. Sussex, *Rise and Fall*, p. 54 (Cavalcanti) and p. 26 (Elton).
24. Harry Watt, *Don't Look at the Camera* (London: Paul Elek, 1974), p. 41.
25. Max Weber, *The Theory of Social and Economic Organization* (New York: Oxford University Press, 1947), pp. 358-63.
26. Rotha, *Documentary Diary*, p. 282.
27. Watt, *Don't Look at the Camera*, pp. 77-78.
28. John Grierson, "Last Interview," *Film Quarterly*, vol. 26, no. 1, Fall 1972, p. 29.
29. Arthur Calder-Marshall, *The Changing Scene* (London: Chapman and Hall, 1937).
30. Gerstein, "English Documentary Films," pp. 114-5.
31. Unnamed critic, q. in Orbanz, *Journey to a Legend and Back*, p. 147.
32. Arthur Calder-Marshall, *The Innocent Eye: The Life of Robert J. Flaherty* (Penguin Books, 1970), pp. 137-8. Calder-Marshall notes that each person he talked to told a different version of the story, but Paul Rotha (*Documentary Diary*, p. 52) corroborates the essence of Calder-Marshall's version. For another version, see Forsyth Hardy, *John Grierson: A Documentary Biography*, pp. 64-5.
33. Watt, *Don't Look at the Camera*, p. 54.
34. Rotha, *Documentary Diary*, p. 117.
35. Ibid., p. 282.

CHAPTER TWO: A MARRIAGE OF OPPOSITES

1. John Grierson, late, undated, unpublished interview.
2. Charles F. Backhouse, *Canadian Government Motion Picture Bureau* (Ottawa: Canadian Film Institute, 1974), p. 10.
3. Vincent Massey, letter to the Secretary of State for External Affairs, November 18, 1937 (Public Archives Canada RG20 B1 236 31670 Vol. 1).
4. John Grierson, "Report on Canadian Government Film Activities," August 1938.
5. National Film Board, *4 Days in May: A Report*, (1975).
6. John Grierson, *Grierson on Documentary*, ed. by Forsyth Hardy (London: Faber and Faber, 1966), p. 367.
7. William M. Baker, "The Anti-American Ingredient in Canadian History," *The Dalhousie Review*, Spring, 1973, p. 57.
8. *Grierson on Documentary*, p. 388.
9. Grierson, unpublished interview.
10. Canada, *An Act to create a National Film Board*, in *Statutes of Canada*, 3 George VI, Ch. 20 (Ottawa: Joseph Oscar Patenaude, 1939).
11. Marjorie McKay, "History of the National Film Board" 1964 or 1965, p.19. (hereafter cited as "NFB Hist.") Available from National Film Board.

216

12. For a more detailed treatment, see Piers Handling, "Censorship and Scares," *Cinema Canada*, no. 56 June-July 1979, pp. 25-31.
13. *Journal of the Society of Film and Television Arts* vol. 2, nos. 4-5, (1972), p. 14.
14. McKay, "NFB Hist.", p. 23.
15. Donald Theall, q. in *Journal of the Society of Film and Television Arts* vol. 2, nos. 4-5, (1972), p. 26.
16. *Cinema Journal*, Fall 1970, p. 7.
17. James Beveridge, q. in *JSFTA*, p. 12.
18. Beth Bertram, q. in *4 Days in May*.
19. Margaret Ann Elton, ibid.
20. McKay, "NFB Hist.", pp. 20-21.
21. This anecdote may have been refined with the passage of time. In other words, it may not be entirely true. The teller insists that it is; the subject cannot remember the incident. If it is not literally true, then it contains "mythic" truth in that it reflects what one old-timer remembers about the Grierson era.
22. McKay, "NFB Hist.", pp. 1-2. This quote is considerably condensed from McKay's lively description of the reactions to Grierson's recruits.
23. James D. McNiven, "The Neatness Syndrome," *Optimum*, vol. 4, no. 4 (1973), pp. 28-37.
24. McKay, "NFB Hist.", p. 23.
25. John Grierson, letter to James A. MacKinnon, Chairman, National Film Board of Canada, November 27, 1940 (Public Archives Canada MG 26 J1, Vol. 288, 244007)
26. John Grierson, letter to James A. MacKinnon, Chairman, National Film Board of Canada, February 11, 1941 (Public Archives Canada MG 26 J1 Vol. 305, 258164)
27. McKay, "NFB Hist.", p. 25.
28. John Grierson, q. in Elizabeth Sussex, *The Rise and Fall of British Documentary* (University of California Press, 1975), p. 112.

CHAPTER THREE: THE BIG BANG

1. National Film Board *Annual Reports*, 1944-45, 1945-46.
2. John Grierson, "The Eyes of Canada," CBC Radio Broadcast, January 21, 1940.
3. National Film Board, *4 Days in May: A Report*, 1975.
4. Graham McGinnis, "One Man's Documentary." Unpublished manuscript available for research purposes at the NFB library.
5. The basic anecdote is from McKay, "NFB Hist.", p. 44. The quote is from Jack C. Ellis, *Cinema Journal*, Fall 1970.
6. National Film Board, *4 Days in May*.
7. *Fortnightly Review* August, 1939.
8. National Film Board, *4 Days in May*.
9. McKay, "NFB Hist.", p. 45.
10. Stuart Legg, q. in ibid., p. 51.
11. Marjorie McKay, q. in *4 Days in May*. The subsequent four quotations are from this source.
12. McKay, "NFB Hist.", pp. 30-31.
13. Richard Griffith's contribution to Paul Rotha, *Documentary Film*, 3d ed. (London: Faber and Faber, 1952), p. 332.
14. Stuart Legg, q. in Elizabeth Sussex, *The Rise and Fall of British Documentary* (University of California Press, 1975), p. 113.
15. John Grierson, CBC radio broadcast, November 30, 1940.

16. *Business Screen*, October 1942.
17. C.W. Grey, *Movies for the People*, National Film Board document, n.d., pp. 38-39.
18. Distribution data from *Business Screen*, October 1942.
19. Grierson, q. in Zechariah Chafee, *Government and Mass Communications*, vol. 2 (University of Chicago Press, 1947), p. 742.
20. National Film Board, *4 Days in May*.
21. Grierson, letter to Tallents, February 16, 1973.
22. Gerald Clark, "Grierson — He's Colossal," *The Montreal Standard Magazine*, January 16, 1943.
23. Unidentified newspaper article.
24. *Canadian Film Weekly*, July 28, 1943, p. 1.
25. *Hansard*, 30 March 1944, pp. 2017-18, Mr. Adamson.
26. Minutes, NFB Board of Governors, 3 February 1945.
27. Ernst Borneman, "Documentary Films: World War II," in *Canadian Film Reader*, ed. by Seth Feldman and Joyce Nelson (Toronto: Peter Martin Associates, 1977), pp. 48-58.
28. Pat Jackson, q. in Sussex, *Rise and Fall*, p. 143.
29. Basil Wright, q. in ibid., p. 110.
30. John Grierson, "The Nature of Propaganda," *Documentary Newsletter*, May 1941, pp. 90-93.
31. Edgar Anstey, q. in Sussex, *Rise and Fall*, p. 116.
32. John Grierson, "The Documentary Idea: 1942," *Documentary Newsletter*, June 1942, pp. 83-6.
33. Erik Barnouw, *Documentary: A History of the Non-Fiction Film* (New York: Oxford University Press, 1974), pp. 146-7.
34. Ibid., p. 64.
35. Sussex, *Rise and Fall*, p. 159.
36. Edgar Anstey, q. in *Journal of the Society of Film and Television Arts* vol. 2, nos. 4-5, (1972), p. 28.
37. John Grierson, unpublished article written in 1939 or 1940.
38. *Documentary Newsletter*, June 1942.
39. *Journal of the Society of Film and Television Arts* vol. 2, nos. 4-5, (1972), p. 7.
40. National Film Board, *4 Days in May*.
41. *Documentary Newsletter*, June 1942.
42. Forsyth Hardy, *John Grierson: A Documentary Biography* (London: Faber and Faber, 1979), p. 115.

CHAPTER FOUR: THE POST-WAR CRISIS

1. National Film Board *Annual Reports*, 1945-46 and 1947-48.
2. John Grierson, "Memorandum to the Staff," National Film Board, 1944.
3. The anecdotes about accounting are based on McKay, "NFB Hist.", p.42.
4. McKay, "NFB Hist.", p. 46.
5. Legg's memorandum, untitled and undated, was circulated under a covering memorandum by Jim Beveridge, National Film Board, March 25, 1946.
6. Kirwan Cox, "The Grierson Files," *Cinema Canada* no. 56, June/July 1979, p. 19.
7. Royal Commission on Espionage in Government Service (Taschereau-Kellock Commission), Ottawa, 1946. Transcripts of testimonies deposited with Public Archives Canada.
8. See Kirwan Cox's article (op.cit.) for a full report on the FBI's interest in Grierson.

9. Interview with Grant McLean by Kirwan Cox and Piers Handling for *Has Anybody Here Seen Canada*? (NFB film, 1979), Feb. 24, 1978.
10. Ross McLean, letter to J.J. McCann, Minister of Revenue, December 1, 1947.
11. For a full report on the Canadian Cooperation Project, see Maynard Collins, "Cooperation, Hollywood, and Howe," *Cinema Canada* no. 56, June/July 1979, pp. 34-36.
12. This clip from *Bend in the River* is included in the NFB documentary, *Has Anybody Here Seen Canada*?
13. Minutes, NFB Board of Governors meeting, March 22, 1949.
14. *The Financial Post*, November 19, 1949.
15. Minutes, NFB Board of Governors meeting, November 29, 1949.
16. Evelyn Cherry, interviewed by John Kramer for *Has Anybody Here Seen Canada*?
17. Arthur Irwin, interview, *Cinema Canada*, June/July 1979, p. 38.
18. "The National Film Board: Survey of Organization and Business Administration" (Toronto: J.D. Woods & Gordon, Ltd., March 1950). Restricted.
19. *Report of the Royal Commission on National Development in the Arts, Letters and Sciences* (Ottawa: Edmond Cloutier, 1951).
20. Vincent Massey, *On Being Canadian* (Toronto: J.M. Dent & Sons, 1948), pp. 52-53.
21. Canada, *An Act Respecting the National Film Board*, in *Statutes of Canada*. 14 George VI, Ch. 44 (Ottawa: Edmond Cloutier, 1950).

CHAPTER FIVE: UNIT B AND AN "ATTITUDE TOWARD THE CRAFT"

1. Charles Augustin Sainte-Beuve, "What is a Classic?" in *Sainte Beuve: Selected Essays*, trans. and ed. by Francis Steegmuller and Norbert Gutterman (Garden City, New York: Doubleday and Company, 1963), pp. 2-3.
2. Peter Harcourt, "The Innocent Eye," *Sight and Sound*, vol. 34 no. 1, Winter 1964-65, pp. 19-23.
3. Public Broadcasting Service, "Nova: The Race for the Double Helix," documentary aired February 24, 1976.
4. Bernard H. Gustin, "Charisma, Recognition, and the Motivation of Scientists," *American Journal of Sociology* 78 (March 1973), pp. 1123-24.
5. James Watson, *The Double Helix: A Personal Account of the Discovery of the Structure of DNA* (New York: New American Library, 1969).
6. Louis Marcorelles, *Living Cinema: New Directions in Contemporary Filmmaking* (New York: Praeger, 1968), p. 7.
7. Henri Cartier-Bresson, *The Decisive Moment* (New York: Simon and Schuster, 1952).
8. Watson, *The Double Helix*.
9. Guy L. Cote, "Living with 'Neighbors': an Interview with Norman McLaren," in *Film: Book 2*, ed. Robert Hughes (New York: Grove Press, 1962), pp. 44ff.
10. Ibid., p. 48.
11. The Film Board has prepared a single screen version of *Labyrinth*.

CHAPTER SIX: THE WORM IN THE APPLE

1. "NFB French Production Organization and Personnel (1941-1964)," NFB memorandum, undated.
2. André Lafrance, *Cinéma d'ici* (Ottawa:Lemeac, 1973), p. 32.

3. Raymond Garceau, "Les carnets d'un p'tit Garceau, no. 5," *Objectif*, August-September 1967, p. 16.
4. Raymond Garceau, "Les carnets d'un p'tit Garceau, no. 4," *Objectif*, May 1966, p. 11.
5. Guy Coté, "Passe Partout in 1956," NFB memorandum, 1956.
6. McKay, "NFB Hist.", p.98.
7. *Cahiers du Cinéma* (June 1968), pp.1-22.
8. Michel Brault, q. in Lafrance, *Cinéma d'ici*, p. 106.
9. André Martin, q. in Gilles Marsolais, *Le Cinéma Canadien* (Montreal: Editions du Jour, 1968), p. 56.
10. Marsolais, *Le Cinéma canadien*, pp. 56-57.
11. Cinémathèque québécoise, La, *Gilles Groulx: le lynx inquiet* (Montreal: La Cinémathèque québécoise, 1971), pp. 22-23.
12. Lafrance, *Cinéma d'ici*, p. 92.
13. *Motion*, January-February 1974, p. 34.
14. Marsolais, *Le Cinéma Canadien*, p. 59.
15. Ibid., p. 62.
16. Lafrance, *Cinéma d'ici*, p. 78.
17. *Objectif*, Winter 1964-65, p. 9.
18. For a detailed analysis of the French-Canadian films of this era, see David Clandfield, "From the Picturesque to the Familiar: Films of the French Unit at the NFB (1958-1964)," *Ciné-Tracts* #4, Spring-Summer 1978, p. 50-62.
19. Lafrance, *Cinéma d'ici*, p. 101.
20. Marsolais, *Le Cinéma Canadien*, p. 64.
21. Arthur Lamothe, q. in Lafrance, *Cinéma d'ici*, pp. 88-89.
22. Peter Harcourt, "The Innocent Eye," *Sight and Sound*, vol. 34 no. 1, Winter 1964-65, p. 23.

CHAPTER SEVEN: LIKE THE MUSK OX, MADDENED BY ITS OWN PERFUME

1. *Grierson* (film), National Film Board, 1974.
2. Quoted from memory by Ronald Blumer, *Cinema Canada* (August, 1974), p. 17. Guy Glover remembers Grierson's talk as a lot less apocalyptic in tone. A partial transcript (undated, unidentified) of a tape of what may have been the same talk is also far milder; it expresses the same point, but without the tone of reprimand that colours Blumer's version. This transcript, however, may not be completely accurate, either. A well-known film, *Fields of Sacrifice*, is transcribed as *Tunes of Sacrifice*, and Guy Glover is called Guy Gloverman. There are numerous parenthetical comments in the transcription, such as "voice too low," "tape stopped," and "cannot make out what he is saying."
3. Ibid.
4. Legg, q. in McKay, "NFB Hist.", p. 51.
5. Grierson, tape of speech given at Poona, India, April 22, 1971.
6. Edwards, Natalie, "Who's Don Owen?" *Cinema Canada* no. 8, June/July 1973, p. 32.
7. Robert Roussil, q. in Howard Junker, "The National Film Board of Canada: After a Quarter of a Century," *Film Quarterly*, vol. 18, no. 2, (Winter 1964), pp.24-25.
8. *parti pris* avril, 1964, p.3.

CHAPTER EIGHT: THE DICTATORSHIP OF THE FILMMAKER

1. National Film Board, "A Summary of Staff Opinion on the Structure and Organization of the English Production Branch" (Montreal: December 19, 1963). Restricted.
2. Ronald Blumer and Susan Schouten, "Donald Brittain: Green Stripe and Common Sense," *Cinema Canada* #15, August-September, 1974, p. 37.
3. Ibid., p. 38.
4. Ibid., p. 37.
5. National Film Board, "Notes on the Role and Responsibility of the Producer and Director" (Montreal: October 28, 1966). Restricted.
6. Blumer and Schouten, "Donald Brittain:," p.38.
7. National Film Board, "Notes on the Role . . . "
8. National Film Board, "Internal Study of National Film Board Management and Operations" (Montreal: May 30, 1968). Restricted.
9. National Film Board, *Annual Report: 1969-70* (Montreal: 1970).
10. Canada, *An Act Respecting Employer and Employee Relations in the Public Service of Canada*, 14-15-16 Elizabeth II, Ch. 72 (Ottawa: Roger Duhamel, 1967).
11. National Film Board, "Report of the Crisis Committee to the National Film Board of Canada" (Montreal: undated). Restricted.

CHAPTER NINE: MIRROR, MIRROR, ON THE WALL

1. *parti pris* avril, 1964, pp. 2-24.
2. *liberté* 8 March-June, 1966, p. 7.
3. *Cinema Canada* no. 9 August-September 1973, p. 31.
4. Paul Rotha, *Documentary Diary: An Informal History of the British Documentary Film, 1928-1939* (London: Secker & Warburg, 1973), pp. 280-281.
5. John Grierson, *Grierson on Documentary*, ed. by Forsyth Hardy (London: Faber & Faber, 1966), p. 322.
6. Calais Calvert-Marty, q. in National Film Board, *4 Days in May: A Report*, 1975.
7. Toronto *Globe and Mail*, 27 December 1972.
8. Montreal *Gazette*, 11 February 1976.
9. Toronto *Globe and Mail*, 27 December 1972.
10. *Québéc-Presse*, 17 December 1972.
11. National Film Board press release, 11 December 1972.
12. *Québéc-Presse*, 6 May 1973.
13. *La Presse*, 8 December 1972.
14. The epithets appeared in *Québéc-Presse* as follows: "imbecile," 10 December 1972; "dictator," 17 December 1972; "idiots," 6 May 1973.
15. Roger Frappier, q. in *Cinema Canada* no. 9 August-September 1973, p. 31.
16. Toronto *Globe and Mail*, 27 December 1972.
17. Pierre Perrault, *L'Art et l'état* (Montreal: Éditions parti pris, 1973).
18. *La Presse*, 8 December 1972.
19. "Corridor" (NFB filmmakers' union newsletter), January 1973.
20. The *Toronto Star*, 23 December 1972.
21. Frappier, q. in *Cinema Canada*.
22. Perrault, *L'Art et l'état*.
23. George Steiner, interview, *Psychology Today*, February 1973, p. 62.
24. Toronto *Globe and Mail*, 27 December 1973.
25. Perrault, *L'Art et l'état*.

CHAPTER TEN: CHALLENGE FOR CHANGE

1. Colin Low, "Media as Mirror," unpublished working manuscript.
2. Paul Rotha, *Documentary Diary: An Informal History of the British Documentary Film, 1928-1939* (London: Secker & Warburg, 1973), p. 277.
3. John Grierson, "Memo to Michelle," *Challenge for Change Newsletter* (Spring 1972), p. 4.
4. Elizabeth Sussex, *The Rise and Fall of British Documentary* (University of California Press, 1975), p. 62.
5. Evelyn Gerstein, "English Documentary Films," in *The Documentary Tradition*, ed. Lewis Jacobs (New York: Hopkins and Blake, 1971), pp. 114-5.
6. *Challenge for Change* (film), National Film Board, 1968.
7. National Film Board, "Proposal for a Programme of Film Activities in the Area of Poverty and Change," March 17, 1967. Restricted.
8. Sandra Gwyn, *Cinema as Catalyst: Film, Videotape, and Social Change* (Memorial University of Newfoundland Extension Service, 1972), p. 6.
9. Ibid., p. 5.
10. James R. Taylor and Elizabeth Van Emery-Taylor, "Using Videotechnology for Social Change: A Report Submitted to the Interdepartmental Committee of Challenge for Change/Société Nouvelle" (University of Montreal, May 23, 1973), p. 7. Restricted.
11. Dorothy Todd Hénaut, "galloping videotis," *Challenge for Change Newsletter* (Spring 1973), p. 3.
12. Taylor and Emory-Taylor, p. 34.
13. Ibid., p. 78.
14. Ibid., p. 139.
15. National Film Board, "Challenge for Change/Société Nouvelle Brief on Community Channels on Cable Television," April 7, 1971. Restricted.
16. Taylor and Emory-Taylor, p. 182.
17. Ibid., pp. 169-180.
18. Boyce Richardson, untitled, unpublished draft manuscript on Challenge for Change, September, 1977.
19. Marie Kurchak, "What Challenge? What Change?" *Take One* vol. 4, no. 1, (January 1974), p. 22.
20. Mark Zannis, "Special Distribution for *Cree Hunters of Mistassini*" (Challenge for Change, 1974).
21. Dorothy Todd Hénaut, "Films for Social Change: The Hammer and the Mirror." Manuscript.
22. Untitled Challenge for Change draft document on the new Challenge for Change programme, October 30, 1979.

CHAPTER ELEVEN: FILM BOARD REGIONALIZATION

1. John Grierson, "Memo to Michelle," *Challenge for Change Newsletter* (Spring 1972), p. 4.
2. Ron Dick, "Regionalization of a Federal Cultural Institution: The Experience of the National Film Board of Canada." Seminar paper, Duke University, March 4, 1980, p. 16.
3. Ibid., p. 8.
4. National Film Board *Annual Report*, 1976-77.

5. Paul Fox, "Regionalization and Confederation," in *Regionalism in the Canadian Community*, ed. Mason Wade (University of Toronto Press, 1969), p. 3.
6. Don Hopkins, "The Next Five Years." Discussion rough draft, July 11, 1979.
7. Programme committee meeting, April 19, 1974.
8. NFB *Annual Report*, 1976-77.
9. Colin Low, "Regionalization." Memorandum, May 28, 1979.
10. George Pearson, memorandum, July 6, 1979.
11. John Grierson, *Grierson on Documentary*, ed. Forsyth Hardy (London: Faber and Faber, 1966), p. 396.
12. Low, "Regionalization."
13. Colin Low, "Some Thoughts on What We're All About." Attachment to NFB memorandum, December 1, 1978.

CHAPTER TWELVE: WEEDPATCH IN A HUNGRY WORLD

1. National Film Board "Internal Study Report," 1968. Restricted.
2. Norman Podhoretz, "Culture in the Present Moment," *Commentary* 58 (December 1974), p.33.
3. Susan Sontag, "Notes on Art, Sex, and Politics," New York *Times*, February 8, 1976.
4. See, for example, Brian Winston, "Documentary: I Think We Are In Trouble," *Sight and Sound*, Winter 1978-79, pp. 3-7, or Jay Ruby, "The Image Mirrored: Reflexivity and the Documentary Film," *Journal of the University Film Association*, Fall 1977, pp. 3-11.
5. Gordon Hitchens, " A Tough Man with an Unbroken Heart," *Vision* 1 (Summer, 1962), p. 75.
6. *Grierson on Documentary*, ed. Forsyth Hardy (London: Faber and Faber, 1966), p. 396.
7. Edwin Markham, "Outwitted," in *The Shoes of Happiness* (Garden City: Doubleday, Page, and Company, 1915), p. 1.
8. T.S. Eliot, "Tradition and the Individual Talent," in *The Sacred Word* (London: Methuen, 1948), pp. 47-59.
9. Toronto *Globe and Mail*, 27 March 1976.
10. Landon Y. Jones, Jr., "Bad Days on Mount Olympus," *Atlantic*, February 1974, pp. 37-53.
11. Chris Argyris, *Behind the Front Page* (San Francisco: Jossey-Bass Publishers, 1974).
12. James Watson, *The Double Helix: A Personal Account of the Discovery of the Structure of DNA* (New York: New American Library, 1969).
13. Tom Burns and G.M. Stalker, *The Management of Innovation* (London: Associated Book Publishers, 1966).
14. W.R. Ashby, "Self-Regulation and Requisite Variety," in *Systems Thinking*, ed. F.E. Emery (Harmondsworth: Penguin Books, 1969), pp. 110-113.
15. I owe this metaphor to James D. McNiven, "The Neatness Syndrome," *Optimum* vol. 4, no.4, (1973), pp. 28-37, but I've substituted "cornfield" for his "manicured lawn."
16. D.G. Hartle, "Operational Performance Measurement in the Federal Government," *Optimum* vol. 3 (1972), pp. 5-15; George S. Odiorne, *Management by Objectives* (New York: Pitman Publishing Corporation, 1965).
17. Max Weber, *The Theory of Social and Economic Organization* (University of Oxford Press, 1947), p. 339.

18. D. Braybrooke and C.E. Lindblom, *A Strategy of Decisions* (New York: Free Press, 1963).
19. E.F. Schumacher, *Small is Beautiful: A Study of Economics as if People Mattered* (London: Blond & Briggs, 1973), p. 41.
20. Louis Fischer, *The Life of Mahatma Gandhi* (New York: Collier Books, 1962), p. 41.
21. "Corridor," no. 9, 1974.
22. John Grierson, interview, CBC, Montreal, 2 April 1969.

SELECTED
BIBLIOGRAPHY

I. BOOKS, ARTICLES, AND OTHER
NON-GOVERNMENT PUBLICATIONS

Adorno, T.W. "The Culture Industry." *Cinéaste* vol. 5, no. 1, Winter 1971-72, pp. 8-11

Argyris, Chris. *Behind the Front Page*. San Francisco: Jossey-Bass Publishers, 1974.

Ashby, W.R. "Self-Regulation and Requisite Variety." In *Systems Thinking*, pp. 110-13. Edited by F.E. Emery. Harmondsworth, England: Penguin Books, 1969.

Backhouse, Charles. *Canadian Government Motion Picture Bureau*. Ottawa: Canadian Film Institute, 1974.

Baker, William M. "The Anti-American Ingredient in Canadian History." *The Dalhousie Review*, Spring 1973, pp. 55-77.

Barnouw, Erik. *Documentary: A History of the Non-Fiction Film*. New York: Oxford University Press, 1974.

Barsam, Richard Meran. *NonFiction Film: A Critical History*. New York: E.P. Dutton, 1973.

_____. ed. *Nonfiction Film Theory and Criticism*. New York: E.P. Dutton, 1976.

Beattie, Eleanor. *A Handbook of Canadian Film*. Toronto: Peter Martin Associates, 1973.

Beveridge, James. *John Grierson Film Master*. New York: Macmillan, 1978.

Blau, Peter. "Decentralization in Bureaucracies." In *Power in Organizations*, pp. 150-74. Edited by Mayer N. Zald. Vanderbilt University Press, 1970.

225

_____ and Scott, W.R. *Formal Organizations: A Comparative Approach*. San Francisco: Chandler, 1962.

Blue, James. "Direct Cinema." *Film Comment*, Fall-Winter 1967, pp. 80-86.

Bluem, A. William. *Documentary in American Television*. New York: Hastings House, 1965.

Borneman, Ernst. "Documentary Films: World War II." In *Canadian Film Reader*, pp. 48-57. Edited by Seth Feldman and Joyce Nelson. Toronto: Peter Martin Associates, 1977.

Braybrooke, D. and Lindblom, C.E. *A Strategy of Decision*. New York: Free Press, 1963.

Burns, Tom and Stalker, G.M. *The Management of Innovation*. London: Associated Book Publishers, 1966.

Calder-Marshall, Arthur. *The Innocent Eye: The Life of Robert J. Flaherty*. Penguin Books, 1970.

Callenbach, Ernest. "Going Out to the Subject: II." *Film Quarterly*, vol. 14, no. 3, Spring 1961, pp. 38-40.

Cartier-Bresson, Henri. *The Decisive Moment*. New York: Simon and Schuster, 1952.

Chafee, Zechariah. *Government and Mass Communications*, vol. 2. University of Chicago Press, 1947.

Cinema Canada, no. 15, August-September 1974. Special National Film Board 35th Anniversary Issue.

Cinémathèque canadienne, La. *How To Make or Not to Make A Canadian Film*. Montreal: La Cinémathèque canadienne, 1968.

Cinémathèque québécoise, La. *Gilles Groulx: le lynx inquiet*. Montreal: La Cinémathèque québécoise, 1971.

Clandfield, David. "From the Picturesque to the Familiar: Films of the French Unit at the NFB (1958-1964)." *Ciné-Tracts* no. 4, Spring-Summer 1978.

Cook, Ramsay. *The Maple Leaf Forever: Essays on Nationalism and Politics in Canada*. Toronto: Macmillan of Canada, 1971.

Coté, Guy. "Living with 'Neighbours': An Interview with Norman McLaren." In *Film: Book 2*, pp. 36-48. Edited by Robert Hughes. New York: Grove Press, 1962.

Cox, Kirwan. "The Grierson Files." *Cinema Canada* no. 56, June/July, 1979.

Crean, S.M. *Who's Afraid of Canadian Culture?* Don Mills, Ontario: General Publishing Company, 1976.

Dibble, Vernon K. "What is and What Ought to Be: A Comparison of Certain Characteristics of the Ideological and Legal Styles of

Thought." *American Journal of Sociology* 79, November 1973, pp. 11-49.

Downs, Anthony. *Inside Bureaucracy*. Boston: Little, Brown and Company, 1967.

Drucker, Peter F. *Managing for Results: Economic Tasks and Risk-Taking Decisions*. New York: Harper & Row, 1964.

Eliot, T.S. "Tradition and the Individual Talent." In *The Sacred Word*, pp. 47-59. London: Methuen, 1948.

Ellis, Jack C. "The Young Grierson in America, 1924-1927." *Cinema Journal*, Fall 1968, pp. 12-21.

_____. "John Grierson's First Years at the National Film Board." *Cinema Journal*, Fall 1970, pp. 2-14.

Epstein, Edward Jay. "Journalism and Truth." *Commentary* 57, April 1974, pp. 36-40.

Evans, Gary. "The Politics of Propaganda: John Grierson." *Cinema Canada*, no. 56 June/July 1979.

Feldman, Seth and Joyce Nelson, eds. *Canadian Film Reader*. Toronto, Peter Martin Associates Ltd/Take One, 1977.

Fischer, David Hackett. *Historians' Fallacies: Toward a Logic of Historical Thought*. New York: Harper & Row, 1970.

Fox, Paul. "Regionalism and Confederation." In *Regionalism in the Canadian Community*, pp. 3-29. Edited by Mason Wade. University of Toronto Press, 1969.

Friendly, Fred W. *Due To Circumstances Beyond Our Control*. New York: Random House, 1967.

Frye, Northrop. *The Bush Garden: Essays on the Canadian Imagination*. Toronto: Anansi, 1971.

Goffman, Erving. *Where the Action Is*. London: Penguin Books, 1969.

Greenberg, Clement. "Avant-Garde and Kitsch." *Partisan Review* 6, Fall 1939, pp. 34-49.

Grierson, John. *Grierson on Documentary*. Edited by Forsyth Hardy. London: Faber & Faber, 1966.

_____. "The Last Interview." *Film Quarterly*, vol. 26, no. 1, Fall 1972, pp. 24-30.

Guback, Thomas H. "Film and Cultural Pluralism." *Cinéaste* vol. 5, no. 1, Winter 1971-72.

Gustin, Bernard H. "Charisma, Recognition, and the Motivation of Scientists." *American Journal of Sociology* 78, March 1973, pp. 1119-34.

Gwyn, Sandra. *Cinema as Catalyst: Film, Videotape, and Social Change*. St John's: Memorial University of Newfoundland

Extension Service, 1972.

Handling, Piers. "Censorship and Scares." *Cinema Canada* no. 56, June/July 1979.

Harcourt, Peter. "The Innocent Eye." *Sight and Sound* vol. 34, no.1, Winter 1964-65, pp. 19-23.

_____. *Movies and Mythologies*. Toronto: CBC Publications, 1977.

Hardy, Forsyth. *John Grierson: A Documentary Biography*. London: Faber and Faber, 1979.

Hartle, D.G. "Operational Performance Measurement in the Federal Government." *Optimum* vol. 3, no. 1, 1972, pp. 5-15.

Hénaut, Dorothy Todd. "Films for Social Change: The Hammer and the Mirror." *McGill University Studies in Canadian Communications*, 1975.

Hitchens, Gordon. "A Tough Man with an Unbroken Heart." *Vision* 1, Summer 1962, p. 75.

Jacobs, Lewis, ed. *The Documentary Tradition*. New York: Hopkins and Blake, 1971.

James, Clifford Rodney. *The National Film Board of Canada: Its Task of Communication*. Ph. D. Dissertation, Ohio State University, 1968.

Jay, Anthony. *Corporation Man*. New York: Random House, 1971.

_____. *Management and Machiavelli*. Harmondsworth, England: Penguin Books, 1970.

Jones, Landon Y., Jr. "Bad Days on Mount Olympus." *Atlantic*, February 1974, pp. 37-53.

Journal of the Society of Film and Television Arts, vol. 2, no. 4-5, 1972. Special Issue on John Grierson.

Junker, Howard. "The National Film Board of Canada: After A Quarter Century." *Film Quarterly* vol. 8, no. 2, Winter 1964, pp. 22-29.

Katz, Daniel and Kahn, Robert L. *The Social Psychology of Organizations*. New York: John Wiley & Sons, 1966.

Kramer, Hilton. "The Age of the Avant-Garde." *Commentary* 54, October 1972, pp. 37-44.

_____. "A Yearning for Normalcy: The Current Backlash in the Arts." *The Montreal Star*, 5 June 1976.

Kurchak, Marie. "What Challenge? What Change?" *Take One* vol. 4, no. 1, January 1974, pp. 22-25.

Lafrance, André. *Cinema d'ici*. Ottawa: Lemeac, 1973.

Leyda, Jay. *Films Beget Films: A Study of the Compilation Film*. New York: Hill and Wang, 1971.

_____. *KINO: A History of the Russian and Soviet Film*. New York: The Macmillan Company, 1960.

liberté 8 March-June 1966. Issue on Quebec cinema.

MacCann, Richard Dyer. *The People's Films. A Political History of U.S. Government Motion Pictures*. New York: Hastings House, 1973.

McNiven, James D. "The 'neatness syndrome.'" *Optimum* vol. 4, no. 4, 1973, pp. 28-37.

Mannheim, Karl. *Essays on the Sociology of Culture*. London: Routledge and Kegan Paul, 1967.

March, J.G. and Simon, H.A. *Organizations*. New York: Wiley, 1958.

Marcorelles, Louis. *Living Cinema: New Directions in Contemporary Film-Making*. New York: Praeger Publishers, 1973.

Marsolais, Gilles. *Le Cinéma Canadien*. Montréal: Éditions du Jour, 1968.

Massey, Vincent. *On Being Canadian*. Toronto: J.M. Dent, 1948.

Merton, Robert K. *Social Theory and Social Structure*. New York: Free Press, 1968.

Mintzberg, Henry. "A National Goals Hierarchy." *Optimum* vol. 5, no. 1, 1974, pp. 5-15.

Morris, Peter. *Embattled Shadows: A History of Canadian Cinema, 1895-1939*. Montreal, McGill-Queen's University Press, 1978.

_____. ed. *The National Film Board of Canada: The War Years*. Ottawa: Canadian Film Institute, 1965.

Odiorne, George S. *Management by Objectives*. New York: Pitman Publishing Corporation, 1965.

Orbanz, Eva. *Journey to a Legend and Back: The British Realistic Film*. Berlin: Volker Spiess, 1977.

Page, Charles Hunt. "Bureaucracy's Other Face." *Social Forces* 25, pp. 88-94.

parti pris, April 1964.

Paulu, Burton. *British Broadcasting in Transition*. University of Minnesota Press, 1961.

Perrault, Pierre, et. al. *L'Art et l'état*. Montreal: Éditions parti pris, 1973.

Podhoretz, Norman. "Culture and the Present Moment." *Commentary* 58, December 1974, pp. 31-50.

Popper, Karl R. "Has History Any Meaning?" In *The Open*

Society and its Enemies, vol. 2, pp. 259-81. Princeton University Press, 1971.

Pugh, D.S., ed. *Organization Theory*. Middlesex, England: Penguin Books, 1973.

Rotha, Paul. *Documentary Diary: An Informal History of the British Documentary Film, 1928-1939*. London: Secker & Warburg, 1973.

_____. *Documentary Film*. London: Faber and Faber, 1952.

Rouch, Jean. "Interview." *Cahiers du Cinema*, June 1963, pp. 1-22.

Ruby, Jay. "The Image Mirrored: Reflexivity and the Documentary Film." *Journal of the University Film Association*, Fall 1977, pp. 3-11.

Sainte-Beuve, Charles Augustin. "What is a Classic?" In *Sainte-Beuve: Selected Essays*, pp. 1-12. Edited by Francis Steegmuller and Norbert Guterman. Garden City, New York: Doubleday and Company, 1963.

Selznick, Philip. "Foundations of the Theory of Organizations." *American Sociological Review* 13, February 1948, pp. 25-35.

Shatnoff, Judith. "Expo '67 — A Multiple Vision." *Film Quarterly* vol. 21, no. 1, Fall 1967, pp. 2-12.

Sheed, Wilfred. *Office Politics*. New York: Farrar, Strauss, and Giroux, 1966.

Shepherd, John R. "The Regionalization of the National Film Board of Canada." *Journal of the University Film Association*, Summer 1979, pp. 13-18.

Simon, Herbert. *Administrative Behavior*. New York: Free Press, 1965.

Snyder, Robert L. *Pare Lorentz and the Documentary Film*. University of Oklahoma Press, 1968.

Spottiswoode, Raymond. *A Grammar of the Film: An Analysis of Film Technique*. London: Faber and Faber, 1935.

Sussex, Elizabeth. *The Rise and Fall of British Documentary*. University of California Press, 1975.

Theall, Donald F. and Joan B. "John Grierson on Media, Film, and History." *McGill University Studies in Canadian Communications*, 1975, pp. 113-130.

Tudor, Andrew. *Theories of Film*. London: Secker and Warburg, 1974.

Vickers, Geoffrey. *Toward a Sociology of Management*. London: Chapman and Hall, 1967.

230

Wadel, Cato. *Community Development and the Enlargement of the Sense of Community on Fogo Island*. St. John's: University of Newfoundland Extension Service, 1969.

Watson, James. *The Double Helix: A Personal Account of the Discovery of the Structure of DNA*. New York: New American Library, 1969.

Watson, Patrick. "Challenge for Change." *artscanada*, April 1970.

Watt, Harry. *Don't Look at the Camera*. London: Paul Elek, 1974.

Weber, Max. *The Theory of Social and Economic Organization*. New York: University of Oxford Press, 1947.

Whitehead, Alfred North. *Modes of Thought*. New York: The Free Press, 1968.

Winston, Brian. "Documentary: I Think We Are In Trouble." *Sight and Sound*, Winter 1978-79.

Wollheim, Richard. "Sociological Explanation of the Arts: Some Distinctions." In *The Sociology of Art and Literature*, pp. 574-581. Edited by Milton C. Albrecht, et al. New York: Praeger Publishers, 1970.

II. NON-NFB CANADIAN GOVERNMENT PUBLICATIONS

An Act to Create a National Film Board. Statutes of Canada, 3 George VI, CH. 20. Ottawa: Joseph Oscar Patenaude, 1939.

An Act Respecting Employer and Employee Relations in the Public Service of Canada. Statutes of Canada, 14-15-16 Elizabeth II, Ch. 72. Ottawa: Roger Duhamel, 1967.

An Act Respecting the National Film Board. Statutes of Canada, 14 George VI, Ch. 44. Ottawa: Edmond Cloutier, 1950.

The Film Industry in Canada. Ottawa: Secretary of State, 1977. (Also known as "The Tomkins Report").

Report of the Royal Commission on National Development in the Arts, Letters and Sciences 1949-1951. Ottawa: Edmond Cloutier, 1951. ("The Massey Report").

III. DOCUMENTS FROM THE NATIONAL FILM BOARD OF CANADA.

A. PUBLIC DOCUMENTS

Access. Early Challenge for Change newsletter.
Challenge for Change (film), 1968.
Challenge for Change Newsletter.
4 Days in May (6 to 9): A Report. 1975.
Grierson (film), 1974.
Hénaut, Dorothy Todd. "Asking the Right Questions"
   November 6, 1975. Mimeographed.
————. "What is Challenge for Change, Anyway?" Undated.
Low, Colin. "Fogo Island Film and Community Development
   Project." 1968. Mimeographed.
"The National Film Board of Canada." Information and Promotion
   Division. Ottawa, 1953.
Pot Pourri. Toronto NFB newsletter.
Zannis, Mark. "Special Distribution for *Cree Hunters of Mistas-
   sini*." 1974. Mimeographed.

B. INTERNAL DOCUMENTS (RESTRICTED OR UNCIRCU-LATED).

"Adaptation to the Future — the Next Five Years." 5 February
   1974.
"Brief Presented to Members of the National Film Board by the
   Film-Makers of English and French Production." Two parts.
   May 1973.
"Budget and Commitment Control." Undated. Early seventies.
"Dossier: Politique d'Emploi." 5 March 1974. Personnel Depart-
   ment.
Employee's Handbook. January 1974.
Glover, Rupert. "An Approach to Film Budgeting at the National
   Film Board of Canada." 11 December 1972.
"Internal Study of National Film Board Management and Opera-
   tions." 30 May 1968.
Litwack, William and Mintzberg, Henry. "Manpower Training in
   the Canadian Screen Industry." 4 April 1973.
"National Film Board Budgetary Control and Reporting System."
   June 1968.

232

"The National Film Board — an Essential New Look."
12 December 1973.
"NFB Meets Doctor Gallup." Undated.
"NFB 1964 ... Some Observations." Undated.
"The National Film Board: A Survey." Information section, 1945.
"Notes on the Psychological Factor in Administration and the
Relation of Public Information to Public Morale." December
1942 (handwritten date).
"Notes on the Role and Responsibility of the Producer and
Director." 28 October 1966.
"A Plan for Consolidation and Renewal 1976-1981. 4 March 1976.
"Pollution: A Survey of Film Possibilities." May 1969.
"Proposal for a Programme of Film Activities in the Area of
Poverty and Change." 7 March 1967.
"Report of the Crisis Committee to the National Film Board of
Canada." Undated. Late sixties or early seventies.
Slade, Mark. "A Working Paper on Audience Needs and Reactions." June 1972.
"Special Environmental Program: Conceptual Analysis and Proposed Working Plan." May 1974.
"A Summary of Staff Opinion on the Structure and Organization of
the English Production Branch." 16 December 1963.
Taylor, James R. and Van Every-Taylor, Elizabeth. "Using
Videotechnology for Social Change." 23 May 1973. Prepared
for the Interdepartmental Committee on Challenge for Change/
Société Nouvelle.
Woods, J.D. and Gordon Ltd. "The National Film Board: A
Survey of Organization and Business Administration." March
1950.

C. UNPUBLISHED DOCUMENTS
"Corridor". Newsletter for members of Le Syndicat Général du
Cinéma et de la Télévision — Section ONF.
Low, Colin. "Media as Mirror." Manuscript slated for publication.
Grierson, John. Talk given at Poona, India. 22 April 1971. Tape
recording. An employee's personal copy.
McGinnis, Graham. "One Man's Documentary." Unpublished
manuscript by an early employee. Undated.
McKay, Marjorie. "History of the National Film Board of Canada". 1964 or 1965. Mimeographed. Written by a former
long-term employee.

INDEX

239

240